Methodist Evangelism, American Salvation

Methodist Evangelism, American Salvation

The Home Missions of the Methodist Episcopal Church, 1860–1920

MARK R. TEASDALE

Foreword by Ted A. Campbell

◅PICKWICK *Publications* · Eugene, Oregon

METHODIST EVANGELISM, AMERICAN SALVATION
The Home Missions of the Methodist Episcopal Church, 1860–1920

Pickwick Publications
An Imprint of Wipf and Stock Publishers
199 W. 8th Ave., Suite 3
Eugene, OR 97401

www.wipfandstock.com

ISBN 13: 978-1-62032-916-0

Cataloguing-in-Publication data:

Teasdale, Mark R.

Methodist evangelism, American salvation : the home missions of the Methodist Episcopal Church, 1860–1920 / Mark R. Teasdale ; foreword by Ted A. Campbell.

xiv + 278 pp. ; 23 cm. Includes bibliographical references and index.

ISBN 13: 978-1-62032-916-0

1. Methodist Episcopal Church—Missions. 2. Methodist Church—United States—History. 3. Home Missions. 4. United States—Religion. I. Campbell, Ted. II. Title.

BX8235 .T42 2014

Manufactured in the U.S.A.

To Ana

Contents

Images

All images are from *Methodism and the Republic, The World Service of the Methodist Episcopal Church*, or *Methodist Centenary Celebration*.

Images

Foreword

Ted A. Campbell

SCHOLARS OF METHODIST HISTORY have expended enormous energy in past decades on the study of the early Wesleyan movement in Britain and the earliest years of the Methodist Episcopal Church in the United States. But the late nineteenth century and the early twentieth century were the periods in which Methodist churches in the US were flourishing and becoming increasingly visible and influential bodies in the nation's social and cultural life. The present study focuses on precisely this critical era in Methodist and American history.

In this study, Mark Teasdale shows in detail how American Methodists by this time—and those of the Methodist Episcopal Church, in particular—had come to think of themselves as a quintessentially American religious denomination with a providential mission in the life of the nation. Teasdale describes this triumphant cultural outlook in practice as "pure American evangelism." Building on the postmillennial vision that had characterized American Protestant communities since the early decades of New England Puritanism, Methodists came to see their evangelistic task in this period as insolubly conjoined with technological progress and the dissemination of American democratic values.

Teasdale's central chapters show how northern (Methodist Episcopal Church) Methodists carried on their home-evangelism work in the South: "white" Southerners needed to be converted to true Americanism by renouncing slavery and secession; "black" Southerners needed to be educated in the ways of America's Christian civilization (chapter 3). The West presented unique challenges to the Methodist Episcopal Church: the challenge of Mormonism and its practice of polygamy, the challenge of traditionally Catholic Spanish-speaking people in the Southwest, and the challenge of Native American peoples and their own religious and cultural traditions in the American West (chapter 4). In their own native territory, leaders of the Methodist Episcopal Church faced the challenge of evangelization of the cities of the east coast and the upper Midwest, especially in a period of growing immigration to these cities of Jews and Catholics (chapter 5). Teasdale shows toward the book's conclusion how the triumphal vision of the period on which he concentrates began to break down in the wake of the First World War, which left Americans as well as Europeans questioning the extent to which technology might be used for human damnation as well as human progress (chapter 6).

This is a work with implications for the study of Methodist churches and their evolution. It is, in a sense, a morality tale about the dangers of wedding one's religious convictions to nationalism and patriotism. But the work that follows also offers a positive assessment of the progressive vision that accompanied this conjoining of religious and nationalistic visions. The period described here was the high point of Methodist post-millennial optimism, which fueled a huge range of reforming efforts including the urban reforms advocated by proponents of the "social gospel" in the early twentieth century. It was a vision that was wounded by World War I and that died—for most Methodists—on that terrible December day in 1933 when Methodists contemplated with horror how a supposedly civilized people could allow something as barbaric as the public sale of alcoholic beverages. Methodists were thus left with the memory of their engagement with reformism, but seriously lacking the theological and inspirational underpinnings that had driven their reform efforts in the past.

Teasdale's scholarship in the following pages challenges us to consider how Christians can engage in genuine evangelism and genuine social and cultural transformation without wedding themselves to a particular nation and its dominant culture. Anyone familiar with the current state of Methodist churches—and other churches, I dare say—know how seriously we continue to struggle with these issues. What follows, then, is a careful historical study, but one that does not allow those of us in churches the option of sitting back and simply observing. It is a narrative that forces us to confront a series of issues with which Christian communities struggle today even as they engage in the practices of evangelization and social transformation.

Acknowledgments

CHARLES DICKENS PENNED THE following brief exchange in *David Copperfield* between David and his aunt. His aunt speaks first. "'I never thought, when I used to read books, what work it was to write them.' 'It's work enough to read them, sometimes,' I returned."

There is no question that much work is necessary to write a book. Gratefully, this work is not one that an author must enter alone. The presence of those who support, strengthen, and improve on the author's efforts helps ease the burden of writing considerably. I am indebted to several people for this. Dr. Ted A. Campbell, who served as my dissertation advisor and now has done me the honor of writing the foreword for this book, remains my guiding star in understanding how to approach the work of a historian. Dr. Doug Strong, who many times encouraged me to publish my research, helped spur me in this work. Drs. Anna Johnson and Barry Bryant, my colleagues at Garrett-Evangelical Theological Seminary, both graciously offered to read this book while it was still in development. I am especially grateful to Dr. Johnson, who kept this commitment in the face of very trying personal times and provided extremely helpful feedback. Likewise, the library staff at Garrett-Evangelical has been a tremendous help in tracking down and digitizing resources that I have needed. Finally, I have great appreciation for the late Rev. Stanley R. Bice. As my senior pastor and mentor when I first entered the United Methodist ministry, Rev. Bice demonstrated the best of Methodist home mission work in his tireless love of his congregations and involvement in the neighborhoods in which his churches were located. He was a living testament to the fact that, when Methodists get it right, they are indeed a blessing to all those around them.

These people have each helped lighten the work of writing this book. I can only hope that Mr. Copperfield's response to his aunt about the onerous work of reading will not apply to your experience of this text.

Abbreviations

BHM&CE	Board of Home Missions and Church Extension
CCWD	The Christian Crusade for World Democracy
CDA	Christian Democracy for America
CES	Church Extension Society
CTCA	Commission on Training Camp Activities
FAS	Freedmen's Aid Society
FA&SES	Freedmen's Aid and Southern Education Society
MEC	Methodist Episcopal Church
MECS	Methodist Episcopal Church, South
NCEU	National City Evangelization Union
UMC	The United Methodist Church
WHMS	Women's Home Missionary Society
WMCNB	"White, Middle Class, Native Born"

Introduction

As I WRITE THIS, the United States is reeling from yet another mass shooting spree, leaving multiple children and adults slain in its wake. The pain of the situation is palpable and only increases with each new photo of grieving parents and stunned survivors posted to the internet news sites. In reading the discussion forums on these sites, the negativity of the comments is striking. Most express outrage at the perpetrator as well as deep sadness and shock at the loss of life. Virtually all share in a wearied resignation over the fact that the once great United States of America has become a place where this sort of violence and the fear it engenders is an all-too-common reality. Hope and peace are far from the public mind and heart.

The disbelief that Americans feel about such events taking place in their own nation is understandable. This is not only because of the horrific nature of these acts, but because Americans have worked hard over their history to insulate themselves from feeling the pain of such brutality. Whether it was the Monroe Doctrine meant to fend off European incursions on the American continents, the isolationism that developed after the First World War, or the creation of suburbs following the return of the GIs after the Second World War, Americans have sought to erect barriers between themselves and the suffering around them. This is not to say that Americans were ignorant of this suffering or impassive toward it. They often were aware of the struggles people faced worldwide and gave generously to help. The Marshall Plan and any number of humanitarian organizations that have their roots in the United States witness to this. Even so, Americans wanted to keep the suffering itself as far from their own daily lives as possible.

Amazingly, many Americans were largely successful in this venture. Aided by a strong economy, a stable and comparatively peaceful location on the globe, and a form of government that allowed for representation and the bloodless transfer of power, certain segments of the American population have been shielded from the worst experiences the world has to offer. Specifically, the white, middle class, native-born (a set of descriptors I will refer to with the initials WMCNB from here on) citizens of the United States have lived in this cushion of relative safety. Within this safety, they have been able to prosper and increase their standard of living.

During the period between the Civil War and the First World War, this particular demographic came to believe that it was not enough simply to enjoy a superior standard of living compared to that experienced by people around the world, but that it had a mandate to share these blessings with others. To do this required that Americans cultivate their own values and patterns of life in others, believing that if people adopted these ways of living they would likewise achieve prosperity. Rudyard Kipling's poem "The White Man's Burden," (1899) written in response to the American conquest of the Philippines during the Spanish American War, articulates this idea. It calls on white Americans to send their best and brightest to overcome the ignorance and moral destitution of the Filipino people. This was a sort of American gospel—the good news of how others could experience the best quality of life possible, premised on the values and patterns of life held by WMCNB Americans.

Chief among those who took up the cause of spreading this American gospel were the WMCNB Americans who were active in the churches. Already committed to the work of evangelism in order to convert people to the Christian faith, it was easy to wed this activity to spreading the American gospel. In combining the two messages, the churches offered hope for people to experience the fullness of God's blessings both in the present life and in the hereafter.

This book is an exploration of how the Methodist Episcopal Church in particular helped shape and manifest this American gospel through its home missions in the late nineteenth century and early twentieth century. It explores the ways the Methodists modified their existing practices of evangelism in order to present the better quality of life that WMCNB Americans enjoyed. I term this work "pure[1] American evangelism" since it represents evangelistic practices that the Methodists formed around an idealized understanding of what the United States was and how its values could be a means of blessing to those who adopted them.

---

1. I use the word "pure" in an attempt to gather the ideal notion of the United States held by the members of the MEC along with what they held to be the purity of the way of life and values they maintained as constitutive of God's salvific work.

AMERICAN METHODISTS AND PURE AMERICAN EVANGELISM

There are several reasons for tracing the American gospel through the evangelistic work of the Methodist Episcopal Church (MEC). The first is that from its beginning the MEC was organically connected to the American people. The MEC was formed in 1784 at the Christmas Conference held in Baltimore. Although it was officially authorized to come into existence by Methodism's founder, the Anglican priest John Wesley, the new church soon charted its own policies and practices in league with the values emerging among the newly independent American people. This was due in part to the fact that the MEC readily drew its leadership from among the ranks of the common people in the United States rather than from the highly educated ranks with closer ties to Europe. These leaders were artisans and merchants—the white, middling class of the early Republic.[2] While Methodists did make allowance for non-whites to participate in leadership on the local levels, the white middling class was the face of denominational leadership. As a consequence of this, the form and presentation of the Christian message propounded by the church was influenced by the values held by this specific demographic.

A second reason for tracing the American gospel through the MEC is that it leaves an especially robust history of evangelistic work in which to view the values it perceived as essential to share with others. Wade Crawford Barclay commented on this at the beginning of his four-volume *History of Methodist Missions* (1949) in which he chronicled the evangelistic outreaches of American Methodism from its founding through the end of the nineteenth century:

> Within the period of early American Methodism it is quite impossible to draw a sharp line of differentiation between the general history of the Church and its missionary activities. The Methodist Movement as a whole was missionary in conception, in motivation, and in method. To attempt to screen out from the totality of activities of the founding fathers, and the three generations of their successors during the three-quarters of a century, 1769–1844, a portion to be labeled missionary in contradistinction to the remainder, would be an artificial procedure, producing a result as unsatisfactory as a tale half told.[3]

2. Wigger, *Taking Heaven by Storm*, 98.
3. Barclay, *History of Methodist Missions*, 1:vii.

3

The effectiveness of this evangelistic work can be seen in the consistently increasing numbers of Methodists over the nineteenth century. From 1800 to 1840, Methodists increased their membership thirteenfold from 65,181 to 855,761. By end of the nineteenth century, the MEC was the largest Protestant denomination in the United States with 4,226,327 members.[4] The vast amount of evangelistic work that lay behind this numerical growth offers a rich means of learning what Methodists thought those they evangelized needed to believe and do in order to share most fully in the blessings of God.

The third reason for working with the MEC is its theology. A large number of people drawn from a specific demographic with an active evangelism program would not be effective to demonstrate the broader cultural values of white, middle-class Americans if the church's theology did not make room for those values to become nested in its existing belief structure.

Methodist theology is uniquely marked by the soteriology articulated by John Wesley. Following Wesley's articulation of what he called "the way of salvation," the MEC understood salvation to be an ongoing process of becoming holy. People participated in this process during their lives on earth in preparation for entering into glory. A critical piece of this soteriology is the high value it places on human agency. While it is only by the grace of God that humans are able to become holy, humans still need to respond to that grace by choosing to live a holy life. Those who became Methodist agreed by the grace of God to reform their lives so that they might exhibit the fruits of holiness. Wesley penned the General Rules to provide a brief description of what a life dedicated to holiness would entail for Methodists.

One of the corollaries of this soteriology is that salvation is available both for individuals and for groups of people. Entire nations might be brought into God's saving work as the people in them agreed to turn their lives toward holiness. As a result of this, Methodists sought to share the gospel in a way that individuals might receive the salvation God offered them through Jesus Christ as well as in a way that shaped the national values. This focus on evangelizing both the individual and the nation is expressed most succinctly in Wesley's call for his preachers to "reform the nation, particularly the church, and to spread scriptural holiness over the land."[5] The leadership of the MEC redacted this to suit their work on

---

4. United Methodist General Commission on Archives and History, "United Methodist Membership."

5. Wesley, "Minutes of Several Conversations," 10:845.

the American frontier: "to reform the Continent, and spread scriptural Holiness over these lands."[6]

This dual focus on bringing the individual and the nation to holiness called for forms of evangelism geared toward convicting people of their sin as well as for evangelism aimed at overcoming structures of evil in society. Methodists engaged in both. They organized camp meetings and formed societies in order to encourage individuals on their way to holiness and they met with government officials to advocate the abolition of slavery. They published various devotional books to help individual Methodists learn about and imitate patterns of holiness and they published newspapers that raised the awareness of the readers about current events in politics, economics, and society that needed to be addressed to draw the nation in the direction of holiness. Both of these forms of evangelism would be used in the work of spreading the American gospel.

The mixture of Methodist theology, the MEC's evangelistic fervor, and the cultural values of the white middle class membership became especially influential in the late nineteenth century, beginning in the midst of the Civil War. During this time, the MEC launched several home missions with the express goal of spreading the American gospel among the various peoples within the borders of the United States who were not yet enjoying the quality of life that the Methodist membership was. These peoples included the African Americans recently freed from slavery, Native Americans, Mexicans, white settlers who had moved West, and the immigrants streaming into the Northern cities. The quality of life the Methodists wanted them to experience entailed the following aspects:

1. Participation in a representative government.

2. Industrious patterns of life.

3. Access to the necessities of life, including medicine, food, education, and housing.

4. A stable and virtuous home life.

5. Adherence to the Christian faith.

Specific activities were necessary to evangelize people into this better life:

1. Education. Only educated people were able to take full advantage of the quality of life that the American gospel promised. Education granted people the ability to engage critically and properly in the

6. Coke and Asbury, *A form of discipline*, 3–7.

political structures of a representative republic. It also allowed people to make proper use of the technology that made life easier.

2. Moral training. Without the necessary moral values to guide decision-making, the powers of the new education, technology, and forms of governance were excessively dangerous. Proper values had to be instilled in people to avoid the misuse of these powerful new tools.

3. Facilities. In order for people to live into the white, middle class patterns of life, they needed structures that supported this way of living. Facilities, especially church buildings and schools, that created a space for these patterns of life were therefore essential.

4. Preaching. More than general education, there was the specific need for inspiration and instruction from the Bible. At the heart of the new life was hope for the ultimate victory of God through Jesus Christ. Preachers were essential to this. They were especially important when called upon to disentangle people from what Methodists deemed to be false versions of the Christian faith, such as Catholicism or Mormonism.

5. An emphasis on women. Following the Victorian values concerning women and domesticity that were prevalent among white, middle class Americans during the late nineteenth century, Methodists both deployed women as a means of spreading the American gospel as well as focused on evangelizing women. Women were essential to maintaining the virtue of the family. Without intentional support and training of women, the quality of life developed by other Methodist efforts would quickly fall apart.

In carrying out these activities, the MEC engaged in pure American evangelism as it sought to spread the American gospel to those who did not fully share in the quality of life that the WMCNB Americans did. In doing this, they brought all their innovation, resources, and courage to bear. Their goal was nothing less than a holy nation inhabited by individuals who enjoyed the salvation of God both through the highest possible quality of life in the present and the hope of glory in the future.

An Opening for Evil

Powerful ideas have the capacity to inspire great good. They also have the capacity to prompt unspeakable acts of evil. The ideas of "America" and "the gospel" have been used for both. The situation was no different when these two ideas were brought together in the formation of the American gospel.

As described above, the MEC certainly did not intend to engage in evil as it spread the American gospel through its home missions. Quite the opposite, it hoped to crush evil, ignorance, and want in order to uplift people to share in the fullness of God's blessings in this life and the next. Notwithstanding these best of intentions, conflict and oppression followed in the wake of this work.

The primary reason for these unhappy attendants to pure American evangelism was that the Methodists were not filling a vacuum with their home missions, reaching out to peoples who had no existing moral compass nor means of organizing their lives. Rather, they were bringing their notion of the American gospel to people who already had clear understandings of the values and patterns of life they found meaningful. The Methodists were not unaware of this, but were so certain of the rightness of the American gospel that they often created a zero sum game in which only one of the two ideals would survive. The role of the home missionary was to find where to plant the American gospel effectively among a specific group of people so that its benefits would become obvious and drive people to accept it in place of their existing beliefs. There was no work to acculturate the missionary message to the new people, since the very culture of the WMCNB Americans was the means by which people would know the fullest blessings offered by God.

This approach inevitably led to conflict, especially when Methodist home missionaries interacted with other white, middle class Americans who held alternative views of the content of the American gospel. These conflicts were regional or theological in nature, with both parties agreeing on the supremacy of the United States and the Christian faith, but disagreeing on the values and patterns of life that each demanded. Initially these disagreements were polemical, with each side launching verbal attacks at the other, as seen in the public debates between evangelists from different denominations in the early days of the Republic. If the conflict persisted, it often became political, such as the MEC's support for constitutional amendments to ban alcohol and polygamy in order to overcome the wealthy "wet" white Americans and the Mormons, respectively. If politics failed, then violence ensued. The disagreement between the northern whites and southern whites leading to the Civil War is the classic example of this. The MEC had been wracked by disagreement over the slavery issue for decades, finally splitting over it in 1844. Incapable of splitting amicably on the level of church politics, the MEC and its southern counterpart, the Methodist Episcopal Church, South, became some of the most enthusiastic supporters of the respective war efforts of the Union and Confederacy.

Oppression occurred when Methodist home missions took the shape of paternalism among peoples who inhabited lower social locations, such as the freed slaves, Native Americans, or the Mexicans in the Southwest. The MEC was so certain that receiving God's blessings required people to embody the values and patterns of life followed by WMCNB Americans that home missionaries easily dismissed the views these groups held as to how they might best flourish in relationship to the United States and the church. For example, the MEC adopted a separate-but-equal system for including African Americans in the denomination by creating racially segregated annual conferences. This reinterpreted the call of African Americans to be brought fully into the life of the church in a way that sustained white authority over the denomination. The pressure placed upon Mexican girls by MEC women missionaries to usurp their mothers' role in the home by fixing American food and keeping house as a good Victorian wife disregarded the value of Mexican traditions touching family relations. The insistence by MEC missionaries that Native American children leave their tribes to attend boarding schools dismissed the value of tribal practices for child rearing. Each of these examples points to Methodist refusal to consider the capacity for the people they evangelized to experience God's blessings through any way of life but those most comfortable to white, middle class Americans.

Beyond the stated desire to uplift non-WMCNB people to share in the fullness of God's blessings, there was a negative motive for this paternalism that Methodists shared with other WMCNB Americans of the late nineteenth century: fear. In spite of their unrivaled position in the social location, whites believed that the remarkable civilization they had built in the United States was fragile. In part, this came from seeing how close the nation had come to destruction in the Civil War. Even with the war over, northern whites continued to fear that the freed slaves who received suffrage through the fifteenth amendment (ratified 1870), might ignorantly vote southern interests back into power and so upset the victory won by the Union. Northern whites had similar concerns about recently arrived immigrants being manipulated by pro-Catholic, pro-liquor interests to strike down the Republic when they became eligible to vote.

Fear also came from questioning the capacity of white men to defend white women from the men of other races, including immigrants from Europe who were white in color, but not native to the United States.[7] White American men feared that they had become so refined by living in American culture that they were no longer aggressive enough to contend with the men of other races. The worst possible outcome of this was that white Americans might, using the term coined by Teddy Roosevelt, commit "race suicide" by diluting their bloodlines through white women bearing children to non-whites or immigrants.[8]

Based on these fears of losing American culture by violence, the votes of an ignorant electorate, or the slow genetic extinction of white people, many white, middle class Americans used social control to strengthen their culture. By the use of monitored playgrounds, the restriction of saloons, and the restraint of public celebrations held by non-whites and immigrants, white Americans sought to force these peoples to assimilate into their vision of America.[9] The MEC's pure American evangelism, which forced those they evangelized to abandon their native patterns of life in order to be educated in Methodist facilities, hear Methodist preachers expound on Methodist moral teachings, and follow Methodist notions of home life, falls in line with this practice of social control.

Ironically, then, the MEC undertook pure American evangelism both because of the duty it felt to share the American gospel as the means by which others could experience the full salvation of God—especially the immediate manifestation of that salvation through a high quality of life in this world—and because of the great fear that it would lose its own share in that salvation if it did not enlist those outside of the WMCNB demographic to accept it. The salvation both of those evangelized and of the evangelists were equally tied to the success of this work. If the evangelism was successful, all would share in the prosperity and peace that

---

7. Unlike today, Americans in the late nineteenth century did not define the categories of "race" and "whiteness" by skin pigmentation alone. These ideas also included what we would call "ethnicity" and cultural achievements. I will treat this issue in more detail in chapter 2.

8. Bederman, *Manliness & Civilization*, 13.

9. Rosenzweig, *Eight Hours for What We Will*, chapters 4–6.

God offered. If it was unsuccessful, the values and ways of life that allowed the Methodists to enjoy God's blessings would be swept away by the unconverted.

Lessons and Outline

For the members of the Methodist Episcopal Church, nothing less than the survival of their culture and participation in salvation was at stake in sharing the American gospel. While we may disagree with this soteriology, there are some important lessons to learn from the Methodist undertaking of pure American evangelism.

On the scholarly level, the evangelistic fervor following the Civil War into the early part of the nineteenth century calls into question a common historiographical trajectory concerning American Methodism, which argues that, as Methodists improved their social location, their appetite for mission abated. A similar point is made about the Methodist Episcopal Church ceasing to be concerned with holiness because of its greater wealth and status. The research in this book suggests such interpretations of history need to be revisited. The home missions described herein demonstrate that Methodists were as desirous of spreading holiness in the early twentieth century as ever, even if their definition of holiness was no longer the same as it had been in earlier in their history.

On a denominational level, this history is needed to speak to The United Methodist Church's current struggle to find a clear identity. In my experience of teaching Methodist history, doctrine, and polity, I find most students want to rush back to the Wesleyan Revival in England and the circuit riders in the United States to find solutions for our current quandaries. There is certainly value in learning about these earliest manifestations of Methodism. However, if we allow our teaching—whether in seminaries, confirmation classes, or Sunday schools—to dwell on these periods of history and minimize the less romantic era of the late nineteenth century and early twentieth century, we leave our students ill-equipped to understand how The United Methodist Church organized itself institutionally in an effort to continue spreading holiness. We essentially ask our students to make the shift from revival movement to modern denominational organization without teaching them to use the clutch. The historical account in this paper offers students the best and worst of how a denomination defines itself and engages in mission. This may suggest new ideas and tools to help Methodists claim their missional identity in the present.

Finally, there is a devotional lesson from this history for those who claim to follow the Christian faith in the United States today. If we would judge the Methodists of this earlier era harshly for letting their understanding of the gospel slip to fit their patriotism and social position, then we must likewise judge ourselves on this same basis. How might the current American church fare based on the ways we have deployed the notion of salvation? Do we fashion our view of God's highest blessing for humanity in ways that reflect or even canonize our ideals, values, and preferred patterns of life? What requirements do we implicitly or explicitly add onto or subtract from the gospel call to be saved by grace through faith? Is there an archetypal picture of what a Christian is supposed to be in our minds against which we compare those we evangelize? Or, have we become so fearful of making the mistakes of the past that we have abandoned evangelism and outreach, not realizing that even our inactivity is still an expression of our own cultural biases toward others?

The devotional lesson does not properly belong to the study of history, so it is up to the reader to consider these questions, as well as to develop others, while reading the text. The text itself focuses on presenting how the Methodist Episcopal Church developed its understanding of the American gospel and then engaged in pure American evangelism by propagating this gospel through its home missions.

Chapters one and two sketch the relationship of the Methodist Episcopal Church with American culture from the beginning of the nineteenth century through the Civil War. Chapter one presents the ways American cultural values shaped the evangelistic messages and practices of the earliest circuit riders. Chapter two describes the explicit adoption of an American gospel by the Methodist Episcopal Church as it rallied to support the Union during the Civil War and became convinced of the unique blessings God bestowed on the values and patterns of life that made up what Methodists called Christian American civilization.

Chapters three through five look in turn at the home missions the Methodist Episcopal Church carried among the various peoples in the United States from the end of the Civil War through the early part of the twentieth century. The chapters are organized by region because the Methodists structured their home missions geographically. Chapter three focuses on the work among African Americans and whites in the South. Chapter four considers the Methodist outreach to white settlers, Mormons, Native Americans, and Mexicans found in the West. Chapter five provides an overview of the efforts in the emerging American cities.

The most complex of the home mission fields, this section touches on mission outreach to the various inhabitants of the city as well as advocacy for moral change in the nation that was ignited by the church's experiences with the city.

Finally, chapter seven describes the ultimate end of pure American evangelism. This occurred as the MEC expanded its home missions to include supporting the First World War and became bitterly disappointed with the failure of the war to bring about Christian American civilization throughout the globe.

Taken together, the home missions of the MEC from the Civil War through the First World War demonstrate how the MEC sought to bring God's salvation to earth by propounding an American gospel through pure American evangelism with all the blessings and sins this work unleashed.

1

For God and Liberty

"I WAS BORN SEPTEMBER 1st, 1785, in Amherst County, on James River, in the State of Virginia. My parents were poor. My father was a soldier in the great struggle for liberty, in the Revolutionary war with Great Britain."[1] So begins the *Autobiography of Peter Cartwright* (published 1856). Cartwright focused the bulk of his autobiography on sharing anecdotes about his years as a frontier circuit rider and opining about the state of the Methodist Episcopal Church throughout the fifty years he served the denomination as a presiding elder. By the end of the memoir, it is clear that Cartwright was a "croaker," a term given to those Methodists who harkened back to what they saw as the heroic days of Methodist ministry marked by camp meetings, frontier living, revivalism, highly emotional conversions, an unfettered itinerancy, and a deep piety evidenced in Methodist worship, Methodist family devotions and Methodist morality against what they perceived to be the laxity of Methodists in the middle and late nineteenth century.

Cartwright and his fellow croakers sounded a chorus against the growing respectability of the Methodists and the ways that the members of their beloved denomination seemed bewitched by the innovations that the culture made available for churches to adopt in their daily operations (e.g., the technology and wealth that made the installation of pipe organs possible). Nowhere is this clearer than in Cartwright's resigned-yet-condemning comments about worshiping in 1852 in a Methodist congregation in Boston, which had adopted all the paraphernalia of denominational and cultural success:

1. Cartwright, *Autobiography*, 25.

I shall not attempt a labored argument here against these evils, for I suppose, where these practices have become the order of the day, it would be exceedingly hard to overcome the prejudice in favor of them, though I am sure, from every observation I have been able to make, that their tendencies are to formality, and often engender pride, and destroy the spirituality of Divine worship; it gives precedence to the rich, proud, and fashionable part of our hearers, and unavoidably blocks up the way of the poor; and no stumbling-block should be put in the way of one of these little ones that believe in Christ.[2]

Yet, as Cartwright's opening lines show, he was no stranger to identifying with American culture. Launching his career in the denomination in 1803, Cartwright was quick to appropriate the core values of the American Revolution, particularly the value of "liberty," as sympathetic to the ministry of the Methodist Episcopal Church. In doing this Cartwright, along with the circuit riders of his era, helped lay the foundation for the denomination to merge Methodist values with the cultural values of the United States over the coming years. In many ways, these early circuit riders established the ability of the denomination to undertake the very changes that they bemoaned later.[3]

This introduction of national values into the message of the circuit riders suggests that during the first half of the nineteenth century the Methodist Episcopal Church was already well on its way to developing an American gospel. Additionally, since the Methodist practice of evangelism sought not only to call people to repentance, but to form people's identities around the core values of Methodism, the Methodist Episcopal Church was creating a structure that would be well-suited to pure American evangelism later in the century.

An Evangelistic Organization

Prior to describing how cultural values began to influence the gospel preached by Methodists, it will be helpful to provide a brief overview of organization of the Methodist Episcopal Church since this greatly facilitated the denomination's practice of evangelism.

2. Ibid., 310.

3. Teasdale, "Peter Cartwright and the Emerging National Identity in Antebellum America," 101–13.

American Methodists structured their denomination around a circuit and conference system they adapted from John Wesley's use of itinerant preachers who gathered to meet once a year. In the American adaptation, the "circuits" were geographical areas to which Methodist bishops appointed itinerant preachers known as "circuit riders." On these circuits the preachers rode from one preaching site to the next to encourage the faithfulness of those already organized into Methodist societies, and to evangelize non-Methodists in the hopes either of drawing them into existing societies or of organizing them into new societies. The "conferences" were regular meetings in which the preachers gathered, worked out administrative, doctrinal, and legal issues for the denomination, and received their new appointments from the bishops. The combination of the circuit and the conferences formed a remarkably flexible-yet-centralized system that was ideal for relating to as many people as possible along the expanding American frontier, while also retaining the uniqueness of the Methodist identity through the accountability of regular meetings among the preachers.

This organizational structure uniquely suited evangelism in several ways. First, it all but guaranteed that the circuit riders understood their primary job to be evangelistic. The denomination deployed them to proclaim the gospel and draw people into both the Christian faith and the Methodist Episcopal Church. That the Methodists who participated in this system during the early nineteenth century understood this evangelistic focus can be seen in the language they used to describe their work. In his history of Methodism, for example, Abel Stevens (1868) often used the words "evangelists," "great evangelists," and "missionaries," interchangeably with such words as "itinerant" and "preacher."[4] It is clear that Stevens understood the itinerant Methodist preacher as involved in evangelistic activity as a matter of course. The Methodist preacher was an evangelist and a missionary precisely because he was a Methodist preacher.

The second way this organizational structure supported Methodist evangelism was by providing the Methodist Episcopal Church the freedom to relate to the American people in a relevant and meaningful way while also allowing the denomination to avoid having its identity become defined as nothing more than a reflection of cultural tastes. In doing this, the Methodists avoided the twin pitfalls of either being so ecclesiastically rigid that they could not be relevant and attractive to potential converts or being so concerned about being relevant that they lost sight of their

4. Stevens, *Compendious History of American Methodism*, 52–53.

denominational identity as handed down in their Wesleyan heritage. The Methodist Episcopal Church's intentional desire to craft a careful balance between preserving identity and forging relevant connections to the American people is seen in 1791 when, even before mass camp meetings began to take place in the United States, the Methodists modified their circuit and conference structure by creating a three-tier system of conferences in order to establish both a greater means of promoting revival on the circuits and a means of providing stronger denominational oversight for those circuits.[5]

The first tier was the General Conference at which preachers and bishops would meet every four years to consider the business of the entire denomination. The second tier was composed of multiple annual conferences in which Methodist preachers appointed to circuits within specific geographical regions would gather to conduct business necessary to the Methodists in their region once a year. The third tier was composed of quarterly conferences that met once every three months. Quarterly conferences would draw together all the Methodists on a specific circuit, providing the opportunity for a religious meeting while also guaranteeing the presiding elder, a preacher who oversaw the preachers on many circuits, an opportunity to ensure good Methodist discipline was maintained.[6] This was a masterful move in the Methodist organization that allowed the Methodists a way to relate to the American people at large while also ensuring that Methodist discipline would not be broached.

A third way the Methodist organizational structure supported Methodist evangelism was by emphasizing evangelistic activity on the local level, including through the work of the laity. Since it would take between four and six weeks for circuit riders to visit all the preaching sites on their circuits, Methodists depended on the laity within their societies to maintain Methodist order and instruction. This most frequently happened within the Methodist class, a subset of the Methodist societies. Methodist classes were small groups in which Methodists would gather for the purpose of reflecting on how they had been living in light of their commitment to Christ through the Methodist Episcopal Church. Without a Methodist preacher in attendance at these meetings, it fell to the lay

---

5. Richey, *Methodist Conference in America*, 51–52.

6. Ibid., 50–51. The 1798 *Discipline* reminds presiding elders "to be present, as far as practicable, at all the quarterly meetings: and to call together at each quarterly meeting all the traveling and local preachers, exhorters, stewards, and leaders of the circuit, to hear complaints, and to receive appeals." Coke and Asbury, *Doctrines and Discipline*, Section V, Q. 5.

Methodists to encourage, rebuke and instruct each other in the class. A layperson served as the "class leader" and was given the responsibility of facilitating the class and looking after the spiritual welfare of the members of the class on a day-to-day basis. Various other laypeople filled roles such as "exhorter" and "local preacher" through which they met the need for Methodist worship services and preaching in the absence of the itinerant preacher. As early American Methodist historian John Wigger (1998) explained it, "Seizing on the democratic and leveling impulses of the age, American Methodists offered new roles to zealous lay men and women as local preachers, lay exhorters, class leaders, and a host of other semi-official positions."[7]

The substantial authority that the Methodist Episcopal Church granted to its laity not only empowered the laity to provide leadership within the Methodist societies and classes, but also to engage in what Wigger called "loosely regulated evangelism."[8] Contrary to the more formal evangelistic preaching of ordained clergymen such as Jonathan Edwards and George Whitefield during the First Great Awakening in the United States, Methodism encouraged its adherents, both men and women, to become evangelists who spread the good work of Methodism through personal persuasion and emotional appeal. David Hempton describes this as the Methodist "mobile laity" who undertook evangelistic endeavors on behalf of the denomination before the denomination was able to create official structures to support those endeavors.[9] William Watters (1806), a Methodist minister from Maryland, summed up this view in his memoirs as he recollected his evangelistic activities as a lay member of the MEC in the late eighteenth century. "In one sense," he wrote, "we were all preachers."[10]

THE PRACTICE OF EVANGELISM:
CAMP MEETINGS AND THE AMERICAN PSYCHE

Complementing the Methodist Episcopal Church's evangelistically-oriented organization were specific practices the denomination deployed to great evangelistic effect. The most potent of these practices, and the one

---

7. Wigger, *Taking Heaven by Storm*, 29.

8. Ibid.

9. Hempton, *Methodism: Empire of the Spirit*, 30.

10. Watters, *Short Account*, 18–19.

that came to be seen as the most emblematic of the Methodist ministry during the early nineteenth century, was the camp meeting.

Originating in Scotland, camp meetings first came to the attention of Americans on a large scale at Cane Ridge, Kentucky in 1801.[11] This particular camp meeting represented an innovative means for American evangelists to reach the masses. According to Sydney Ahlstrom (2004), not only evangelists, but whole denominations were quick to make use of this new format for evangelizing: "The organized revival became a major mode of church expansion—in some denominations the major mode. The words evangelist and evangelism took on this connotation."[12] When discussing the Methodists specifically, Ahlstrom noted that one of the factors that led to the rapid numerical growth of the Methodist Episcopal Church in the antebellum era was the Methodists' "appropriation of the camp meetings, which they made an instrument for satisfying both the social and the religious impulses of a scattered, though naturally gregarious people."[13]

Ahlstrom's analysis is worth further consideration. The success of the Methodist camp meeting was because it demonstrated a profound capacity to relate to the real life situations of Americans on the frontier. It was especially effective in meeting the deep need many frontier dwellers felt for relationship. On this point William McLoughlin (1978) explained that camp meetings, "were communal in nature . . . Frontier dwellers had nowhere else to get their children baptized, to pray and sing together, to have weddings performed by ministers, or to give vent to pent-up feelings . . . The fact that people went to great effort to attend camp meetings, traveling miles by wagon over rough roads and camping out when they arrived, indicates a craving for human fellowship and spiritual consolation."[14]

As Ahlstrom put it, "underlying every other conditioning circumstance was the immense loneliness of the frontier farmer's normal life and the exhilaration of participating in so large a social occasion."[15]

In addition to offering solitary inhabitants of the frontier an opportunity to gather, McLoughlin also observed that the camp meetings provided participants with the potential to have powerful religious experiences along with the emotional release that often attended such experiences. Nathan Hatch (1989) suggested that "American camp meetings were

11. Schmidt, *Holy Fairs*, xi–xxix.

12. Ahlstrom, *Religious History of the American People*, 435.

13. Ibid., 437.

14. McLoughlin, *Revivals, Awakenings, and Reform*, 132.

15. Ahlstrom, *Religious History of the American People*, 433.

awesome spectacles indeed, conjuring up feelings of supernatural awe in some."[16] Ahlstrom recorded a lengthy passage from Barton Stone's journal in which Stone named several of the outward manifestations people exhibited when impacted by the presence of God. These included falling like dead, a rapid jerking of the body ("the jerks") sometimes accompanied by a barking or grunting noise, dancing in ecstasy, laughing in rapturous joy, running away from fear of being convicted of sin, and heavenly singing of praise to God.[17] Contrasted with the restraint and discipline settlers had to demonstrate in order to survive in the frontier wilderness, the evangelistic camp meeting provided a safe, indeed a sanctified, setting in which settlers could release pent up anxiety and receive a sense of hope and joy.[18]

These analyses of the camp meetings make it clear that "the churches were made for people rather than the people for churches."[19] Wigger agreed with this assessment, suggesting that after the Revolution "Christianity in America was popularized…by allowing the people to become the final arbiters of religious taste."[20] This analysis points to the same tension between identity and relationship that the Methodist Episcopal Church sought to balance in how it organized its circuit and conference system for evangelistic activity. At times, it undoubtedly became tempting for the denomination to mirror the identities and values of those it evangelized. This move toward the values of the evangelized could decrease the firmness of the denomination's identity, but could potentially increase the denomination's appeal to the evangelized.

While the denomination kept a healthy tension between its identity and its relationship with the American people during the early part of the nineteenth century, keeping this tension required significant internal accountability and unanimity within the denomination. As the nineteenth century moved ahead, this internal fortitude became increasingly more difficult for the denomination to muster. As a result, the organization of

16. Hatch, *Democratization of American Christianity*, 55.

17. Ahlstrom, *Religious History of the American People*, 434.

18. It is worth noting that this is not the universally accepted reading of what these various activities meant. In his autobiography, Peter Cartwright mused on the meaning of the jerks and concluded they were "a judgment sent from God" meant to convict sinners and to prove God's power working in people's lives and bodies whether they desired God to do so or not. Additionally, Cartwright was wary of other extravagant demonstrations in his revivals, such as jumping and barking, realizing that these were sometimes the antics of weak-willed individuals rather than the genuine movement of the Holy Spirit in people's lives. Cartwright, *Autobiography*, 46.

19. McLoughlin, *Revivals, Awakenings, and Reform*, 133.

20. Wigger, *Taking Heaven by Storm*, 11.

the Methodist Episcopal Church and the evangelistic practices of the denomination would change.

Two-Part Evangelism: Conversion and Denominational Loyalty

If the organization and practices of the Methodist Episcopal Church implicitly promoted evangelism through providing excellent means of the denomination retaining a clear understanding of its own identity while it related to the American people, the content of Methodist preaching and teaching was explicitly evangelistic. It was in these verbal connections with the American people that the Methodist preachers clearly laid out the Methodist message and called their hearers to respond to it.

The message of the Methodist preachers aimed primarily at bringing their hearers to a conversion experience. Conversion, for Methodists, was a three-step process, which followed "the Scripture way of salvation" articulated by John Wesley. The first step was the "awakening," in which a person became aware of his or her sins and of the impending judgment that the person would face as a result of those sins. The second step, which was the actual moment of conversion, entailed a renunciation of those sins and a declaration of allegiance to Jesus Christ. The final step was sanctification, which encompassed the lifelong process of the converted individual resisting sin and seeking to live a holy life through engaging in Christian practices.

That facilitating this conversion was a central task of Methodist preachers was made plain by Bishops Francis Asbury and Thomas Coke in the 1798 *Discipline*. Under Section VIII, which covered the duty of preachers, they began by quoting Wesley: "You have nothing to do but to save souls. Therefore spend and be spent in this work. And go always not only to those that want, but to those that want you most. Observe! It is not your business only to preach so many times, and to take care of this or that society: But to save as many souls as you can; to bring as many sinners as you possibly can to repentance, and with all your power to build them up in that holiness, without which they cannot see the Lord."[21]

Offering further observations on these words, the bishops reiterated this: "The salvation of souls should be your only aim. The zeal of the Lord's house should eat you up. O that we could but feel a little of what Jesus felt

21. Coke and Asbury, *Doctrines and Discipline*, 59, 65.

for immortal souls, when he offered up himself on Calvary!" In Section XII, entitled "Of the Matter and Manner of Preaching, and of other public Exercises," the bishops offered practical advice on how to carry out the mandate to save souls through the work of preaching, specifically enumerating the three steps of conversion.

> The preaching of the gospel is of the first importance to the welfare of mankind; and consequently *the mode* of preaching must be of considerable moment. . . . The preacher must: 1. Convince the sinner of his dangerous condition. . . . He must set forth the depth of original sin and shew the sinner how far he is gone from original righteousness; he must describe the vices of the world in their just and most striking colours, and enter into all the sinner's pleas and excuses for sin, and drive him from all his subterfuges and strongholds . . . ; 2. He must set forth the virtue of the *atoning blood.* He must bring the mourner to a *present* Saviour: he must shew the willingness of Christ *this moment* to bless him, and bring a present salvation *home* to his soul. Here he must be indeed *a son of consolation* . . . ; 3. He must, must like a true shepherd, feed the lambs and sheep of Christ [i.e., those already converted]. He must point out to the newly justified the wiles of Satan, and strengthen them if they stagger under unbelief. He must set before them the glorious privileges offered to them in the gospel.[22]

The way American Methodist preachers put their bishops' exhortations into practice in the antebellum era was to preach sermons that pressed people into a crisis situation in which they had to choose between continuing with their sins, recognizing damnation was the result of that, or accepting forgiveness through Christ with its hope of eternal glory. Often a conversion occurred when people who were fully awakened to their perilous spiritual position suddenly and radically repented of their sins and felt the assurance of forgiveness offered through Jesus Christ. Following this crisis conversion, the preachers offered the people a means of engaging in the process of sanctification through inviting them to become members of the Methodist Episcopal Church.

What is critical to recognize here is that denominational commitment was a central feature of Methodist preaching, tied directly to the Methodist understanding of conversion. This denominational commitment took the form of converts first assenting to the discipline of the Methodist Episcopal Church and then joining a Methodist class on

22. Ibid., 85–86.

probation. Methodist classes would meet regularly to provide a place for Methodists to support one another in discerning and living out the moral and ethical implications of their new commitments to Jesus Christ and the Methodist Episcopal Church. While full membership was reserved for those who attended Methodist classes for at least six months and demonstrated a transformed life, the fast-swelling ranks of the Methodists in the early and middle part of the nineteenth century show that once a person became active in a Methodist class, full membership was highly likely to follow.[23] After a period of time on probation, the convert was welcome to join a Methodist society and participate in such events as love feasts, which were Eucharistic gatherings reserved only for Methodists who were members of societies in good standing.

In his autobiography, Peter Cartwright provides an example of how this instruction leading toward denominational commitment operated in his ministry as a frontier circuit rider. In one vignette he recounts how he began preaching in a neighborhood where a large number of the residents were members of the local Presbyterian congregation. The Presbyterian pastor received Cartwright's preaching cordially; however, he made it clear to Cartwright that he did not want any Methodist denominational instruction attached to the more general evangelistic preaching, saying that, "this neighborhood was in the bounds of his congregation; that I was heartily welcome to preach but, said he, you must not attempt to raise any society. I told him that was not our way of doing business; that we seldom ever preached long at any place without trying to raise a society."

True to his word, Cartwright returned to the neighborhood a few weeks later over the objections of the Presbyterian minister. Then, "At the close of my sermon I read our General Rules, and explained our economy. I then told them . . . if there were any there that day that believed the Methodist doctrine, and were willing to conform to the Discipline of the Methodist Church, and desired to join us, let them come and give me their hand, and I would form them into a class and appoint them a leader. There were twenty-seven came forward; thirteen of them were members of this minister's Church."[24]

Clearly, for Cartwright, an allegiance to Christ was best connected with an allegiance to the Methodist Episcopal Church. As such, he felt he could appropriately evangelize even those who were already converted to Christ but who were not Methodist.

23. Kirby et al., *Methodists*, 177–78.
24. Cartwright, *Autobiography*, 90–91.

Nathan Bangs included a similar situation in his biography of Freeborn Garrettson (published 1845), a circuit rider during this era. What is striking in this passage is the amount of energy it required of Garrettson to receive his converts into the Methodist Episcopal fold. Quoting from Garrettson's own journal, Bangs recorded:

> Monday, April 5th, I preached still nearer the sea; and the same convincing power ran through the audience. Some of them thought but little of walking ten or twelve miles to hear the word. I appointed a day to read and explain the rules of our society; and many came together. I preached with great freedom; then explained the nature and design of our society, and desired such of the weeping flock as desired to join, to draw near and open their minds. I examined and admitted about thirty; but being weary, I declined taking any more at that time. Weeping and mourning were heard among the people.[25]

The Methodists had reason to press denominational commitment as a necessary second step for converts. The chaotic religious and intellectual situation in which churches operated in the early United States created an atmosphere in which conversion experiences that occurred under a specific denomination's ministrations were no guarantee of that denomination gaining new members among those converts. Hatch suggested that the combination of anxiety over the possibility that the Republic would fail, the mobility of Americans—which cut them off from any traditions—and the democratic spirit—which allowed for an infinite number of variations of Christianity—meant that "people veered from one church to another [while] religious competitors wrangled unceasingly, traditional clergy and self-appointed preachers foremost in the fray."[26] Left to their own devices, without guidance as to how to join a church community that would help them remain faithful to their newly proclaimed Christian faith, those who became converts under Methodist auspices would likely drift toward one of the established churches, especially the Presbyterians or Congregationalists, or would be ripe for the picking by other frontier evangelists who urged converts to declare loyalty to the various denominations they represented.

Cartwright's autobiography offers a window into how he had to deal with the sheep-stealing tactics of other denominations, specifically of Baptists who sought to woo away those who had experienced conversion

25. Bangs, *Life of the Rev. Freeborn Garrettson*, 81–82

26. Hatch, *Democratization of American Christianity*, 63–64.

under Cartwright's preaching. Following several days of preaching, Cartwright recorded:

> There were twenty-three very clear and sound conversions . . .
> I was young and inexperienced in doctrine, and especially was
> I unacquainted with the proselyting [sic] tricks of those that
> held to exclusive immersion as the mode, and the only mode,
> of baptism. I believe if I had opened the doors of the Church
> then, all of them would have joined the Methodist Church, but I
> thought I would give them time to inform themselves. Accord-
> ingly, I told them that when I came again, I would explain our
> rules and open the doors of the Church, and they could join us
> if they liked our rules and doctrines. In the meantime I left them
> some copies of our Discipline to read. After doing this I started
> on my circuit round, and although the Baptist preachers had left
> this place, without preaching in it for years, yet, in a few days
> after I was gone, there were sent on appointments for the next
> Sabbath three of the Baptist preachers . . . When they were done
> preaching, they opened the way for persons to join the [Baptist]
> Church by giving in their experience.[27]

Cartwright agonized over hearing the Baptist preacher declare his converts fit for membership in the Baptist Church as a result of the conversion experiences they had under his own Methodist preaching. Only quick thinking and subterfuge on the part of Cartwright allowed him to reclaim his converts for Methodist membership before they underwent full immersion baptism.

Garrettson noted in his journal that he not only had to contend with those who desired to sway his converts away from Methodism,[28] but with state and local officials who were members of more established denominations using their authority to restrict his preaching.

> Monday, July 20th, . . . After sermon, being much spent, I with-
> drew. Shortly after a person came to me and said "two men
> wanted to see me." I told him to desire them to walk up, thinking
> they were persons in distress, and wanted instruction; but when
> I saw them I discovered wickedness in their very looks. One of

27. Cartwright, *Autobiography*, 55–56.

28. Immediately following the acceptance of thirty new Methodists, Garrettson recorded that "a man started from his seat, saying 'Sir it is a shame for you to go on as you do; why do you think you can make us believe your doctrine is true?'" Bangs, *Life of Freeborn Garretson*, 82. In a separate episode, Garrettson reported that his "work was greatly hindered by the Baptists, who came among the people, drew off a few, and set others to disputing about the decrees, and their method of baptizing." Ibid., 90.

them was a magistrate, and he was a Churchman; the other was
a Presbyterian, and he was a disputant. The magistrate brought
him out in order to confute me in the points of religion: and
then his intention was to send me to prison.[29]

Fortunately for Garrettson, he was able to overcome the religious argumentation of the Presbyterian and, gaining the sympathy of the sheriff sent to arrest him, allowed to proceed unmolested to his next preaching appointment.

By the mid-nineteenth century, the practice of early Methodist preachers instructing their converts in how to become members of Methodist classes was codified in a genre of books known as convert's guides.[30] These guides, often published by annual conferences, offered practical advice on how converts could remain faithful to their new allegiance to Christ through participating in Methodist spiritual practices. These practices, of course, were much easier to undertake if the convert would join the Methodist Episcopal Church and so be surrounded by like-minded individuals.

A representative example of these guides is *The Convert's Counsellor Respecting His Church Relations*, published in 1856 by the Methodist Book Concern. The book's subtitle spoke directly to the purpose of bringing those who had experienced conversion under Methodist ministry to membership in the Methodist Episcopal Church: *Popular Objections to Methodism Considered and Answered: with Reasons Why Methodist Converts Should Join a Methodist Church*. The text begins by commenting on how vulnerable the new convert is to advice about joining churches, especially when that advice is prejudiced against Methodism:

> I address you as recently converted, but as undecided concerning your church relations. You have been led to Christ, I will presume, through the instrumentality of Methodism. If left to your own unbiased judgment, you would unhesitatingly unite with the Methodist church. But your associates, relatives, or personal friends are hostile to Methodism. Perhaps you reside in a community where Methodism is crushed down and trodden under foot by proud, influential, sectarian men. False views of Methodism, the offsprings of a prejudice which is willingly ignorant of the true character and spirit, are whispered in your ears. So much is said to you, by persons you have ever esteemed, that your mind is perplexed and unsettled. You hesitate and

29. Ibid., 94.
30. Kirby et al., *Methodists*, 179.

wait. You do not feel entirely free to relinquish Methodism. You are too deeply indebted to it to turn from it readily; yet in consequence to what has been said to you by others, your mind is not satisfied with respect to your duty to enter into church relation with it. Like a weaver's shuttle, you are tossed to and fro, and amid these perplexities, you are tempted to join no church at all.[31]

After overcoming this temptation to avoid any sort of denominational membership, the text then seeks to woo converts to Methodism by suggesting that Methodism alone would offer converts true understanding and support in working through their conversion experience. This contrasts to other denominations, which would look askance at having such an experience at all, and which might even put converts in danger of losing their conversion experience altogether.

> I hail you, dear reader, as a *child of Methodism*…having been converted to Christ through Methodist instrumentalities, *you* are a child of Methodism! God sent Methodism to you, as he sent Ananias to Saul of Tarsus, that it might become your spiritual parent. It found you a poor unawakened sinner. It alarmed you, persuaded you, led you to the cross, taught you how to believe, encouraged your first acts of trust, and led you, with the solicitude of a mother, through the earliest steps of your experience in the way of faith. Under God, you owe your spiritual life to it. . . . Remember, that being a child of Methodism, you will be but an *adopted child* in any other branch of the Christian church. You will feel this fact painfully, if you leave your true home. So long as you are the object of a zealous proselytism, the confidence and sympathy of those who seek to win you to their ranks will appear strong and deep. But when you have once crossed the Rubicon, and stand among them as a candidate for church membership, a change will be visible in the spirit of your new friends. Having lured you from Methodism, they will seek to divest you of every shred of the Methodistic garment, and to shape the manifestations of your experience in their own denominational mold. They will scrutinize your conversion, and challenge its genuineness, because it was obtained among the Methodists. It will be well if they do not lead you to cast it aside as mere excitement and leave you to grope through mist and unbelief after new light, so that, after all, you may date your new

---

31. Wise, *Convert's Counsellor*, 12–13.

birth from the period of your connection with them, and thus lose your sense of obligation to your true spiritual parent.[32]

As this guide points out, one of the deep concerns Methodists had for their new converts was that they would be wracked with doubts concerning the authenticity of their conversion experience. A Methodist society was critical in helping them claim their experience absolutely. According to David Hempton (2005), "the spiritual lives of most members of Methodist societies began with keenly remembered conversion experiences. Indeed, the conversion narrative is a common Methodist genre in which is stressed the drama of the second birth as a means of escaping a world of sin and licentiousness, and of entering a world of faith and godly discipline . . . Once the decision is made, there are the customary doubts and episodes of self-examination. It is at this point that the Methodist machinery of class meetings and prayer groups offers crucial community support."[33]

DENOMINATIONAL LOYALTY AND AMERICAN IDENTITY

Undoubtedly, Garrettson, Cartwright, and the authors of the various convert's guides genuinely believed Methodism offered the most effective doctrines, polity, and practices for supporting converts in their new lives as Christians. However, their denominationalism also had a pragmatic edge. In the free marketplace of American religion, if the agents of any particular denomination could not convince a sizable portion of the American people to accept and commit to their vision of the Christian church, then their denomination was doomed to obscurity and, potentially, to disappear forever. It was precisely the Methodist insistence on connecting converts to the Methodist Episcopal Church that allowed for the Methodist Episcopal Church to become the largest Protestant denomination in the United States by the end of the nineteenth century.

At the same time, it was the Methodist effort to be relevant to American culture as circuit riders called for denominational loyalty that led Methodists to become progressively more wedded to American cultural values. The very practice of competing in the religious marketplace demonstrated that Methodists, if only implicitly, were already taking marching orders from American values. Their emphasis on accruing loyal adherents

32. Ibid., 23–24, 26–30.
33. Hempton, *Empire of the Spirit*, 61–62.

who accepted Methodism to the exclusion of all other denominations had strong sympathies with the work of merchants who hoped to win over customers that would remain loyal to only their particular products. Wigger explained this point in observing that one of the central reasons Methodists were so successful in convincing Americans to join the Methodist Episcopal Church was that they were "'packaging' American Methodism to suit the tastes and demands of a new kind of consumer."[34] Specifically, American Methodism was attractive to the middling and artisan classes because it was "enthusiastic, individualistic, entrepreneurial, and lay-oriented,"[35] all of which were traits that could be just as easily applied to the marketplace for pecuniary rewards as they could to organizing a church. This was a significant attraction for Americans who, now free from the hierarchical system that would have kept them in a specific socio-economic bracket regardless of their personal industry, intelligence or talents, were electrified with "an unprecedented sense of entrepreneurial energy."[36]

Wigger stated that Methodists also connected with American aspirations through their lay leadership and their morality. The people Methodist preachers often tapped to become the class leaders, those individuals who held direct authority over the Methodist laity during the times in between the visits of itinerant preachers, "were the more successful members of their peer groups, both in terms of worldly accomplishments and spiritual progress." This sent the clear message that the values that led to wealth and status were of equal importance to the Methodists as the values leading to holiness of life—or rather, that these two sets of values were essentially the same. The morality of the Methodists made this same point. "The church's *Discipline* condemned indebtedness, intemperate drinking, swearing, ostentatious dress, gossiping, discord, gluttony, gambling, bribery, and taking 'treats' when voting." While these moral dictates certainly fit with the Methodist identity, they also proclaimed a message that "would make sense" to the American striving to do well financially for himself and his family through self-discipline and diligence.[37] More than that, the Methodist practices could help him attain the financial success he sought. As a result, "Methodism simply appealed to and nurtured the kinds of people likely to do well in the fluid social environment of the time. It did so by encouraging individual initiative, self-government, optimism, and even

34. Wigger, *Taking Heaven by Storm*, 26.
35. Ibid., 7.
36. Ibid., 8.
37. Ibid., 98.

geographic mobility . . . In short, Methodism accepted and encouraged the new values necessary for 'improvement in a market-driven society."[38]

In addition to appealing to the desire of Americans to improve their social and economic stations, the Methodists of this time also felt comfortable weaving national values together with their call to conversion. As noted at the beginning, Peter Cartwright explicitly engaged patriotic themes and values to buttress his preaching. He was specifically fond of the value of liberty. In Cartwright's thinking, becoming a Methodist epitomized the liberty America had purchased in the Revolution. When a person became a Methodist, that person declared his or her personal liberty to worship according to his or her conscience rather than the person worshipping in a specific church because of familial, societal or other external forces compelling the person to do so.

Cartwright raised this point on numerous occasions when dealing with preachers from other denominations that resisted the influence of the Methodists. In the case of the Presbyterian minister mentioned above who forbade him from forming a Methodist society, Cartwright recorded that he told the minister, "the people were a free people and lived in a free country, and must and ought to be allowed to do as they pleased." Later, speaking directly to the people of the neighborhood, Cartwright prefaced his invitation to join the Methodist Episcopal Church by expressing a similar sentiment, "I then told them my father had fought in the Revolution to gain our freedom and liberty of conscience; that I felt that my Presbyterian brother had no bill of sale on the people."[39]

Effectively, then, in its organization, practices, and preached message, Methodism was already forming an American gospel even as it emphasized conversion and denominational loyalty as its primary goals. The fact that so many Methodists drew close connections between the Methodist understanding of a holy life with the life of a good citizen, a hard worker, and an economically-successful individual, suggests that the denomination's strategies for retaining an identity that had some independence from the American culture would soon fail. Conferences of preachers and calls to denominational loyalty can only maintain a distinct identity for a church so long as the preachers going to the conferences and the existing members of the denomination do not accept parity between national values and the values handed down by the denominational heritage. Given that even such ardent croakers as Peter Cartwright showed a penchant

---

38. Ibid., 12.
39. Cartwright, *Autobiography of Peter Cartwright*, 90–91.

for baptizing national values, it was all but certain that those Methodist leaders who were glad to adopt the innovations made available by wealth and higher social status would do the same. The arrival of the Civil War would provide many opportunities for the Methodist Episcopal Church to do just this.

2

Forging an American Gospel

To CONSTRUCT AN AMERICAN gospel by acculturating the Christian faith to American cultural values is one thing; mobilizing the evangelistic forces of the Methodist Episcopal Church around that American gospel is another. For the latter to happen the Methodist Episcopal Church needed to be convinced of the holiness of the American culture itself. Initially, this would have been impossible, since the Methodist understanding of holiness called for the reformation of people's manners according to the General Rules propounded by John Wesley.[1] Such a defined view of holiness often led to a poor fit between Methodists and mainstream culture because the General Rules overtly challenged many socially acceptable practices, including charging usury, reading books or singing songs that did not expressly glorify God, wearing costly apparel, self-indulgence, speaking evil of others, and drunkenness.[2]

However, as the decades passed, the members of the MEC began to reconsider whether their countercultural values were necessary to promote a life of holiness. This took place for two reasons. First, the Civil War created an explicit and popular connection between the MEC and American cultural values as the denomination threw its full support behind the

---

1. The General Rules, which continue to be printed in the *Book of Discipline* of several of the Methodist denominations today, state the basic requirements that John Wesley laid out for those who desired to be Methodists. The Methodists were "to continue to evidence their desire for salvation First by doing no harm, by avoiding evil of every kind . . . Secondly: by doing good; by being in every kind merciful after their power; as they have opportunity, doing good of every possible sort, and, as far as possible, to all men . . . Thirdly: by attending upon the ordinances of God."

2. All of these examples come directly from the General Rules.

Union war effort. Second, as the Civil War came to a close the Methodists became aware of the increasing quality of life in the United States contrasted to the rest of the world. Methodists came to believe that this quality of life was a result of Americans constructing a Christian civilization that reflected the character of God's Kingdom. The combination of these two items led the Methodists to believe that the patterns of life and the values related to American culture, particularly white, middle class, native born, northern culture, were the God-given means for participating in the fullness of salvation. As a result of this, Methodists began to propagate these cultural values by wedding the American gospel to their evangelistic activities.

METHODIST UNIONISTS

During his presidency, Ulysses S. Grant is said to have remarked "that there were three great parties in the United States: the Republican, the Democratic, and the Methodist Church."[3] It is likely his observation came from seeing how the Methodists rallied in huge numbers to aid the cause of the Union during the Civil War. At the same time the Methodist Episcopal Church was making its mark on the Union, however, the American culture as defined by the Union made a significant imprint on the Methodist Episcopal Church. Indeed, what made the denomination so capable of wielding the influence that it did during the Civil War was the willingness of its leaders and laity alike to adopt the Union agenda. Such an adoption earned the admiration and gratitude of Union leaders. It also had significant implications for the evangelistic ministry of the denomination by explicitly connecting the church to a specific ideal of the United States.

Those who were a part of the MEC had a deeply personal reason for claiming the Union's interests as their own. From its inception until 1844, the MEC had included members from throughout the United States, including in the southern states. A byproduct of the Methodists being open to the culture in which they were set was that the Methodists in the various regions of the United States began to hold to the respective values of those regions. This meant that as the regions began to develop different value systems from each other, the Methodists in these regions followed suit. Most potently, the same conflict over slavery that was occurring within

3. Carwardine, "Methodists, Politics, and the Coming of the American Civil War," 309.

the American populace as a whole during the early and mid-nineteenth century was mirrored in the church.

At the General Conference of the MEC in 1844, delegates clashed over the fact that one of the bishops had become the owner of slaves by marriage and inheritance. The northern delegates demanded the bishop recuse himself until he was disentangled from slave ownership. The southern delegates countered that doing so would send a signal to Methodists in the South that the church did not honor southern values. The result was a tentatively agreed upon Plan of Separation that would allow the annual conferences in the southern states to withdraw amicably from the MEC and form the Methodist Episcopal Church, South (MECS) as a separate denomination. The plan was approved by the delegates.

Over the ensuing four years, however, the consensus surrounding the plan dissipated. The northern conferences, believing that they needed to ratify the plan for it to be legitimate, roundly defeated it. The southern conferences, believing that the plan empowered them to form the MECS independently of northern approval, proceeded to do this, holding their inaugural General Conference in 1846. The result of this was that, when the MEC held its next scheduled General Conference in 1848, it repudiated the Plan of Separation, refused to admit emissaries from the MECS, and claimed that those conferences that had formed the MECS to be secessionists. This inflammatory rhetoric along with what the southerners perceived to be a reneging of support for the creation of the MECS generated significant ill-will between the Methodists in the North and the South.

The animosity between the Methodists grew further when the MEC refused to honor stipulations in the Plan of Separation for splitting denominational funds with the new MECS. This resulted in two lawsuits being brought against the MEC by the MECS. One of these eventually made its way to the Supreme Court, which ruled in favor of the MECS in 1854. This legal loss along with the perceived secession of the southern conferences created a strong sentiment against the MECS among the remaining members of MEC, laying a sturdy foundation for the support of the Union when the war started.

In addition to this background, the MEC found commonality with the moral values held by the Union. The Union was anti-slavery, anti-secession, and pro-liberty. These values fit well with Methodist teachings on holiness, making it easy for the Methodists to baptize the Union. Likewise, any alternative set of values, particularly a set that allowed for slaveholding and secession, was something the Methodists agreed needed to be over-come at any cost. Just as the Methodists had counseled their converts not to abandon the Methodist fold for other denominations that would wreck their conversion experiences, so Methodists could also claim during and after the Civil War that Americans should not abandon the Northern vi-sion of the United States lest *both* their denominational and national iden-tities falter. The interests of the Union became the interests of the MEC.

With the church's own bitter memories of dealing with the South and the common morality between the MEC and the Union, it is little surprise the MEC turned to its powerful evangelistic organization to support the Union once the Civil War began. As historian James May (1964) stated, "The nature of its [the Methodist Episcopal Church's] organization, the distribution of its membership, the vigor of its press, and the aggressive personal leadership of its bishops served the nation as well as the church."[4]

The first place this pro-Union evangelism made its appearance was in the content of the sermons from the MEC preachers to existing Method-ists, calling them to commit substantial resources to support the Union. This in-house evangelism was highly effective. According to Abel Stevens (1868) the Methodist laity enthusiastically complied with the urgings of their preachers having "not...a momentary doubt of the issue of the struggle, or of the destiny of the country."[5]

This enthusiasm manifested itself as members gave generously of both their lives and funds to support the Union. They gave their lives through massive numbers of Methodists joining the Union Army. William Warren Sweet (1933) recorded that approximately fifteen percent of the Union Army was Methodist,[6] and that the Methodist Episcopal Church lost 61,188 members to death in battle. They gave their money by opening their pocketbooks as never before in the history of the denomination. This giving first and foremost benefitted the YMCA and the Sanitary Com-mission, both of which cared for Union soldiers. However, Methodists did not just give to war-related causes. Between the years 1860 and 1865 Methodists substantially increased their annual giving to denominational foreign missions work ($340,000 more given in 1865 than 1860), to the American Bible Society ($61,000 more given in 1865 than 1860), and to

4. May, "War Years," 216.

5. Stevens, *Compendious History of American Methodism*, 574.

6. May disputed this, suggesting that at most 125,000 Methodists served as soldiers throughout the course of the war, which would be far less than fifteen percent of the total Union Army. May, "War Years," 226.

the American Tract Society ($6,000 more given in 1865 than 1860).[7] It is notable that all of the causes that received these significant increases in contributions were evangelism-related. Methodists seemed to equate the advance of their faith and the advance of the Union army, giving generously to support both.

The capacity of the Methodist Episcopal Church membership to sustain this level of commitment to the Union during the war can be traced to the Methodist practice of evangelism throughout the early and mid nineteenth century. As previously described, this evangelism produced a large number of converts among middling Americans who displayed a high level of denominational loyalty as a result of Methodist evangelism connecting the message of salvation to the importance of joining the Methodist Episcopal Church. As such, when the denominational leaders exhorted their members to adopt the Union cause as their own in the name of the church, these loyal American Methodists provided a vast resource that willingly yielded enormous sums of money and manpower. This was a lesson that the leaders of the denomination quickly grasped, and it gave them new, highly optimistic visions of how they might position the denomination after the conclusion of the war to expand the evangelistic outreach of the Methodist Episcopal Church. In this way, the church was poised to launch the home missions through which it would engage in pure American evangelism during the late nineteenth century.

It was not only the lay members of the Methodist Episcopal Church who joined in the war effort under the promptings of Methodist evangelism. In addition to advocating that their members go to war as soldiers in the Union Army,[8] Methodist preachers engaged in a new practice of evangelism by heading to the Union camps with a total of 510 Methodist preachers commissioned as chaplains in the Union Army. Their duties included organizing evangelistic services and revivals within the camps, distributing Bibles and tracts on moral living to the troops, reporting to the commanders on the morality of the soldiers, and often raising funds to purchase necessities for the camps.[9] In addition to chaplains, 458 Methodist preachers served in the United States Christian Commission, an evangelical relief agency primarily overseen by the YMCA, which dispatched preachers for six-week stints in the Union camps to provide for the spiritual

---

7. Sweet, *Methodism in American History*, 287–97.

8. May, "War Years," 226.

9. Ibid., 220–22.

and physical needs of the soldiers.[10] These activities brought Methodist evangelism under the banner of national values, since the clergy engaged in evangelistic activities on behalf of the Union Army rather than as circuit riders who were American, but who itinerated and preached only at the behest of the Methodist Episcopal Church.

The MEC also rallied its denominational press behind the Union cause. Traditionally used to remind Methodists of their unique Wesleyan soteriology and to discuss how to be faithful to that soteriology in the course of daily life, the Methodist publications willingly added to their job descriptions the need to denounce the South and to laud President Abraham Lincoln. The denomination was intentional in this with the delegates of the General Conference ousting editors of the denomination's periodicals who printed more conciliatory articles concerning the South and replacing them with individuals who took an adamantly pro-Union, anti-Confederacy stance. In claiming this more strident, pro-Union message the denomination put in place critical pieces of what I am terming the American gospel and pure American evangelism by espousing a specific vision of the American nation over against other visions. As James May, who studied Methodist involvement in the Civil War extensively, explained, "the victory of Northern arms would vindicate Northern principles and validate the North's assumption of cultural superiority. Since Methodism was believed to carry with it the highest civilization of all times, its mission to the South was now clearly revealed, and only the defects of Southern character stood in the way of the rejuvenation of the vanquished territory."[11]

While this vision was sectional in nature, the way the Methodists actively promoted their denominational identity along with the Union identity opened the door for far deeper connections between the Methodist Episcopal Church and American culture following the war. The specific tenets of the American gospel were taking shape, as was the evangelistic practice that would spread that gospel later in the nineteenth century.

The most explicit connection between the nation and the MEC during the Civil War was in the bishops' cultivating close ties with Union leaders, including Bishop Matthew Simpson's friendship with President Abraham Lincoln and Bishop Edward R. Ames' friendship with Secretary of War Edwin M. Stanton.[12] May observed that "Methodists were

10. Ibid., 222; and Deverell, "Church and State Issues in the Period of the Civil War," 12.

11. May, "War Years," 220.

12. Norwood, Story of American Methodism, 243–44.

especially proud of the political leadership of Matthew Simpson, who more than any of the wartime bishops symbolized the Methodist struggle for status. Simpson believed in the ultimate triumph of Christianity and in the peculiar destiny of the American nation. He also believed in the greatness of the Methodist Episcopal Church and was jealous of its claim to distinction."[13]

Nor was Simpson disappointed in his desire for distinction. Lincoln gratefully acknowledged the Methodists in his communiqué to the 1864 Methodist Episcopal General Conference. Lincoln wrote: "Nobly sustained, as the Government is, by all the churches, I would utter nothing which might in the least appear invidious against any. Yet, without this, it may fairly be said that the Methodist Episcopal Church, not less devoted than the best, is by its greatest numbers the most important of all...the Methodist Church sends more soldiers to the field, more nurses to the hospital, and more prayers to Heaven than any."[14]

While Lincoln's message certainly conveyed the importance of the Methodist Episcopal Church to the Union, it also made clear the extent to which (1) Lincoln did not claim a Methodist identity for the Union, and (2) leaders of the denomination accepted the Union identity as nearly synonymous with their Methodist identity. To be a good Methodist was to be a loyal citizen of the Union dedicated to the advancement of the Union's vision of the United States against any rival visions.

In sum, the Civil War was an essential catalyst in the MEC articulating an explicit American gospel through the Union providing the church with clear values that they could propound over and against competing values. It also mobilized the church in new ways that would allow it to undertake the large scale home missions through which it would call people to accept that American gospel. More than that, it created an excitement about what the church might be able to accomplish through these new evangelistic apparatuses.

Even with all this, more than the Methodist Episcopal Church's unwavering support of the Union was needed for the denomination to practice pure American evangelism. Evangelism requires not only challenging alternate beliefs or calling people to live by certain values, but a sense of the ultimate. It was not enough to reform how people lived, the church had to provide hope that this new life was a means of participating in

13. May, "War Years," 228.

14. Lapsley, *Writings of Abraham Lincoln*, 138.

salvation. It was the rising notion of Christian American civilization that would provide this in the years following the Civil War.

A Christian American Civilization

By the end of the nineteenth century, it was common for WMCNB Americans who lived north of the Mason-Dixon Line to think of themselves as having the pre-eminent civilization in the world. The overarching reason for this was that the quality of life in the United States was improving substantially for those within their demographic. Peace and prosperity seemed to be the order of the day in a time when Europe was in political and economic turmoil and the rest of the world was far behind in its development. One of the favorite pastimes of Americans during this era was musing over what made the United States so remarkable. I will focus on three reasons that featured prominently in these considerations: technology, race, and the political/economic structure of the United States.

Technology provided the capacity for the American civilization to demonstrate its greatness by accomplishing feats thought impossible in most other parts of the world, such as allowing people miles apart to speak to one another through the telephone or allowing people in New York and Chicago to visit one another by riding only a few hours on a train. Americans were deeply impressed with the power of their civilization's technological capacities and delighted in exhibiting what they could do. As an example of this, historian David Nye (1990) pointed to the world's fairs, which generated a great deal of hope among Americans as to the possibilities for the future.[15]

Technology also provided a means for the United States to become an economic powerhouse by vastly increasing the nation's prosperity. While the United States ranked fourth in manufacturing output in the world in 1860, by 1894 the nation's manufacturing nearly equaled that of Great Britain, France and Germany combined. According to technology historian John Kasson (1976), "celebrating the stupendous achievements of America's 'triumphant democracy,' the steel magnate and Scottish immigrant Andrew Carnegie thumbed his nose at European rivals, 'The old nations of the earth creep on at a snail's pace; the Republic thunders past with the rush of the express.'"[16]

---

15. Nye, *Electrifying America*, 34–35.
16. Kasson, *Civilizing the Machine*, 183.

While Carnegie gloated over American economic superiority in reference to American technological capacities, other Americans saw the technology their nation wielded as a great responsibility. With it, Americans could carry their own orderly civilization to the rest of the world with ease and effectiveness. William Jennings Bryan was a chief proponent of this. He exhorted college graduates on this topic at both Nebraska State University and Illinois College by declaring,

> And what an opportunity for service this age presents! If I had my choice of all the ages in which to live, I would choose the present above all others. The ocean steamer and the railway train bring all the corners of the earth close together, while the telegraph—wire and wireless—gives wings to the news and makes the events each day known in every land during the following night. The printing press has popularized knowledge and made it possible for each one who desires it to possess a key to the libraries of the world. Invention has multiplied the strength of the human arm and brought within reach of the masses comforts which, until recently, even wealth could not buy. The word "neighborhood" no longer describes a community; that "all ye are brethren" can be more readily comprehended than ever before. It is easier for one to distribute blessings to the world today than it was a few centuries ago to be helpful to the residents of a single valley. A good example set anywhere can be seen everywhere, so intimate has become the relation between man and man.[17]

Historian James H. Moorhead (1999) explained this enthusiasm over American technology was buttressed by an increasing belief among American evangelicals in the coming millennial reign of God. Technology was what Christian Americans could use to transform the world to be the image of the Kingdom of God.

> Increasingly, millennialists enumerated more sophisticated technology, greater prosperity, and the flourishing of the arts and sciences as signs of the millennium. Just as the polity of the Republic bore an intimate relationship to evangelicalism, so, too, other secular advances went hand in hand with the triumph of Christianity. Thus . . . a writer for a Methodist women's magazine had drawn . . . explicitly millennial conclusions from telegraphic communication: "This noble invention is to be the means of extending civilization, republicanism, and Christianity

17. Bryan, *Speeches of William Jennings Bryan*, 2:309–10.

over the earth . . . Then shall come to pass the millennium." . . .
Improvements in printing had permitted the inundation of the
nation with religious tracts and newspapers; the steamboat and
the merchant opened the doors of foreign lands to the missionary; and affluence made possible the host of Christian colleges
from which evangelical influences emanated.[18]

So it was that the emerging power of American technology was
bound up to American culture as well as to transcendent aspirations to
achieve God's Kingdom "on earth as it is in Heaven." Not surprisingly,
this potent mixture spurred evangelism as those who were native to the
American culture felt a deep desire to spread their exceptional civilization
to those without such technological power at their disposal. Technology
was both a hallmark of the superiority of American civilization and also
the primary means of conveying that civilization to others.

Race served as a second hallmark of Christian American civilization.
During the late nineteenth century and early twentieth century scientific racism came into its heyday, as Americans sought an objective way
to understand the differences that existed among the various races they
encountered at home and abroad. These races included not only African
Americans, who became even more diffuse in American culture after the
liberation of the slaves, but the races of the various peoples immigrating to
the United States, including those from China, Japan, Mexico, and Central
and Southern Europe. Invariably, the scientific studies conducted on these
races proved the superiority of the white American "race" over all others.

One of the critical reasons white Americans concluded their race was
superior to those in other nations was because of their penchant to mix
biology and cultural achievements. As historian Gail Bederman (1995)
explained, "Lacking the conceptual framework to differentiate between
physical morphology and cultural traits, educated Victorians subsumed
both in a gestalt which they termed 'race.'"[19]

White Americans argued that they were the superior race biologi-
cally because they represented the ultimate mixture of the bloodlines of
the greatest civilizations on earth. Notably, all of these civilizations were
European. G. Stanley Hall (1844–1924), a professor of pedagogy and
psychology who focused his work on the development of white American males, "believed their very racial mix made it possible for them to
achieve the most complete manhood ever evolved—to become, in fact,

18. Moorhead, *World without End*, 9–10.
19. Bederman, *Manliness & Civilization*, 29.

the 'super-men' who could lead the nation to a millennial future."[20] Believing that both cultures and humans evolved to become more advanced over time, Hall deployed the notion of race recapitulation to explain how American males could revisit each successively more evolved human culture, all of which were bred into their biological natures. Having unlocked the best from each of these civilizations, American men were equipped to surpass them all as they became the next link to an even higher form of human and cultural evolution. That this idea found traction with the larger public is clear from a speech entitled "America's Mission" delivered by William Jennings Bryan. In it he stated baldly, "Great has been the Greek, the Latin, the Slav, the Celt, the Teuton and the Anglo-Saxon, but greater than any of these is the American, in whom are blended the virtues of them all . . . The American people can aspire to a grander destiny than has opened before any other race."[21]

These grand notions about the greatness of white Americans notwithstanding, it is also possible to read these ideas and detect a hint of fear in the dominant white, middle-class Northern breast. As already described in the introduction, this demographic became convinced that, powerful as they were, the less civilized races might overthrow them. Moorhead explained this fear thusly:

> Anglo-Saxonism or Teutonism became an intellectually fashionable ideology. Scholars stressed the superiority of the people and institutions of Germanic and British origins, associated the strength of America with that heritage, and buttressed the argument with appeals to pseudo-Darwinian racialist theories of the survival of the fittest. At first glance a smug assertion of the supremacy of old-line Protestant Americans, the new racialism was in fact the desperate cry of the people who feared that they were about to lose control of their country and were determined to preserve "race purity" at all costs. It signified a massive loss of confidence in the ability of the nation to assimilate the foreign born.[22]

As a result, Moorhead opined, the subsequent move to preserve and expand American civilization might be seen in part as a rearguard action. The white, middle-class, Northern Protestants were battling to keep the

---

20. Ibid., 105.
21. Bryan, *Speeches of William Jennings Bryan*, 15.
22. Moorhead, *World without End*, 82.

cultural hegemony they felt was theirs by right lest the various other races present in the United States decimate Christian American civilization.

In addition to the technology Americans wielded and their claimed racial superiority, Americans pointed to how their political and economic structures allowed for them to enjoy their peaceful and prosperous way of life. Bryan specifically lauded the wonders of a republican government and the ways in which it protected and encouraged human rights. While acknowledging that the nation might occasionally fail in its obligation to maintain the rights of all its citizens, he protested that there was no better form of government in the world to seek the equal rights of all.[23] Historian Matthew Frye Jacobson (2000) claimed that it was less the American form of government than the American capacity to produce and consume varied industrial goods that was the cause of American prosperity.[24]

More than just prosperity, by the late nineteenth century, many American Protestants began to understand the political and economic structures of the United States to be millennial, that is, to be indicative of the Kingdom of God.[25] As an example of this, Moorhead noted that following the Civil War the popular view of heaven began to look like an extension of WMCNB, northern American culture. To support this claim he cited popular fiction author Elizabeth Stuart Phelps, who sold over 100,000 copies of her novels about heaven during the late nineteenth century. He explained that in these novels, "she advanced the notion of heaven as an idealized New England projected in the sky . . . Persons live in pleasant middle-class homes . . . People continue the employments which they began on earth. Museums, universities, and concerts provide cultural improvement . . . Never does God intrude to mar the earth-like quality of heaven, and Jesus moves about unobtrusively, sometimes unrecognized by the inhabitants."[26]

The result of this was to give evangelistic imperative to the spreading of American civilization, not only because it was superior to every other civilization, but because it was the means of bringing heaven to earth. As historian Robert Handy (1984) stated, "however and whenever the kingdom was to come, for many Protestants the millennial expectancy provided a goal for civilization as well as for religion; it provided a religious coloration to their thought about civil society. For them, the religious

23. Bryan, *Speeches of William Jennings Bryan*, 330–34.

24. Jacobson, *Barbarian Virtues*, 16–17.

25. Handy, *Christian America*, 29–31.

26. Moorhead, *World without End*, 59–60.

quest and the civil process, though clearly distinct, moved toward the same happy climax."[27] Consequently, all the successes of American civilization offered glimpses of both human and divine activity.

Although non-white and/or non-American races could not hope to attain the biological traits of the American race, it was possible for other races to emulate the political and economic patterns of WMCNB Americans. Educating these other races to do this was to help them participate in Christian American civilization. Not only was it possible to train others in the political and economic ways of the United States, it was a necessity. The substantial blessings WMCNB Americans in the North enjoyed charged members of this elite racial group with the responsibility to share the blessings of American civilization with others. Bryan expressed this in a speech he entitled "The Price of a Soul": "Our nation is the greatest in the world and the greatest of all time . . . It is giving the world ideals in education, in social life, in government, and in religion. It is the teacher of nations, it is the world's torch-bearer . . . No material considerations should blind us to our nation's mission, or turn us aside from the accomplishment of the great work which has been reserved for us."[28]

Joining Bryan in this belief about the potency of America's mission was Theodore Roosevelt. Roosevelt stated quite grandly in his speech "True Americanism" (1894), "Our nation is that one among all the nations of the earth which holds in its hands the fate of the coming years."[29] The fact that these two individuals, who faced one another in the presidential election of 1904, could agree on this basic point (if not on how to carry out the mission, as shown by Roosevelt's far more imperialistic wording) underscores how prevalent this belief was.

WMCNB Americans explicitly connected the possibility of instilling American political and economic designs among the lesser races with evangelistic outreach to these other races. Jacobson, using his economic analysis of this era, argued how Josiah Strong, in his famous publication *Our Country*, wove the attempt to civilize others together from the joint processes of developing them as consumers and evangelizing them.

> Isolation is the mother of barbarism, wrote Josiah Strong in his popular tract of nationalism and Christianity, *Our Country*. For Strong, as for many of his compatriots, the notion of American grandeur entailed not only establishing a global presence by

27. Handy, *Christian America*, 31.

28. Bryan, *Speeches of William Jennings Bryan*, 367.

29. Roosevelt, "True Americanism," § 4.

reaching out to other regions and peoples of the world, but fully transforming the ways in which those people lived. The transformation, rather loosely envisioned under the imprecise rubric of "civilization," would be both spiritual and material: conveniently, the export of Christian ideals would go hand in hand with the export of finished textiles and manufactured goods. "The mysteries of Africa are being opened," wrote Strong; "the pulse of her commerce is beginning to beat. South America is being quickened, and the dry bones of Asia are moving; the warm breath of the Nineteenth Century is breathing a living soul under her ribs of death. The world is to be Christianized and civilized." Lest the reader miss the crucial connection between the nation's roles as both spiritual savior and industrial supplier to these benighted nations, Strong went on to ask rhetorically, "What is the process of civilizing but *the creating of more and higher wants?*" Commerce, he concluded, would follow the missionary: The millions of Africa and Asia are someday to have the wants of a Christian civilization.[30]

Bryan, in a less commercial vein, argued that uplifting other races required providing them with universal education, a republican form of government, and the Christian religion.[31]

Even as WMCNB Americans were looking at taking the blessings of a Christian American civilization to other lands, they were also deeply concerned about connecting the various non-white and/or non-native born groups within the United States with the civilization that already existed there. Indeed, as mentioned in the introduction, they believed it was necessary to reach these groups in order to safeguard the genius of the republican government that had provided the environment necessary for the flourishing of the American race. From the nation's founding Americans understood that public virtue and education were necessary to maintain a republican form of government.[32] This lesson remained forefront in the white Americans' minds during the late nineteenth century, especially as they considered the large number of people streaming into the nation who hailed from non-republican backgrounds. White Americans feared that immigrants-turned-citizens and freedmen-turned-citizens, all of whom lacked the natural proclivities toward virtue that the white Americans carried in their blood, would quickly bring the Republic to ruin by the misuse

---

30. Jacobson, *Barbarian Virtues*, 17.

31. Bryan, *Speeches of William Jennings Bryan*, 327, 367.

32. Bailyn, *Ideological Origins of the American Revolution*, 379.

of the vote. They believed that the freedmen, many of whom continued to work on the plantations as sharecroppers or tenant farmers, would be influenced to vote according to their former masters' wishes, thus opening the door for Southern infidelities to enter back into the Union. Likewise, white Americans believed the machine politics of the city would co-opt the votes of the immigrants. Thus, a strange mixture of millennial excitement that God was bringing about the Kingdom in the United States and fear that those evangelized could bring the nascent Kingdom of God in the United States to ruination if not quickly assimilated into it, motivated the political and economic outreach of white Americans.

In sum, the late nineteenth century and early twentieth century was a time in which white, middle-class Americans of the North became increasingly aware of their unique values, patterns of life, and material blessings. Awakened to this by the fires of the Civil War, which forced them to articulate their vision of America in contrast to the rebel South, they further refined their understanding of themselves in terms of a Christian American civilization. They premised their view of their civilization on what they believed to be superior technology, racial bloodlines, and political and economic structures in relation to the rest of the world. They imbued all of this with millennialism, believing that God was establishing the Kingdom of God in the advanced civilization of the United States.

By making the connection between Christian American civilization and the Kingdom of God, WMCNB Americans not only sought to articulate a specific vision of the United States, but to advocate for others to accept the vision that it set forth as the divinely mandated way to be blessed. In doing this, members of this demographic recognized how the work of evangelistic missions fit with its desire to help others participate in Christian American civilization. Indeed, the notion of a Christian American civilization is at the heart of both the American gospel and pure American evangelism. It provided the content for the American gospel and the impetus for engaging in evangelistic outreach.

It is not surprising that members of the Methodist Episcopal Church, who largely were white, middle-class, and almost exclusively from the North, and who had committed themselves with fierce abandon to the preservation of the Union during the Civil War, were attracted to the idea of Christian American civilization. Methodists came to believe that Americanization was central to their work of evangelism. Thus, they became some of the most outspoken advocates of both protecting the domestic Christian American civilization within the Union and expanding that civilization to encompass the rest of the world. Methodists desired to win people both to Jesus and to their ideal view of white, middle-class, Northern civilization.

METHODISTS AND THE SPREAD OF A CHRISTIAN AMERICAN CIVILIZATION

Already primed to understand American culture as being in line with God's will because of their support of the Union during the Civil War, the eschatology connected to Christian American civilization offered the Methodist Episcopal Church the necessary ingredient to make American cultural values part of their evangelistic endeavors. They could readily accept that they could invite people into Christian American civilization and God's salvation at the same time.

What made Methodists especially open to this work was their belief that the Methodist Episcopal Church could claim credit for bringing civilization to the United States in the first place. This meant that the lauded Christian American civilization was, more precisely, a *Methodist* American civilization. The fact that by the late nineteenth century the Methodist Episcopal Church was the largest Protestant church in the United States corroborated this fact for them. To call people to participate in this civilization, then, was simply a continuation of calling people to holiness by inviting them to join the MEC. Indeed, they believed that the MEC was uniquely fitted to be the primary instrument through which Christian American civilization could extend to all people because of its evangelistic organization and tradition of calling people to live reformed lives.

These claims may seem remarkably prideful to present day readers. However, Methodists of this era did not have any qualms about placing themselves at the center of American history from the very beginning. Thus the Board of Home Missions and Church Extension of the Methodist Episcopal Church opined in a 1908 publication, "Who can read the story of the rise of the Republic and the rise of Methodism without believing that God was raising up a great spiritual force that should aid largely in molding the thought and sentiment of the young Nation?"[33] The same idea is in Matthew Simpson's panegyric for Francis Asbury in his *A Hundred Years of Methodism* (1876): "As an apostle to the Churches of America he has had no equal. He shunned no toil or sacrifice which lay in the pathway

33. Forbes, "Methodism and the Republic," 12.

to duty. Enfeebled and diseased, he kept ceaselessly on his way, crossing mountains and traversing forests, seeking the lost, and inspiring young ministers with missionary zeal. To no other man does American civilization owe so much as to Bishop Asbury. He is worthy of a place among the heroes of '76."[34]

Simpson argued further that Methodism alone preserved the civilization of the American people as they migrated westward even as other denominations looked on and mocked the Methodist preachers.

> Who can tell what would have been the condition of western society, as it poured its streams of population over mountains and valleys, if the itinerant preacher had not accompanied or soon followed them? Had no minister preached until the towns and cities were built, and until congregations were formed and called, who can describe the moral desolation? Ministers may stand to-day in the pulpits of fine city churches, and declaim about apostolic succession; they may deny the validity of the ministerial orders of the heroic itinerant preachers, and consign them and their congregations to the uncovenanted mercies of God; but the thousands of happy and useful Christians on earth, and the thousands of the redeemed in heaven, who, but for them, had not heard the name of Jesus, will rise up and call them blessed. The blooming fields once a wilderness; the towns and cities of yesterday, which rival in population the old cities of Europe; the masses of an industrious, thriving, well-ordered, and happy population; the beautiful and thronged school-houses, the numerous and tasteful churches; and the multitudes of devout worshipers, all attest to the power of the Gospel which was proclaimed in their midst. To them it was a gospel of humanity, in strengthening them for their labors, and comforting them in their sorrows; it was a gospel of peace, in revealing a Saviour full of compassion and ready to forgive; it was a gospel of holy triumph the dying inmate of the lonely cabin to the mansions prepared by the Son of God.[35]

Simpson regularly cited the fact that the Methodist Episcopal Church was the largest Protestant denomination in the United States at the end of the nineteenth century as evidence for the MEC being the best representative of Christian American civilization. He pressed this point home in his commentary accompanying the various statistics he presented comparing

34. Simpson, *Hundred Years of Methodism*, 101.

35. Ibid., 351–52

the Methodist Episcopal Church to other denominations in the United States: "A review of the events connected with the Churches of the last century shows that, when compared with other Church organizations, Methodism has been pre-eminently successful . . . To-day it ranks first among all the religious bodies in the number of its communicants, in the number and capacity of its church buildings, and in the value of its Church property."[36] Clearly, he implied, given the numerical success in all these areas, how could the MEC be anything less than the ideal candidate to lead the charge for spreading God's Kingdom.

Stevens made a similar comment in reference to the growing influence wielded by the Methodist preachers within the United States as the years passed: "From the beginning not a few of the itinerants had, by their moral energy and natural talents, wielded more than a denominational sway over the popular mind; but the new class were to attain a sort of national rather than denominational recognition, and to give their Church the highest vindication before the American people."[37]

According to such writers as Simpson and Stevens, the Methodists, in effect, held controlling interest in the American people, so the denomination could claim not only to have been a primary force in shaping American civilization, they could also claim to best represent the civilizing force Americans could offer the world. Holding such a prestigious position, it is understandable why the Methodists would be so open to aligning their denominational identity and the national identity by adopting the civilizing mission of the United States. The membership of the MEC was not only the demographic of Americans who held to the supremacy of American culture, they were the ones who had shaped that culture in the first place!

With both the content and structures in place to articulate a Methodist understanding of the American gospel and to propagate that gospel through pure American evangelism, the Methodists were prepared to undertake a vast home missionary effort during the period from the end of the Civil War through the end of the First World War. In these home missions, the MEC home missionaries would seek to inculcate the values of WMCNB Americans into various groups who were not part of the Christian American civilization by virtue of their race, place-of-birth, or religious convictions. These included white Southerners who had participated in the secession, the African American freedmen, the inhabitants of the American West, and the urban dwellers who were quickly becoming

---

36. Ibid., 339.

37. Stevens, *Compendious History of American Methodism*, 552.

the largest demographic in the United States. This list reads the same as the list of groups that white, middle-class Americans in the late nineteenth century and early twentieth century found the most potentially dangerous to the potency of Christian American civilization. Thus, evangelizing these groups with the American gospel was both a means of uplifting the fortunes of these peoples and also protecting white American supremacy in the culture of the United States.

In chapters three through six, I will deal with each of these groups in turn, considering how the Methodist Episcopal Church's home missions in relation to each one is best described by my definition of pure American evangelism. In each case, the regional contexts surrounding these groups elicited and, in some cases, modified, the pure American evangelism of the Methodists.

3

The South

FROM ITS ESTABLISHMENT IN 1784 through the late nineteenth century, the Methodist Episcopal Church was in the process of evolving alongside of American culture, forging an American gospel by linking cultural values to the biblical faith. Especially during the Civil War, the Methodists recognized how significantly their own constituency of WMCNB Northerners was in sympathy with the cultural values of the Union, and this resulted in an unabashed effort by Methodist leaders to tie the fortunes of the MEC to those of the United States. Added to this was the Methodists' identification of their own cultural norms with a Christian American civilization, which they believed heralded the coming Kingdom of God. While the racial aspect of Christian American civilization was out of reach for those who were non-native born whites, it was at least possible for other groups of people to participate in this civilization through learning the values and patterns of life that were common to the WMCNB Northerners.

All of this had significant implications for how the MEC understood and practiced evangelism. It began to merge its call to eternal life with a call to share in the quality of life that WMCNB Northerners enjoyed, believing that both were essential to God's work of salvation. The new form of evangelism that emerged from this is what I have termed pure American evangelism, and it found its primary outlet through home missions that the MEC launched to reach peoples who lived within the borders of the United States but were not WMCNB or from the North.

The first groups to garner the attention of these home missions were the whites and the freedmen in the South during and following the Civil War. In the thinking of the WMCNB Methodists, the former needed evangelism because, even though they were white, they held to a heretical view of what the Christian American civilization should be, as demonstrated by their support of slavery and secession. The latter needed evangelism because of their race and their lack of education.

Civilizing the Southern Whites

Disintegration and Absorption

The MEC's evangelistic outreach to white southerners can best be seen in how the church related to its southern counterpart, the Methodist Episcopal Church, South. For over a decade prior to the Civil War, the MEC had nursed an increasingly negative view of the MECS because of the bitter way the two denominations had parted. The fact that the MECS placed its benediction on the Confederacy's twin evils of slavery and secession only inflamed this.

Even as the Civil War was raging, the MEC began developing plans for reclaiming the southern conferences it believed had unlawfully seceded both from the true Methodist church and from civilization. These plans found their genesis in a communiqué from a Methodist chaplain in the Union Army to the Methodist bishops. According to Methodist historian Daniel Stowell (1998), in 1863, when the it became clear the tide of the war was turning in the Union's favor,

> A chaplain with Federal forces in Nashville wrote to northern Methodist bishop Matthew Simpson that most of the [MECS] local pastors had deserted their congregations; the church buildings were either empty or occupied by the army. The MEC could "regain" the churches "if the matter could be properly presented to the government authorities." Bishop Edward R. Ames hurried to confer with his friend, Secretary of War Edwin M. Stanton. On November 30, 1863, Stanton issued an order instructing generals in the Departments of Missouri, Tennessee, and the Gulf to "place at the disposal of Bishop Ames all houses of the MECS, in which a loyal minister, who has been appointed by a loyal Bishop of said Church does not officiate." The generals were also directed to "furnish Bishop Ames and his clerk with transportation and subsistence when it can be done without prejudice to the service and will afford them courtesy, assistance, and protection." On December 9, the War Department issued the same order concerning Methodist churches in

the departments of North Carolina, Virginia, and the South, over which the northern bishops Osmon C. Baker and Edmund S. Janes had authority. On December 30, Stanton repeated the order for Kentucky and Tennessee under the direction of Bishop Simpson.[1]

As Stowell further reported, the bishops took full advantage of this governmental largesse:

> The northern Methodists engaged in the most extensive campaign of church occupation in the South. Believing that thousands of southern Methodists were eager to rejoin the northern Methodist church, Methodist missionaries and several of the bishops themselves entered the South to seize buildings and organize local, loyal churches. Bishop Ames left for the lower Mississippi valley almost immediately after Stanton issued the order. Within a few weeks he had "appropriated, under the order of the War Department" and supplied a dozen churches formerly belonging to the MECS in Memphis, Little Rock, Pine Bluff, Vicksburg, Jackson, Natchez, Baton Rouge, and several in New Orleans. Bishop Simpson traveled to Nashville in January 1864 to establish loyal Methodism there; he placed Michael J. Cramer in charge of the churches in Nashville and authorized Chaplain Calvin Holman to occupy churches in Chattanooga. Cramer, after appealing over the heads of local officials to his brother-in-law, Ulysses S. Grant, secured both McKendree Chapel and the German Methodist Church in Nashville. Chaplain H. A. Pattison acquired an order from General George H. Thomas granting possession of the Methodist church in Murfreesboro, Tennessee. Northern Methodist agents also occupied churches in Norfolk and Portsmouth, Virginia; Fernandina, Jacksonville, and St. Augustine, Florida; and Beaufort and Charleston, South Carolina.[2]

As a precondition for worshiping in the occupied Southern Methodist church buildings, Bishop Ames required those in the congregation to profess loyalty to the Union.[3] It is little wonder that one historian noted, "Methodists in the military found it difficult to separate their commitment

---

1. Stowell, *Rebuilding Zion*, 30.
2. Ibid., 30–31.
3. Buckley, *History of Methodism in the United States*, 2:177–78.

to the Union from their commitment to plant the flag of Northern Methodism in the South."[4]

Even though President Lincoln later rescinded the orders by Stanton because they overstepped the boundaries of the military's authority, the die had been cast. The MEC, under this initial charge to occupy the rebel church buildings, was committed to the South as their new field for evangelism. So it was that the bishops, equating the work of the Union Army to the providence of God, declared in their episcopal address to the 1864 General Conference, "the progress of Federal arms has thrown open to the loyal Churches of the Union large and inviting fields of Christian enterprise and labor . . . And now that the providence of God has opened her way, she should not be disobedient to her heavenly calling, but should return at the earliest practicable period."[5]

The same conference delegates who heard this stirring call to evangelism in the South soon provided the church a potent new tool for accomplishing it: the Church Extension Society (CES). The CES was an arm of the denomination tasked with raising money for the purchase and/or construction of new church buildings in the United States. Now, not only would the Methodists have the ability to occupy existing Southern Methodist church buildings, but to establish new MEC outposts in the South from which to spread their American gospel. In the same vein, the delegates also voted to change the constitution of the Missionary Society to allow for resources to be sent to the South as a mission field.[6]

With these new evangelistic tools in place, the MEC's idea of occupying the South grew in intensity with the ending of the war and the dawning of Reconstruction. The MEC was especially emboldened as the Radical Republicans took control of Congress and enacted harsher penalties against the South in an attempt to crush the southern value system, replacing it with its northern counterpart. Reginald Hildebrand (1995), a historian who studied the MEC engagement in the South following the Civil War, commented:

> Methodist missionaries saw themselves as the rear guard of the
> Union Army and the vanguard of Republican Reconstruction.
> The denomination and the Republican party entered the South

4. Hildebrand, *Times Were Strange and Stirring*, 79.

5. Harris, *Journal of the General Conference of the Methodist Episcopal Church, Held in Philadelphia, PA, 1864*, 278–79.

6. They did this by allowing the Mission Society to establish mission districts "in the United States and Territories not included in the bounds of any of the Annual Conferences." Ibid., 387.

together, protecting each other's flanks as they attempted to establish themselves in hostile territory. Northern missionaries helped prepare the soil in which the Republican party could take root. The party mobilized the government and military in ways that helped the racially iconoclastic denomination survive in the South. But the match between the denomination and the party was more than a marriage of convenience. The social gospel of the M. E. Church meshed with the civil religion of the Republican party.[7]

MEC support for reforming the South went beyond just participating in the official work of Congress. It extended to all northern attempts to stamp the image of northern civilization onto southern whites and their structures. Even the often-unscrupulous carpetbaggers found the approbation of the MEC, as seen in a sermon preached by Bishop Haven, an Episcopalian invited to address a group of MEC leaders who were concerned about mission work in the South.

> O ye ribald revilers of that sacred word, take heed to your ways and words! Pronounce it reverently, for it is the word of Christ and Christianity to-day. "Carpet-bagger" is the true knight-errantry of the age. Of old they went forth on horse and in armor. To-day, with less than David's sling, with less than the disciple's staff, with a simple carpetbag, they go forth to conquer. Deserted by the Government he has elected, and the nation he has recreated, the carpet-bagger will yet save that nation, will again restore a true and honest and patriotic government that shall protect every citizen in his every right by every force at its command.[8]

Not surprisingly, with this broader missionary goal of overcoming southern resistance to northern values, the MEC adopted a policy toward the MECS that came to be known as "disintegration and absorption." Believing that God had struck the South, specifically the MECS, with divine wrath through the blighting work of the Union Army, the MEC was ready to reclaim the territory it lost when the southern conferences had separated from it. As Stowell explained, "God, in righteous indignation against the sins of secession and slavery, had not merely chastened the South, but had brought His fierce judgment upon it. Because secession from the Union was a sin, northern Christians reasoned, secession from

---

7. Hildebrand, *Times Were Strange and Stirring*, 106.

8. Freedmen's Aid Society, *Eleventh Annual Report* .

the national church bodies was also sinful. Now that the Union was restored, national denominational structures should also be reconstructed."[9]

Beyond this claim to theodicy, the MEC believed the disintegration and absorption policy was simply pragmatic. The Southern Methodists were disorganized and impoverished after the war, and the MEC had already occupied many of the MECS church buildings with its own preachers thanks to the order of Secretary Stanton. It only made sense that the MEC should reassert both itself and the civilization it championed in the South by drawing into itself the remnants of the MECS. Accordingly, the MEC made clear through its missions into the South that it would welcome MECS members who were ready to repudiate slavery and secession. Those who held to their heretical American gospel that allowed for these evils would be left to disintegrate. Those who foreswore them could be absorbed back into the true church. The same held true for the MECS denomination as a whole. It could be reconciled with the mother church of American Methodism when it was ready to give up its wicked notions of what America entailed or it could wait to crumble and have the MEC claim whatever was left.

The MEC was encouraged in this strategy by the seeming ease with which it was able to form new conferences in the South with the aid of the newly created CES. As early as 1 June 1865 the MEC added the Holston Annual Conference, which covered the eastern part of Tennessee. By 1869 it claimed nine new conferences. The members of these conferences were largely made up of African Americans and southern white scalawags who had never been loyal to the Confederacy. These groups were ready candidates to swear allegiance to the American gospel and receive its benefits by joining the MEC.

Southern Reactions

White southerners recognized and reacted against the MEC's efforts to spread Northern civilization in the South. At best, they treated the MEC as alien, at worst, as a despised occupier. As Southern Methodist historian Hunter Dickinson Farrish (1938) explained, the white Southerners, especially in the upper class, resented that the Methodist missionaries rejected "the 'Bourbonism' of the old South" especially by condemning what they

---

9. Stowell, *Rebuilding Zion*, 6.

saw as "manifestations of it under various forms, such as Southern historical societies, anniversary celebrations, and Confederate monuments."[10]

Farrish argued that at first the Southern Methodists were open to reconciliation with the MEC because they accepted that God had indeed judged the South for its sins.[11] However, the Southern Methodists, as well as white Southerners in general, refused to believe that slavery and secession numbered among those sins.[12] As a result, when the MEC pressed Southern Methodists to repent of these specific sins as a precondition for reconciliation and ultimate reunion between the denominations, this proved to be too much.[13] These requirements not only transgressed the theology of the Southerners, they transgressed the foundation of Southern identity.

It was this conviction that spurred the Southern Methodists to rebuild their fortunes, fearing that the MEC would sweep away their southern civilization with a northern one. As Farrish opined, "The aims and policies of the MEC were at all times opposed on the ground that they were the outgrowth of Northern ideas and prejudices. Representatives of the Southern Church addressed their pleas to sectional prejudice in various forms, convinced of the correctness of the attitude of their Church toward all efforts to convert them to Northern views."[14]

To combat this, the MECS quickly moved to strengthen its own southern civilization through making strong evangelistic efforts among the upper-class white Southerners who still held to southern values,[15] distancing itself from the freedmen who were too easily swayed by northern missionaries through the formation of the Colored Methodist Episcopal Church,[16] launching numerous periodicals that would allow for a public bolstering of southern civilization in print,[17] and establishing both primary schools and institutions of higher education to help inculcate southern values in the rising generations.[18] Finally, the Southern Methodists made their own declaration, through an episcopal letter to the MEC, on

---

10. Farrish, *Circuit Rider Dismounts*, 78.

11. Ibid., 78.

12. Hildebrand, *Times Were Strange and Stirring*, 7.

13. Farrish, *Circuit Rider Dismounts*, 41.

14. Ibid., 146.

15. Ibid., 90–92.

16. Ibid., 171–72.

17. Ibid., 148.

18. Ibid., 242, 258–59.

the issue of possible reunion. In it they not only repudiated, but hurled back the charges the Methodists leveled at them. They argued that there had been no secession, only a mutual parting that the General Conference of 1848 refused to honor. They further asserted that radical abolitionist involvement in politics by Methodists in the North, not slavery, had been the key issue causing the separation of the denomination. Finally, they called on the MEC to repent of its occupation of Southern Methodist houses of worship as part of a disintegration and absorption policy. Only once the MEC leaders were enlightened enough to accept these claims could reunion move forward.[19]

These reactions make sense only when seen as an attempt to stand against pure American evangelism. The issue was not that the southern whites disagreed that there was an American gospel to spread; it was that the southern whites could not accept the content of the American gospel that the MEC home missionaries brought with them.

Having just completed a bloody struggle in which each church had endorsed the slaughter of the other's members in their respective backing of the Union and Confederate armies, tensions flared afresh and might well have led to deeper animosity between the two denominations. However, a more urgent need for spreading Christian American civilization was brewing in the aftermath of the Civil War that would call these two erstwhile combatants together.

"Civilizing" Freed Slaves

Early Relations between the MEC and African Americans

Entangled in the sectional divide between the MEC and MECS was the African American population. While the African Americans obviously were a group in need of the American gospel, since they were not white, nor were they properly educated to use the technology or the vote, relating to them was a complex affair for the MEC. This complexity was a result of the MEC evangelistic outreach among African Americans prior to the Civil War combined with the racist attitudes harbored by many MEC members.

The MEC forged strong ties with the African American community during the denomination's early years. According to John Wigger, the widespread Christianization of African Americans in the United States did not begin until the Methodists and Baptists began to preach to the

19. Ibid., 57–59.

slaves. He provided three reasons that the slaves particularly warmed to Methodist evangelism: First, Methodists earned the respect of the slaves by willingly suffering persecution at the hands of pro-slavery whites in order to lead the slaves in worship. Second, the Methodists preached the gospel in a passionate way using the vernacular. This allowed slaves to understand and appropriate the message readily. Third, the Methodists made room for African Americans to take authority in the denomination as lay leaders and even as itinerating preachers. As such, African Americans found a community that offered them respect and a measure of equality in the MEC.[20]

The result of this outreach was a growing population of African Americans within the ranks of Methodism. However, this inclusion of African Americans in the MEC in no way meant that the Methodists were free from racist attitudes. The rise of the African Methodist Episcopal Church and the African Methodist Episcopal Church Zion, both founded by former African American members of the MEC because of the racism they experienced in local MEC congregations during the early nineteenth century, is witness to this. So is the fact that nearly a third of the Methodists in the United States chose to leave the denomination in 1844 to form the MECS because of their pro-slavery stance.

Even after the departure of the southern annual conferences, racism continued to haunt the MEC. The church remained officially ambivalent in its view of slavery, fearing the loss of more members who lived in the Border States where slavery was legal and widely accepted.[21] It was only with the outbreak of the Civil War that the MEC passed legislation declaring its abolitionist stance, and it was only after the need arose for MEC home missionaries to head South to evangelize the newly freed slaves that the General Conference granted African Americans the right to be ordained.[22] Even then, the so-called anti-caste (i.e., anti-racist) stance of the MEC only extended as far as granting equality under church law, not to equality of whites and African Americans as human beings. In all cases, the actions seem spurred more by political considerations than a genuine desire to promote equality between the races.

In many ways, the MEC was simply showing its own cultural connections to the WMCNB North in its simultaneous abhorrence of slavery and maintenance of racist attitudes. A comparison can be made with the Buffalo

20. Wigger, *Taking Heaven by Storm*, 127–30.

21. May, "War Years," 209.

22. Hildebrand, *Times Were Strange and Stirring*, 75–77.

National Free Soil Convention in 1847. Attended by a variety of people who championed an anti-slavery stance, the convention was thrown into turmoil when Frederick Douglass and other African Americans attended. Ultimately they were seated at the convention, but not without significant backlash by some of the white attendees. As American historian Sean Willentz (2005) observed, some of the Free Soilers "despised blacks as well as slavery."[23] The later fears of race suicide among the WMCNB northerners would only intensify this feeling.

While the MEC remained institutionally racist in these ways, this did not decrease its desire to help African Americans participate in the better quality of life provided by a Christian American civilization. Especially after the abolition of slavery in the United States, the MEC was deeply concerned that the newly freed slaves would have the tools made available for them to share in the salvation that this sort of civilization offered them. To this end, the General Conference of 1868 sanctioned the Freedmen's Aid Society (FAS) as an official denominational agency.[24] The FAS, in turn, helped spark the formation of the Women's Home Missions Society (WHMS) in 1881. Both groups became heavily involved with providing money, supplies, and missionaries to the South.

The Work of the Freedmen's Aid Society

African American students doing lab work at Rust College in Mississippi

23. Willentz, *Rise of American Democracy*, 623–24.
24. Hildebrand, *Times Were Strange and Stirring*, 81.

African Americans learning cabinet making
at Morristown Industrial College, Tennessee

The work of the FAS can be understood entirely in terms of the MEC seeking to establish the American gospel among African Americans in the South. Initially, the way the FAS did this is through founding primary schools for African American children and recruiting missionaries to teach in those schools.

The traditional Methodist concern for awakening people to the grace of Jesus Christ and leading them to conversion was a necessary part of this work given the fact that adherence to the Christian faith undergirded all the values and patterns of life held by WMCNB Northerners. In a section of the third annual report describing the work of the FAS missionaries, there was a note on this specific point: "Special attention has been devoted to the spiritual welfare of the pupils by the teachers. They have taught in schools the truths of the Bible, preached Jesus, and sought by their example to allure their pupils to a higher and purer life, and God has made them the honored instruments of awakening and leading more than one thousand souls to the Savior."[25]

This "purer and higher life" was not simply a matter of saving souls, however. The FAS understood that education would go hand-in-hand with

25. Freedmen's Aid Society, *Third Annual Report*, 12.

evangelization to help African Americans live the kind of life God desired for them in this world as well as in the next. The society explained this when it also stated in its third annual report, "we engage in the humbler work of educating the children, and in preparing them for the important duties of this life, and for happiness in the life to come."[26]

That the "duties of this life" entailed being catechized into a WMCNB Northern civilization is visible in how the leaders of the FAS described the specifics of the organization's work. For example, the FAS declared that they hoped to start a trend in the South in which free schools on the "New England plan of teaching"[27] would become easily accessible for African Americans. Even more telling are the before-and-after accounts of students attending FAS schools. These equate the results of religious conversion and education with participation in civilization. Two such descriptions make this point well. The first is from the third annual report of the FAS. It exclaimed, "Nine years ago he [the student] saw this [Freedmen's Aid] school in linsey-woolsey gowns, and ragged jackets and trousers, without shoes, without knowledge, without culture, almost without a consciousness of humanity. How changed! So handsomely appareled, so comely of countenance, so intelligent, so self-reliant. They were urged to grow in these graces, and be worthy of the vocation wherewith they were called."[28]

The second is from the eighth annual report.

> It is a pleasant sight to watch the gradual change which comes over a student who comes to us fresh from his log-cabin in the woods. His hair soon gets an extra touch—his linen and his clothes soon show and breathe a little more of the air of civilization, and often a few months finds him stepping ahead of his city cousins in his daily tasks. But best of all is to see strong young men bow at the altar as penitents and rising promise to go back to their companions at home and tell them of Jesus. The seeds of good that are sown in these schools are scattered widely over the land, and bring forth fruit more than with human wisdom we can calculate.[29]

---

26. Ibid., 6.
27. Ibid., 5.
28. Freedmen's Aid Society, *Eighth Annual Report*, 19–20.
29. Freedmen's Aid Society, *Twelfth Annual Report*, 39.

Original caption: "If we-uns could only go to school"

Original caption: Plenty More on the Way

The assumption was that, prior to the FAS schools' evangelistic work, the African Americans were poor, uncivilized, and without faith. Following the work of the MEC home missionaries at the schools, these same African Americans were ready to share in the fullness of God's blessings, having professed faith in Jesus Christ and learned to adorn themselves with the trappings of WMCNB northern civilization. Particularly noteworthy in these descriptions are the ways in which the students' participation in civilization is visible through the students' outward appearances. This includes the students' clothes and shoes (something that also points to the students participating in the growing consumer economy of the United States), as well as the students' hair. Additionally, the students' transformation to being genuine converts to the American gospel is obvious through the students' usefulness; of being "so self-reliant" to preach on their own or otherwise engage in a meaningful vocation.

As with all pure American evangelism, lurking behind this altruistic work of uplifting those in need was the fear of what would happen if this work was not accomplished. The FAS opened its fourth annual report with the caution: "The importance of this work can scarcely be overrated. The welfare of the nation, the prosperity of the Church, and the salvation of missions of a long-neglected race, are closely connected with it. To neglect it is to peril interests vital to Christian civilization. It is to fling away one of the grandest opportunities ever presented to save a race, and bind it with indissoluble bonds to the Church and the republic."[30]

In a keynote address to the FAS the following year, Bishop Janes declared, "I say to this audience, this country can not *afford* to have such a mass of our population uneducated and untrained; we can not afford it; it will *peril every interest* of this grand and glorious Republic."[31]

The following year, the FAS directors repeated this point in even starker language, "Patriotism, philanthropy, and religion, with united voice, urge us to consider this subject and make provision that this calamity which threatens us may be averted. Four millions of ignorant citizens in a national crisis may wreck a Republic! These must be educated and Christianized, or all that we hold dear in Church or State will be imperiled."[32]

However, this fear was outshone by the great promise of missionary work among the freed slaves. The FAS believed that civilizing the African

---

30. Freedmen's Aid Society, *Fourth Annual Report*, 3.

31. Freedmen's Aid Society, *Fifth Annual Report*, 31. This speech proved so popular that the Society reprinted it two years later in its Seventh Annual Report.

32. Freedmen's Aid Society, *Sixth Annual Report*, 40–41.

Americans would not only save the Republic, but create opportunities for expanding the influence of the Republic around the world. As early as 1869, the spokesmen for the FAS articulated how evangelized and civilized freed slaves could become missionaries who carried Christian American civilization to Africa. Bishop Thompson stated in his address to the third annual meeting of the FAS: "As you penetrate into the interior [of South America and Africa] you find a people rude, and almost nude, knowing nothing of electricity or steam, and living in huts more artless than the nests of the birds. Why have not these regions been cultivated by the white men? The climate forbids. Christian colonies of the black race are needed to carry thither our civilization and religion."[33]

Six years later, an address at the FAS reiterated this point, arguing that it at the very core of the FAS's purpose was "to give a Gospel Vocation to a Heathen Race and a Heathen Continent" by helping African Americans rise above their deplorable circumstances in the United States through instilling in them a desire to civilize Africa.[34] J. P. Newman, the concluding keynote speaker for the FAS at its fourteenth annual session, re-stated this idea:

> I hope that from the South shall come forth an evangelizing power that is to transform the only continent that remains to receive the touch of Christian civilization. Perhaps the historian, one hundred years hence, will simply record this astounding fact, that inasmuch as time is an element in the administration of Almighty God in the elevation of humanity, Africa was reserved until out of the issues of our war should come a race identical in blood and bone, but with an intellect emancipated and with a heart purified, with all the attributes and agencies of civilization, inspired with a divine religion to go there and lift that continent, until like a black diamond it shall shine resplendently in the crown of the Redeemer of the world![35]

One critical means of making certain that the freedmen would be promoters of Christian American civilization rather than a menace to it was for the MEC to help them develop strong home lives; a concern born from the Victorian belief that a strong nation required strong families. The FAS initially took on this work as part of the mission to educate the African

---

33. Freedmen's Aid Society, *Third Annual Report*, 17.

34. Freedmen's Aid Society, *Ninth Annual Report*, 25–39.

35. Freedmen's Aid Society, *Fourteenth Annual Report*, 79. Sadly, this historian, writing over 100 years after this address, can report no such thing.

American population in the South. Focusing primarily on women, since women were the pillars to creating happy and healthful family homes, the society helped African American women learn how to respect their own womanhood by conducting their domestic work with dignity.[36] The FAS specifically called for women missionaries to go to the African Americans in the South to help in this effort. In its twelfth annual reported, it stated:

> In no mission effort is woman's influence, tact, and Christian zeal more needed than among the freed people. The absence of all the refinements of home-life and the degrading influences that surround them afford but little hope of elevation. Our schools are doing a good work among the Freedmen, and our pupils reflect the highest credit upon their teachers by their intelligence and uprightness. But if the homes, to which these youth return, and in which their time is spent, except the few hours each day that they are under the influence of Christian teachers, could be reached, how much more rapidly the work of elevating this people could be carried forward.[37]

It was this part of the FAS's mission that spurred the formation of the WHMS.[38]

The Work of the WHMS

The WHMS was the creation of several "great-souled" Methodist women who became convinced they had to respond to the need for Christ and civilization among poor women and children in the United States.[39] While the WHMS would quickly move beyond providing domestic missionary work in the South alone,[40] it was in reference to the needs of African American women and children in the South that the agency first organized. The impetus for this organization came from two directions. First, Jennie C. Hartzell, the wife of a Methodist pastor assigned to a large, white

36. Freedmen's Aid Society, *Eleventh Annual Report*, 16–17.

37. Freedmen's Aid Society, *Twelfth Annual Report*, 54.

38. Freedmen's Aid Society, *Thirteenth Annual Report*, 16.

39. Tomkinson, *Twenty Years' History of the Women's Home Missionary Society*, 8.

40. The Constitution of the WHMS adopted at the first annual meeting stated "The aim of this Society shall be to enlist and organize the efforts of Christian women in behalf of the needy and destitute women and children of all sections of our country without distinction of race, and to co-operate with the other societies and agencies of the Church in educational and missionary work." Women's Home Missionary Society, *First Annual Report*, 15.

congregation in New Orleans, attracted the attention of several prominent Methodist women in the North because of her work among the African American women and children in the city during the 1870s.[41] Most of this work was traditionally evangelistic in nature—going house-to-house to share the gospel and pray with small groups of women. The surprisingly fruitful results of this work, including numerous conversions, an ever-growing number of requests by the African American women for Hartzell to visit their homes, and, by 1879, the founding of a regular school and eight sewing schools overseen by Hartzell and staffed by seven female missionaries she employed, convinced the northern women of the importance of this endeavor.

This evangelistic effort came at precisely the time when the FAS was most in need of help constructing a Christian American civilization in the South. As the 1870s wore on, the directors of the FAS became discouraged at the slow pace of African Americans becoming practitioners of WMCNB values and patterns of life. As a historian of the WHMS put it, "Something more, evidently, was needed to cope with the appalling social conditions existing than the teachings of the schools, or even the preaching of the gospel."[42] It was, the women who founded the WHMS concluded, the unique power of women to extend Christian civilization that was missing. To make this point, the WHMS historian approvingly cited Emerson's quote "Civilization is simply the influence of good women."[43]

With the help of sympathetic and influential clergymen (who often were also the husbands of these women), Hartzell and a group of similar-minded women were able first to gain official recognition for Hartzell's work through the FAS and, in 1880, to found the WHMS. Anchoring the agency's connection to the Northern (and explicitly Republican) civilization was the woman selected to be the first president of the WHMS: Lucy Webb Hayes, or as the minutes of the first annual report of the WHMS recorded her name, Mrs. Rutherford B. Hayes.

The WHMS was explicit that imparting civilization was central to its mission. This was a point that Rev. Isaac J. Lansing, the keynote speaker at the inaugural meeting of the WHMS, reminded the members of in his oration to them. "[T]his Society is composed of Christian women who, prizing their own homes and perceiving in contrast, with sorrow and pity,

41. Tomkinson, *Twenty Years' History of the Women's Home Missionary Society*, 15–17.

42. Ibid., 7.

43. Ibid., 8.

the degradation of thousands of families throughout the United States, have banded themselves together to elevate the sunken and degraded to a Christian plane. This they propose to do by sending representative women into these miserable families, whose work, begun with the female members of the household, shall be directed to making a home of cleanliness, order, intelligence and piety."[44]

He specifically pressed the importance of the emphasis on the home and family as critical to this work, stating, "In attempting the salvation of the family as a whole, the Woman's Home Missionary Society gives the best and largest culture to every individual . . . to lift each person to the highest plane of life."[45] He then brought this point to bear specifically on the freedmen.

> If you call to mind the great work among the freedmen made necessary by emancipation, to which work this Society directs special effort . . . The heaviest, deadliest, sorest curse of slavery was this, that the slave had no family, no home . . . When slavery thus destroyed the home, it degraded slave and master, black man and white, so that their morals were rather those of heathens than Christians. And by what means can the moral degradation resulting from slavery and still existing be removed? Not by the ballot, not by the civil rights bill, not by increased wealth, nor through the spread of primary schools and education, but only by the restoration and purification of the family. When the freedmen learns to be a loyal husband and a loving father, when his children and wife are to him a holy family, then and not till then will the Southern problem by effectually humanely and righteously solved.[46]

What is especially notable in this passage is that Lansing not only saw instilling proper home life among the freedmen as central to uplifting African Americans, but to civilizing the entire South, including the whites who had enslaved Africans and African Americans. Also notable is the extent to which women could accomplish this work beyond anything that men could do in the traditionally male realms of politics and economics.

C. H. Fowler, who was deeply involved with the FAS, sent a letter of greeting to the women at the same meeting Lansing addressed. It also pointed to the concern of uplifting African Americans and white southerners alike. "There are a million homes in the South among the colored

44. Women's Home Missionary Society, *First Annual Report*, 50.

45. Ibid., 53.

46. Ibid., 58.

people, and twice as many more among the poor whites of the South that need some one to enter with new ideas and new spirit, that they may be elevated into Christian homes."[47] Clearly, the WHMS and its supporters, male and female, saw the spread of Christian civilization through the power of training women to run good, Victorian homes as crossing all racial, class, and sectional boundaries.

The goal of uplifting the freedmen through creating better homes was something that found sympathy among the freed slaves themselves. Historian Leon F. Litwack (1979) stated that soon after emancipation many former slaves desired to possess the "graces of civilized life." This specifically led many African American men to take the role of being the breadwinner and demanding that their wives exit the labor force to keep up the home and the children. African American women, who did not necessarily want to trade slavery for subservience to their husbands, often chose not to leave off working altogether, but spent "more time in their own households and made labor arrangements that would permit them to do so."

Most African Americans also agreed that women should prepare for marriage by learning to "knit, sew, mend cloths, bake bread, keep a clean house, cultivate a garden, and read and write . . . that black women should aspire to be like their white counterparts and abide by the conventional wisdom and experience of mid-nineteenth century American society."[48] This is precisely what the FAS and, especially, the WHMS hoped to inspire African American women to do in order to bring African Americans as a race to the place of being full participants in a Christian American civilization.

Like the FAS, the WHMS was mindful of the dangers if they failed in their mission of spreading American Christian civilization. Not only, as the above addresses to the ladies implied, would the existing state of degradation continue for vast numbers of people in the United States, but the WMCNB Northern Christian civilization would itself be threatened by the products of those degraded homes. So it was that the executive board of the WHMS raised the alarm to its membership by explaining in its first report that, "multitudes of helpless children are coming into these miserable homes to enter surely upon lives of vice that will be continual menaces to our civilization."[49] Two years later, the board made the same point:

47. Ibid., 56.

48. Litwack, *Been in the Storm so Long*, 244–46.

49. Women's Home Missionary Society, *First Annual Report*, 39.

"We must give all these people our help, because it is the most economical investment we can make to suppress crime; because it is necessary in self-defense to keep *our* homes intact."[50]

Both the FAS and the WHMS, then, demonstrate the MEC's commitment to spreading the American gospel through pure American evangelism. The American gospel was a message of a better life in heaven with Jesus as well as a better quality of life now through the adoption of northern WMCNB values and patterns of life. African American men and women alike could learn their proper roles, the former being cleaned up and dressed properly as they entered into respectable vocations, the latter by setting up virtuous homes in which they raised civilized children. As the entire race grew in civilized ways of living, they would become a vast army of evangelists to carry this civilizing American gospel to parts of the world where white missionaries had been ineffective. The alternative to all this was the race becoming an army of poor, uneducated brutes that would overthrow the Republic through criminal activity.

Nativism over Sectionalism

As profound as the promise of successful evangelism among the African Americans was, and as fearful the prospect of failing, by the beginning of the 1870s the MEC began shifting its attention away from its work in the South, particularly from the African Americans. There are numerous reasons for this. First, the Federal Government began to withdraw financial support to agencies working with freed slaves. In 1870 the government shuttered the Freedmen's Bureau, and in 1872 federal grants given to the FAS and other Protestant-run organizations with the goal of providing primary education among freed slaves ceased. For Methodists, who were so closely tied to the United States Government in the aftermath of the Civil War, this shift in federal policy had a ripple effect. It drove significantly lower giving to the FAS among Methodists. Indeed, the years 1870–1873 saw the lowest giving to the FAS of its existence.[51] FAS reports are replete with sniping about the ever-diminishing amounts of dollars it received from denominational coffers in contrast to other denominational agencies, such as the Mission Society and the Church Extension Society. It also caused the FAS to shift its attention from primary education, which

---

50. Women's Home Missionary Society, *Third Annual Report*, 19; italics added.

51. Freedmen's Aid Society, *Fourteenth Annual Report*, 67.

no longer had federal funding, to higher education, focusing its efforts on establishing a few universities and seminaries that could produce African American preachers and teachers who could uplift their own people.[52] This new emphasis decreased the need of the FAS to confront the social dynamics of the South because its missionaries now only operated within private denominational schools with relatively small student bodies rather than through primary schools opened to all comers.

The second reason for the decreased emphasis on evangelizing the South was a general desire on the part of northerners to forget about the Civil War and forge ahead with southern whites as a united nation. Historian David Blight (2001) described how, as the Civil War receded into the past, white Americans in the North increasingly chose to adopt a "reconciliationist" view of the war, which downplayed the moral concerns of slavery and secession in favor of healing sectional wounds.[53] Methodists, as those who prided themselves on being the very quintessence of northern civilization, were certainly adherents to this view. As a result, fewer MEC pulpits blazed with calls to bring justice to the freed slaves and fewer MEC leaders waved the bloody shirt to demand the repentance of the southern whites because of their complicity with slavery and secession.[54]

Part of this broader move toward reconciliation may well have come from the success of the church's evangelism in terms of establishing annual conferences in the South and attracting tens of thousands of freed slaves into the MEC fold. With a greater northern presence in the South, there was less threat of the South rising again in its errors. Moreover, the need for missionaries to go to the South decreased.[55] The number of MEC missionaries working in the South peaked in 1870 at one hundred ten and settled back to seventy-five for the balance of the decade.[56]

The third reason was so that the Methodists could muster their resources to deal with the newly resumed influx of immigrants in northern cities following the Civil War. These immigrants, many of whom were Catholic, drank alcohol, and did not adhere to other values of WMCNB northerners, were of great concern to the MEC because they threatened to weaken the potency of Northern civilization from the inside. As dangerous as the unrepentant white southern rebel and the uneducated

52. Benjamin and Scott, "Methodist Episcopal Church in the Postwar Era," 366.

53. Blight, *Race and Reunion*, 2–3.

54. Stowell, *Rebuilding Zion*, 142.

55. Ibid., 140.

56. Benjamin and Scott, "Methodist Episcopal Church in the Postwar Era," 370–71.

freedmen-citizen in the South might be to the Republic, these threats were external to the North. The immigrant moving unimpeded within the North carried even more potential for damage by undoing the very seat of civilization from whence Christ's Kingdom would come. As a result, an evangelism defined by the values of WMCNB northerners would set its sights on evangelizing and civilizing these immigrants as its first priority.

White American Solidarity

Original caption: Mountain woman, hand to plow

Original caption: This lad, they say,
thought the World War was a mountain feud

Whereas throughout Reconstruction the MEC had little use for white southerners apart from their willingness to make an ardent confession and repent of their support of secession and slavery, the church found reason to appreciate this demographic in the light of immigration. Specifically, the MEC discovered the importance of the "Mountain People" who lived in the Appalachians in the Southeast. While this specific group does not match with the aristocratic southern slave-owners, since the Mountain People were too poor to own slaves, lived in Border States, and often remained loyal to the Union, the critical piece to recognize is that the MEC acknowledged these people to be 1) southern and 2) necessary to Northern civilization. Chiefly, the MEC's appreciation for this group came from the "purity" of their white American stock, which was untainted by immigrant blood.

Wilbur P. Thirkield, a white Methodist from Pennsylvania who served as President of Howard University in Washington, D.C. prior to being elected a bishop in 1912, stated this case most explicitly in an article he wrote in 1908 for the Church Extension and Home Missions Society (the successor of the Church Extension Society). Specifically describing the whites found in the Southeast, he extolled "the character and life of the several millions of sturdy, high-souled, clean-blooded Anglo-Saxon highlanders of the border and central South" and declared them to be "of pure, clean blood, uncontaminated by the vices."[57] Having amply raised up the "cleanness" of their blood, he pressed Methodists to make use of this remarkable resource. He demanded that the denomination "must contribute to the uplift and strength of these people, who with their pure Americanism have in them capacity for immense service to the Nation. The Nation with its millions of foreign immigrants who now dominate certain sections, needs this strain of pure Anglo-Saxon blood to reinforce the depleted blood of our people."[58]

While he acknowledged the unique need of the South to be civilized in describing the mountain people, he suggested this civilizing process was actually a means of saving the Christian American civilization found in the North: "In our churches and schools we are training the future teachers, ministers, mothers and home makers, who are to mold the civilization of the new South. By giving them wider knowledge, loftier ideals, broader and more Christlike views of humanity, they are to become an important factor in the peaceful solution of the greatest problem of the races ever given to any nation to solve."[59]

A later publication put forward by the MEC in 1924 used similar language to describe the inhabitants of the Southeast: "The faddist in 'undiluted Americanism' will find in the 13,990,272 people who live in that sweep of the Atlantic Coast from Maryland to the southern tip of Florida, a situation to delight his heart, so far as nationalities are concerned. It is populated by an almost exclusively native people, of the white and black races. Only 315,290, or 2.3 per cent, are foreign born, one of the lowest percentages in the United States."[60]

It is notable that the author of this piece is willing to include African Americans as part of the "native" people in the South. However, later in

57. Thirkield, "Mountain Whites of the South," 13–14.

58. Ibid., 14–15.

59. Ibid., 14–15, 15–16.

60. Wade, *World Service of the Methodist Episcopal Church*, 323–24.

the article it becomes clear which race is more important to American bloodlines when the author narrowed the focus to the Appalachian whites:

> the purest strain of American blood to be found today is in the most backward section of the United States. Hidden away in the picturesque slopes and ravines of the Appalachian mountains, these descendants of a "lost race" live in their log cabins, run barefooted, marry in childhood, cherish their superstitions, fight out their feuds, and talk in the language and live by the customs of pre-Revolutionary days. Nowhere in American life are [sic] more romantic people to be found, and their quaint ways and manners have been sung in story until they are familiar to nearly every mind.[61]

As with Thirkield, this article ends with a push to help these highly promising native whites to enter civilization through evangelism that includes "an unusual emphasis upon education and social service."[62]

While written several decades after Reconstruction, the ideas explained in these two articles already were having an impact during the 1870s. The relationship of the MEC to the MECS offers a picture of this. Fearing the encroachment of the immigrants, and believing in the purity of white southern blood, the MEC began to rethink its reticence to fraternal relations with the Southern Methodists. In doing this, its leaders willingly accepted several changes to their evangelistic strategy in the South, which, in turn, impacted the organization of the denomination.

The first official change came in August 1876 when, after a lengthy process of delegates being sent between the General Conferences of the MEC and the MECS, the two denominations agreed to a joint commission that would meet in Cape May, New Jersey to "adjust all existing difficulties" between the two denominations.[63] The result of this meeting was a document entitled "The Declaration and Basis of Fraternity." In it, the two denominations agreed that each was a legitimate expression of the one, true Wesleyan heritage. In making this statement, the MEC expressly agreed with the statement that the MECS did not secede but had, instead, separated based on the mutually agreed upon Plan of Separation set forth at the General Conference of 1844.[64] The document also outlined a means of resolving outstanding disputes on the ownership of local church prop-

---

61. Ibid., 331.

62. Ibid., 332.

63. Kirby et al., *Methodists*, 136.

64. Tigert, *Constitutional History of American Episcopal Methodism*, 458.

erty that arose because of the Methodists occupying the South after the Civil War.

With these changes, the MEC, in effect, ceded the moral victory to the MECS by abandoning the positions that it had established as necessary for reunion with the South and capitulating entirely to the Southern positions that their bishops had set forth a decade earlier. More than that, the MEC also substantially transformed its evangelistic strategy toward the South. White southerners no longer needed to be evangelized by calling them to repent of their participation in secession and slavery. Rather, they were equals with whom the MEC should join in building a Christian American civilization. So it was that the Cape May declaration pictured the denominations as apostles sent out two-by-two to evangelize the world, striving with each other to "wave the banner of the Cross in this western world."[65] Likewise, in the fraternal address delivered by H. B. Ridgeway of the MEC to the MECS at the latter's General Conference in 1882, it was possible for him to state, "I can not think of my denomination as apart from yours. First of all, the conversion and conservation of this Christian nation is committed to us . . . The heathen at our own doors, nay, inside our doors—the numerous people pouring into our bosom from foreign lands, West and East, and who come too often without vital knowledge of God, must be saved and made good Christians and good citizens."[66]

Given this common cause of defending the nation against the immigrants, it was not even too much for Ridgeway to commend the work of the Southern Methodists concerning their ministry with the slaves. He declared, "You of the South have done much for the colored people. It is doubtful if history has done you full justice in this respect, I personally . . . know that your efforts for the slaves . . . were accompanied in thousands of breasts by the purest benevolence." It is little wonder that Stowell concluded "the Cape May conference marked the end of religious reconstruction for Methodists. Northern Methodists recognized the permanence and legitimacy of the southern church, which they had hoped in 1865 would disintegrate in the face of their intensive missionary efforts."[67] According to Morris L. Davis (2008), this new attitude on the part of the MEC lasted well into the second decade of the twentieth century due to the larger concern of sustaining and propagating Christian American civilization. He stated, "MEC periodicals and publications were

---

65. Neely, *American Methodism: Its Divisions and Unification*, 230.

66. "Fraternal Address."

67. Stowell, *Rebuilding Zion*, 174.

filled with references to American Christian civilization, but there were no references to 'the North.' Political and regional identities among white MEC members were subsumed by national identity, but they were nearly always willing to play the part of the spoiler in the southern drama. White MEC members, in deference to their peers in the MECS, assented to the accusations of northern aggression and shared in southern hand-wringing over the tragedy of the loss of 'the old plantation.'"[68]

With the MEC acceptance of southern whites as essentially good co-laborers in the construction of American civilization, it undertook a dramatic reallocation of its resources for evangelizing the South. First, it began to back away from its anticaste position, in which it declared that all races should have equal opportunities before both civil and ecclesiastical law. The denomination had heralded this position following the Civil War as a sign of its moral superiority to the MECS in an attempt to attract more African Americans into membership.[69] As popular as this position had turned out to be with African Americans, it was equally unpopular with Southern Methodists who retained their notion of African Americans being inferior to whites.[70] The MECS was particularly displeased with the steps the MEC had taken to educate and ordain African Americans. Given the pressure to regain the pure, white stock from the South, the concern for retaining fraternal relations with the Southern Methodists took precedence over working toward equality between the races, causing the MEC to embark on a period of segregation.

James Buckley (1898) chronicled the decision of the General Conference of 1876 to allow for annual conferences to separate on the basis of race. If a majority of both African American and white clergy in an annual conference agreed, two separate annual conferences could be formed in the same geographical area—one for whites and one for African Americans. Within the African American conferences, African Americans would fill all the ecclesiastical positions except the episcopacy, since bishops were voted on by the church-at-large. According to Buckley, a group of delegates did oppose this decision on the basis that it promoted a caste system. However, the majority of delegates overruled them, arguing from a position of pragmatism by claiming 1) that the annual conferences were already internally segregated in how they operated and 2) that separation was necessary to sustain the evangelistic work the denomination was now

68. Davis, *Methodist Unification*, 39.

69. Hildebrand, *Times Were Strange and Stirring*, 86.

70. Stowell, *Rebuilding Zion*, 143.

committed to among (and with) Southern whites.[71] As a result of this decision, by 1884 twenty-five of the twenty-eight MEC annual conferences in the South were either entirely white or entirely African American.[72]

The *Central Christian Advocate* articulated the pragmatist position in an article written a few years later in which it sought to reconcile the anticaste stance of the denomination and its willingness to allow for racial segregation:

> The conviction and faith of the MEC is as strong, and her practice as nearly in accord with her faith, as that of any Protestant Church; but her faith and practice are not, and never have been, in harmony in regard to the colored people. The simple fact is, that wherever the colored people have become Methodists, and are found in any considerable number, they have been formed into separate societies; when a number of societies have been formed they have been organized into a separate district, and in the end into separate conferences. The line of procedure has been the same in the North, where slavery has not prevailed for generations, and the rights of the colored people are fully recognized, as in the South where the prejudice against them is the greatest . . . It does not mean that we intend to be unjust or unchristian, nor that we harbor secret prejudice against our colored brethren, but simply that the condition of things about us makes it impossible, as we say, to put our theory in practice. We are not hypocrites, nor are we consciously faint at heart in contending for the equal rights of all men; but we have learned that the leaven of Christianity has not yet leavened society. We find our theory and the practical reason not in accord, and we follow reason. For we are not propagating a theory but engaged in obtaining actual benefits for men. The object we have in view is itself a step towards the overthrow of error and sin and prejudice. It is not a surrender, but accepting what we can not at once change that we may yet reach the object in view.[73]

71. Buckley, *History of Methodism in the United States*, 2:223–24.

72. Stowell, *Rebuilding Zion*, 145.

73. "Theory and Practice," 2.

The Transformation and Fall of the FAS

New Community Center constructed by the MEC
for White Residents of Appalachia

In addition to reorganizing its conference structure in a way that suited southern tastes on racial issues, the MEC began to reallocate its resources for evangelism among the southern whites and African Americans. This is especially visible in the career of the FAS, which saw its mandate change dramatically as fear over immigration waxed.

For the first ten years of its existence, the FAS board members heard reminders of the reasons why it was critical to the welfare of the United States for the MEC to invest significant wealth and energy in uplifting the freed slaves. For example, the organization marked its ninth anniversary by providing nine major reasons that the work of the society was essential. Of the nine reasons, three spoke to the dangers inherent to northern civilization if they failed to uplift the freed slaves, three spoke to the specific obligations the MEC had to care for the freed slaves, and three spoke to the ways in which the uplifted freed slaves could further spread Methodist missions by influencing yet more African Americans to accept WMCNB northern values. With such potent arguments in favor of uplifting the freed slaves, the mission of the FAS would seem to have been secure.

However, the specter of immigration and its dangers began to be sounded even at the FAS meetings. The result of this was not to bring an end to the work of the FAS, but to change the motivation for that work. No longer was the FAS concerned with uplifting African Americans because of the potential boon or bane they could be to American civilization, but because engaging with this demographic connected with the needs of a northern civilization under assault from the immigration of numerous non-Protestant foreigners. One way the FAS made this connection was by imagining Catholicism sweeping into the South and claiming the loyalty of African Americans through providing education that would indoctrinate them into accepting the anti-civilization promoted by the pope. As early as 1870 one FAS report luridly declared,

> If we abandon this field so full of promise, and give up the schools that we have taught with so much success, the Roman Catholics will enter into our labors and continue them. They stand ready to enter several localities, where we have for years sustained schools, if for the want of funds, zeal, or any other cause, we shall abandon them. If Protestants realized the danger threatened from this quarter, they would cheerfully contribute to this enterprise the money essential to its continuance, and thus avert so fearful a calamity. Methodism, with the funds at her disposal, can hold this field against Catholicism, or any other system of error that may assail it.[74]

Only a year later, the FAS included a lengthy section on how to defeat "Romanism" among African Americans. It concluded that the primary strategy for this entailed instilling WMCNB values and patterns of life by instituting free schools and a free press through which the FAS could teach the Bible and respect for the Sabbath. The denomination ultimately deployed these same solutions in relating to Catholic immigrants, as we will explore later.[75]

In addition to this shift as to why the FAS needed to evangelize African Americans, the FAS began to develop a more positive view of southern whites. This shift did not take place quickly or easily because of how ardently the members of the FAS believed in the American gospel of the north in contrast to the heresies of the South. The FAS made this clear in 1881 when it described the Civil War as "the conflict of two civilizations, each rooted and grounded in the profoundest convictions of millions of people," and then went on to declare

> if any one believes that when General Lee handed his sword to General Grant, that the political and social convictions of the

74. Freedmen's Aid Society, *Fourth Annual Report*, 7.

75. Freedmen's Aid Society, *Fifth Annual Report*, 9.

South passed over with that sword to the civilization of freedom, as distinguished from the civilization of slavery, such a one has not read history aright or knows not the power of strong conviction. The abolition of slavery is accepted, but the conviction which preached from every Southern pulpit that slavery was a divine institution still demands that the relative positions of the white and black man shall be as distinctly marked as when the former bought and sold the latter.[76]

Still, this sort of description of the South was tempered by other comments that were far friendlier. In 1877, four years earlier than the above quote, the FAS proved that it was not above lauding the Southern Methodists' evangelistic work among the freed slaves. As Dr. Matlack, an ardent supporter of the FAS, declared:

Somebody had been with them [the freed slaves] and aided them before our Aid Society was organized. Thousands and tens of thousands were being converted, and exhibited a true religious life; and besides were so imbued with a love for antislavery Methodism that they flocked to the open doors of their "old mother Church" in great crowds. Whom have we to thank for such a preparation of material, all ready to our hands, and for such an opportunity to organize Churches and conferences, that the first quadrennium thereafter gave us an increase of membership numbering nearly three hundred thousand—one-third of which was from the ranks of the freedmen? The answer presents to us the Southern Methodists . . . Honor to whom honor is due . . . Sir, it is not wise, neither is it just, that we should boast beyond measure. If they of the South neglected to do all their duty in the past years of formidable difficulties, our present well doing with our more favorable surroundings is too recent and too imperfect to warrant much self-laudation. If they will wink at our past inconsistencies, we can honorably compromise by omitting all allusion to their past short-comings. "We be brethren."[77]

The leadership of the entire MEC took a step beyond acknowledging the positive impact the Southern Methodists had on the freed slaves, claiming that the white southerners could be an even greater aid in civilizing African Americans and immigrants alike if they had greater opportunities to deploy their untainted white heredity. Accordingly, at the General Conference of 1880, the denomination renamed the Freedmen's Aid

76. Freedmen's Aid Society, *Fourteenth Annual Report,* 50.
77. Freedmen's Aid Society, *Ninth Annual Report,* 68–70.

Society the Freedmen's Aid and Southern Education Society (FA&SES) and mandated that the new FA&SES begin to distribute its funds to both whites and African Americans in the South. The directors of the FA&SES sought to put a good face on this dramatic change in the mission statement of the agency through wrapping it in anticaste language in their annual report for the year 1880.

> The General Conference instructed the Directors of this Society to aid schools for whites in the South all it could without embarrassment to its work among the freedmen, and they are following its instructions to the best of their ability . . . [I]t is thought that, by a judicious enlargement of our work among the whites in the South, we may reach a large class of our people who have never taken much interest in this movement, and have never contributed much, if any, to its wants; so that, instead of diminishing, we may hope to increase our funds for the elevation of the freedmen as well as for the neglected white people of the South. In the accomplishment of this purpose donors may name the object to which they desire their benefactions to be applied, and all funds concerning which donors do not give specific directions will be appropriated by the Society in accordance with the instructions of the General Conference . . . The enlargement of our school enterprise among the poor whites will strengthen the colored work . . . We seek to instruct and save the people of the South, without regard to race or color.[78]

The call to save Northern civilization took on a new and more strident tone in the society's communications following the inclusion of whites in its work. The report the following year carried a potent admonition to Methodist pastors to take the financial support of the FA&SES seriously by weaving traditional arguments for support of the freed slaves together with the need to protect northern civilization. It did all of this by identifying the MEC as "the Christian Church of America," stating:

> O! How God calls the Christian Church of America to save them! How he piles up the arguments: *gratitude*, for out of their toil we have grown rich; *self-interested*, for their redemption is our own; *Christian charity*, for they are in want and we are rich; *patriotism*, for the Christian civilization of this nation in its conflicts with Rome, rum, and communism may very soon need every one of their votes, it certainly will be safer with them; *philanthropy*, for they are our brothers; *the judgment*, for "inasmuch

78. Freedmen's Aid Society, *Thirteenth Annual Report*, 11–12.

as ye did it not unto one of the least of these my brethren, ye did it not unto me."[79]

Later in the same report a reprinted speech by J. P. Newman made the relationship of the inclusion of white education as part of the FA&SES mission to protecting northern civilization startlingly clear.

> I am more concerned in regard to the future of the white people of the South, because I do not know but what in the changing fortunes of nationalities, the South will yet prove to be the sheet anchor of this republic. We know it may be in the order of divine Providence that the tide of immigration has swept by the Southern States—gone to the North, the East, and the West. New England has largely ceased to be Yankee, and is being rapidly populated by foreigners. The foreign population of Massachusetts, Connecticut, New Hampshire, Vermont, and Maine, will soon outvote the native population. I would utter no word to create prejudice against the foreigner. He is welcome here, but I remember that selfishness underlies emigration, true of all history in regard to those who come to our shores. They come not for love of liberty, not for our institutions; they come to improve their material condition. It is not until the second, and sometimes the third generation, that we can trust them to stand fast by those principles held sacred by the fathers of the republic . . . But in the South is the American to the manor born. And it may be that the pride of blood flowing down from father to son may yet prove to be the life blood of the republic, that when the cosmopolitan population of your city and of my own city, caring for nothing but itself, shall disregard the traditions of the republic—the fundamental principles on which the Union rests, and especially the divinity of our religion—from the savannas of the South shall come forth an American citizenship imbued with the spirit of the fathers, reverently cherishing their sentiments and clinging to the eternal principles of our religion. And it may be that the *"boys in gray" may yet save the flag and save the Church.*[80]

So it was that the Confederacy would save the Republic!

Over the following decades the FA&SES continued to see its mission among African Americans de-emphasized by the MEC as a primary focus of saving American civilization. In 1907, as a result of a massive

---

79. Freedmen's Aid Society, *Fourteenth Annual Report*, 53.

80. Ibid., 78–79.

organizational move made by the General Conference of 1904 to create a centralized set of missions agencies within the denomination, the
MEC discontinued the FA&SES as one of the independent societies of
the denomination. Instead, it absorbed it underneath the newly formed
Methodist Episcopal Department of Education. With this stroke, the great
evangelistic effort to uplift the freed slaves so that they might participate
in Christian American civilization was sunk to a bureaucratic sub-level.

The denomination did repent of this move in successive years. The
General Conference of 1908 severed the white work in the South from
the work among African Americans, once again creating the Freedmen's
Aid Society. The new FAS was still under the auspices of the Board of
Education, but was free to focus only on the educational needs of African
Americans. The General Conference of 1916 took a further step by setting
the FAS free to be a stand-alone agency once again.

While the actions of the General Conferences in 1908 and 1916
might seem to suggest a growing support for evangelization among African Americans by the MEC in the early twentieth century, this was not the
case. Historian Morris Davis argued that during the 19-teens the primary
concern for the MEC in its relationship to African Americans generally,
not just through the FAS, had to do with the delicate meetings of the Joint
Commission on Unification the denomination was holding together with
the MECS and the Methodist Protestant Church.

According to Davis, race was the primary issue of division during these meetings, which served as the precursor to the merger of the
three denominations in 1939. Specifically, the question of how to include
the African American members of the MEC in any merger was of serious concern. The five meetings of the Joint Commission began with the
participants approaching the issue from the perspective of what would
be appropriate social interactions between the races in the unified church
and ended with an emphasis on "American nationalism and patriotism,"
especially in light of the First World War.[81] Given the MEC's soteriological
relationship with WMCNB civilization and the denomination's belief that
only southern whites could help sustain this civilization against the immigrants, the direction of the conversation made it progressively easier to
give way on racial issues. Segmenting out the FAS as a separate organization made it easier for the MEC to identify and marginalize it as needed in
its negotiations with the MECS.

81. Davis, *Methodist Unification*, 106.

This segmentation policy became more evident when the merger finally occurred. The MEC was willing to compromise with the MECS on a separate-but-equal policy, which created regional conferences for all whites in the newly formed denomination and placed all African Americans in a single, nation-spanning Central Conference. This allowed the African Americans to continue in the denomination, but not as members who would interact regularly with the whites. It also secured the northern and southern whites together.

Another reason for segmenting out the FAS had to do with the distribution of denominational resources. During the early twentieth century, Methodists gave their primary attention and resources to the major denominational boards and departments. By removing the FAS from the Department of Education, the Methodists were effectively de-emphasizing it. Rather than have the advocacy of one of the corresponding secretaries of these major denominational agencies whose portfolio included overseeing the FAS, the FAS was forced to compete with these major agencies. The fact that it did not always fare well in this competition is seen by how far back in the General Conference Journals its reports are placed compared to the reports of the major agencies.

The decreased denominational support for the FAS, in terms of attention, resources, and advocacy for racial equality, may point to the fact that by the early twentieth century the MEC concluded that African Americans had been successfully civilized. As a result, the FAS did not need to engage in the same level of evangelistic and educational activity that it did immediately after the abolition of slavery.

The Methodists measured the civilization of the African Americans in two ways. One was by way of historical comparison. FAS representatives delighted in reminding delegates to the General Conference about the growth of wealth, professionalism, religiosity and patriotism among African Americans since the days of slavery. One example of this is found in the FAS report to the General Conference of 1912.

> The first half century in the education of the Negro furnishes a record unmatched in the history of any race. More than six out of ten can read the Bible as compared with seven out of ten emancipated Russian serfs yet in illiteracy. Thousands of trained ministers now give their lives with efficiency and a high sense of consecration to Christian service. Forty thousand churches, built at a cost of over fifty million dollars, are standing testimony to the religious and moral earnestness of the Negro race. More than two thousand well-equipped physicians are giving higher

vitality to the race and an ethical uplift to home and personal life. A host of Christian teachers trained in our colleges have become centers of intellectual energy. Multitudes have acquired homes and farms, giving every assurance of an ever-advancing economic future for the race.[82]

The FAS report to the General Conference of 1920 offers another good example of this:

> Dear Fathers and Brethren: For fifty-four years the Freedmen's Aid Society has been engaged in solving the most difficult, perplexing, and intricate of our national problems. Four millions of people of African descent, just out from 250 year of slavery, and a thousand generations of savagery, were left to shift for themselves, without property, without education, and worse than all, without experience in taking care of themselves. Two elements of hope rose above the surface of this mass of ignorant black humanity. They spoke the English tongue, and were imbued with the elements of evangelical Christianity. These were the sure signs of democracy and progress. To put the spelling book and the Bible into the head and heart of the Negro was the aim of the men who organized the Freedmen's Aid Society. How well they did it is evidenced by the fact that, while the race had nothing to begin with, to-day with its numbers increased to twelve millions, eighty or more out of every hundred can read and write. They that were once homeless slaves now own 500,000 homes, have 35,000 Christian churches, besides farms and other property valued at over a billion dollars. From these homes and churches 300,000 stalwart Negro soldiers responded to the call of the Nation [during the First World War], and proved the patriotism and bravery of their race in defense of democracy, side by side with other valorous Americans, who died that "government of the people, by the people, and for the people shall not perish from the earth.[83]

Taken together, these passages demonstrate that the FAS believed that the seeds of civilization were already sown in the African American race, and the help of the MEC through the FAS had produced a significant yield of WMCNB virtues. These included loyalty to the Republic, Methodist morality, and capitalistic financial success—all of which were

82. Hingeley, *Journal of the Twenty-Sixth Delegated General Conference*, 714.
83. Mills, *Journal of the Twenty-Eighth Delegated General Conference*, 1131.

critical markers for demonstrating participation in Christian American civilization.

This historical success tied into a second indicator of civilization among the African Americans: the use by African Americans of their new-found wealth and citizenship to better themselves, particularly through providing generous financial and capital support to the educational institutions maintained by the FAS. Routinely, the FAS included comments on "self-sufficiency" in their reports to General Conference when their representatives appeared to seek more funding from the denomination. Sometimes these remarks pointed to the ingenuity and diligence of the students and faculty in improving and maintaining the FAS-supported schools where they were located. In one such instance, the students at Wiley University in Texas built the new central building, making the bricks themselves, and a professor at Wiley procured the parts for an electrical plant, built it, and lit the entire campus.[84] More often, the FAS proudly pointed to the generous contributions by African Americans for the work of the FAS over and above their regular giving toward MEC missions. The FAS noted that it gained substantially in contributions from the African American conferences, especially as soon as it broke free of its association with the white work in the South. Even the bishops recognized this in their Episcopal Address of 1912.[85]

The ironic result of this generosity on the part of African Americans was for the white Methodists to relegate the work of the FAS to the MEC's African American membership, expecting them to put forth the lion's share of the means the FAS needed to operate. This expectation was made explicit in the fundraising drive launched by the FAS to celebrate its fiftieth anniversary of existence in 1916. The FAS reported to General Conference that

> the friends of Negro education and the Negroes themselves in the Church are requested to use this opportunity to help this most worthy cause by a semicentennial gift of $200,000, one hundred thousand to come from the white people and one hundred thousand from the colored people ... [In addition] we recommend the efforts of colored Methodists in America in their federated and cooperative plan of raising one dollar per member for Christian education in the next four years, and express the hope that our 350,000 colored members may rally loyally to the plan and may have every encouragement, by conditional

84. Hingeley, *Journal of the Twenty-Fourth General*, 851.
85. Hingeley, *Journal of the Twenty-Sixth Delegated General Conference*, 225.

gifts of funds, to do their part in raising during these four years $350,000 for the educational advance of their own people.[86]

In spite of the fact that the African American membership of the MEC was less than one tenth of the white membership, the FAS, with the concurrence of the General Conference of 1916, called on African American Methodists to raise an equal amount of money as the whites for a base gift, and then 3.5 times as much as an additional gift. Clearly, by this point in history the denomination saw work among African Americans as an essentially African American responsibility.

Such an assumption, regardless of how inequitable it might have been, demonstrates that the white MEC leadership believed that the African American members of the church were fully civilized. They were capable of handling money and carrying forward the mission of further evangelizing and educating their own race with little aid from whites. The extent to which the white Methodists believed this was ultimately shown in the General Conference of 1920 when the FAS was renamed "The Board of Education for Negroes" and requested that at least two of its board members be African Americans.[87] This sort of inclusion was a powerful indication of the white Methodists believing they had accomplished their work among the African Americans so well that they could entrust whatever work remained to the African Americans themselves.

With all of this success, it might be asked why the MEC needed to maintain the FAS at all by the early twentieth century. The reason, according to the FAS, was because neither the southern state governments nor the Federal Government had stepped in to guarantee that these civilized African Americans, who had faced terrible hardships, would receive equal educational opportunities to continue their advancement. As stated in the report of the FAS to the General Conference of 1912:

> The time has not yet come when the church can turn over the education of the colored people to the States wherein they reside. In most of these States the public school facilities are wholly inadequate to their educational needs. In some places little or no provision at all is made for them, and where such provision is made it is but a poor excuse. The work of the Christian churches is still necessary to supplement the work of the States, and to provide for that higher training for Christian leadership which is absolutely necessary to these people in their

86. Locke, *Journal of the Twenty-Seventh Delegated General Conference*, 657–58.
87. Mills, *Journal of the Twenty-Eighth Delegated General Conference*, 639.

formative stage. Left to themselves, with their present poverty, their social and industrial handicaps, and their lack of experience, they are unable to produce sufficient competent leaders to direct the growth of the young life of their people into moral and religious channels. This must be done through the Christian schools established by the great churches of the land, or it will not be done at all. A not unimportant phase of the work of these schools is the preparation of young men and women as Christian teachers to serve in the public schools in the Southland. In this manner the moral and religious influence of these schools is felt, not only in the churches, but by these Christian teachers, in is carried into the humblest homes of the masses of the Negro people.[88]

This southern disregard for the African American population to have equal opportunities to share in the blessings of Christian American civilization still had to be overcome, necessitating the continued existence of the FAS. So long as this existed, the dangers of uneducated African Americans held for the Republic still maintained. However, the tacit indication is that as soon as state governments were ready to step into the current void by allowing African Americans to be educated well, the FAS would disengage. There would be no more use for its work since government would remedy the external "handicaps." Notably, none of these handicaps were attributed specifically to racial inferiority or lack of civilization on the part of African Americans. The MEC was no longer concerned with these issues, both because it felt it had nearly completed this work and because it had left off fighting for social equality among whites and African Americans. The denomination simply wanted to finish what it perceived as the nearly completed work of evangelizing and, thereby, civilizing the South. The FAS was tolerated as that organization supported by the civilized African American members of the MEC as the means to finish this work.

In the end, the midwife that brought the MEC's concern for evangelizing the freed slaves into existence and the attending physician that signed that concern's death certificate were one and the same: the desire to establish a Christian American civilization through evangelism. Using my terminology, pure American evangelism drove the MEC to charge into the South to civilize the freed slaves for the sake of the Republic and then drove the MEC to declare that they had accomplished this mission so that they could reallocate their resources to deal with other peoples they felt were a greater threat to the Republic. The result was to leave the African

88. Hingeley, *Journal of the Twenty-Sixth Delegated General Conference*, 1285.

Americans who had joined the MEC to take care of the African Americans who continued to struggle for the equality they had hoped would follow on the heels of emancipation.

The WHMS Expands Its Concerns

The WHMS followed a similar path as the FAS. Although it traced its origin back to the inspiring evangelistic work of women among freedmen, it quickly shifted its attention away from this. As early as its second annual meeting, even as it developed a bureau to oversee its work with "colored people in the South," it also developed a bureau for "illiterate white people in the south." In the Corresponding Secretary's report for the same meeting, while describing in detail the work the agency was sponsoring in the South, there was not a single mention of work specifically among the freedmen. This contrasted with the very clear message the secretary enunciated about immigrants and Mormons. Concerning immigrants she wrote, "the refuse of all nations is drifting to this country. These immigrants bring more of the vices, superstition, infidelity, and irreligion of the Old World with them than they bring of its culture, its graces, or its art . . . It is a work of no little importance to resist the evil influences of these multitudes flocking to our shores, and to mold them into harmony with our free institutions and the Christian faith."[89]

These words ring loudly against the silence of the secretary on the issue of evangelizing the freed slaves. Already there is a hint that the agency, which began out of specific concern for the domestic betterment of the women and children among the freed slaves, was repositioninig itself to become a protectress of Christian American civilization against the far greater danger of immigration. Accordingly, the secretary looked to the importance of focusing the WHMS's resources on immigrants in order to promote WMCNB values in them.

This is not to suggest that the WHMS completely abandoned work among African Americans. As late as 1901 the Annual Presidential Address to the WHMS meeting declared,

> Many are still touched with the curse which slavery left upon them: they have not yet emerged into the full light of our gospel day; they are superstitious; ignorant, without God, without the Bible. Do you realize the vast number of these dusky sisters looking towards you with pleading eyes from their Southern

89. Women's Home Missionary Society, *Second Annual Report*, 25.

cabins? There are millions of them; some far advanced in Christian civilization, but thousands of them are not. The masses are as yet unreached, unchristianized, and they must depend on us for their elevation and salvation. What an inheritance do they possess! For hundreds of years they knew degradation, in its awfulest forms. No marriage, no home. No true motherhood and wifehood. At any moment were the bonds snapped, and all home ties destroyed. From such an inheritance, from such associations can we expect even now that *all* should show purity of home, Christliness of character? . . . Their lives have no continued thread, and forty years are not enough to bring a race to perfection. Those cabins, one room and windowless, can not be fountains of purity. The "debased motherhood" of the race must be reached, uplifted, redeemed. We must begin at the home, the center of national life and strength.[90]

Strident as this call to action was, it ceased to be the norm as the WHMS entered the twentieth century. Instead, as with the FAS, the WHMS began to place its emphasis on those African Americans who the home missionaries believed already were civilized. In 1905, for example, the former superintendent of a WHMS home of girls in Tennessee was able to report the story of a little African American girl. This girl preferred to stay at the home than to live with her own family and "became expert in the use of the needle." Upon graduating, she went to Puerto Rico to serve as a missionary because, the girl claimed, "The Winchester Auxiliary has spent $280 for me; I can never be happy until I pass out to others something of what has been done for me."[91] In so doing, the girl showed she had a good, American character. She had recognized the importance of a domestic education even as a child, and as an adult she became a fully active WHMS missionary. It would be hard for the WHMS to find a better example of an African American being civilized than this!

The WHMS further claimed to see the civilized nature of African Americans in the generosity that African American conferences showed toward the WHMS coffers. In 1907, the Corresponding Secretary of the WHMS happily reported, "We have much to expect from the help of the colored people when they understand the needs and their responsibility."[92] The consistently increasing financial gifts of the African American conferences, totaling $2,377.71 the previous year, an increase of $400.68 from

90. Women's Home Missionary Society, *Twentieth Annual Report*, 97.

91. Women's Home Missionary Society, *Twenty-Fourth Annual Report*, 29.

92. Women's Home Missionary Society, *Twenty-Sixth Annual Report*, 73.

the year before, made this clear. Likewise, a number of African American women were presenting themselves as possible candidates for the position of deaconess, a form of ministry created for women by the WHMS that we will consider in more detail in a later chapter. In these selfless acts, the African Americans showed themselves to be civilized in the eyes of the WHMS. Much like the General Conference, the WHMS saw the growing finances and generosity of the African Americans as a sure indicator of the civilized virtues imparted to the African Americans attained under the auspices of Methodist evangelism.

Based on this perceived success, during the second decade of the twentieth century the WHMS took the final steps in de-emphasizing the threat of the African Americans to the Republic while also calling for greater giving to help the African Americans who suffered from poverty and lack of opportunity. In 1915 the WHMS instituted several bureaus entitled "Colored Work in . . ." naming the state in which the work took place. In 1917 these were renamed "Negro Work in . . ." And, in 1920, in a move that simultaneously solidified the WHMS agenda with that of the MECS's view of African Americans while also pointing to the successful participation of African Americans in Christian American civilization, the President of the WHMS quoted at length a passage from *Our Brother in Black: His Freedom and His Future.* This text was a treatment of race relations authored by Southern Methodist Atticus Haygood in 1881. She proclaimed, "plant these Industrial Homes all over the South; send out one well-trained woman from such a Home. She will be worth a regiment of trained lady missionaries and their visitations. She will live among the people who need her, the knowledge of her, will itself be the beginning of home education to these people . . . she will pay her own way and something over to start her sisters on the march to the 'promised land' of homes for the Negro race; she will be a wife and mother worthy of these holy names." In response to this passage, the president exulted, "Great is this tribute, and to-day are seen the results of such seed-sowing."[93]

That the president of the WHMS claimed the words of a Southern Methodist penned thirty-five years prior as a tribute to the work the WHMS accomplished among the African Americans in the South is a clear indicator of the drift in the agency's own thinking. While the women of the WHMS continued to see importance in helping the African Americans just as they saw the importance of helping anyone who was underprivileged or needy, they no longer needed to place particular focus on

93. Ibid., 61.

African Americans. This was because, as they saw it, the African American women were now taking the uplifting work of the WHMS into their own hands to reach whoever among their own race was still uncivilized. Pure American evangelism had thus taken root and blossomed among African American women by bringing them to adopt the values of WMCNB northerners and then sending them out to share those values with others. As such, the WHMS was free to turn its attention to the scourge of immigration, which all Christian Americans needed to address immediately to save the civilization.

AN EVANGELISTIC REACTION

Original caption: Am I not a man, and a brother?

It is worth recognizing that not everyone approved of the MEC's swing away from the freed slaves and toward the southern whites. One unique analysis of this came from Rev. L. M. Hagood, an African American medical doctor who became an ordained member of the MEC. Hagood penned a thoughtful book entitled *The Colored Man in the MEC* (1890) in which he sought to correct what he perceived as the misperceptions of many African Americans about the MEC following the creation of separate annual conferences based on race and the expansion of the FAS to the FA&SES. In his book, Hagood wanted "to show that, so far as the question goes, the heart of the MEC has always been right; and that, though errors may have been committed, they have been in most instances, from the head and not from the heart of the church; and it has come as near reaching the proper solution to the question 'What shall be done with the colored man?' as any other organization that has had to do with the question."[94]

To make this case, Hagood spent several pages reminding his readers of the ways that the MEC reached out to and honored African Americans during its early history in the United States. Based on this, he roundly castigated the founders of both the African Methodist Episcopal Church and African Methodist Episcopal Zion Church. Calling these groups the incendiary term "secessionists," he argued that they did more to promote the notion of caste by refusing to work with the white members of the MEC than they did to alleviate it by forming their own denominations.[95] The insidiousness of these denominations became obvious to Hagood prior to the Civil War when they duped honest white MEC preachers to believe that it would be better for African Americans to be among their own race at church rather than surrounded by potentially oppressive whites. As such, Hagood contended that many white MEC ministers welcomed AME and AMEZ preachers into their pulpits and exhorted the few African Americans in their own congregations to join these denominations rather than inviting them into the MEC.[96] All of this drew members away from the MEC, which Hagood believed was willing "to make concessions to the colored man, to train, protect, and elevate him . . . It has in every case, as far as practicable, tried to remedy the wrongs perpetrated upon him as well as lessen his burdens."[97]

94. Hagood, *Colored Man in the Methodist Episcopal Church*, 4–5.

95. Ibid., 46–47.

96. Ibid., 72–74.

97. Ibid., 62.

Based on this duplicity by the African Methodist denominations, Hagood argued that the MEC had no choice but to offer conferences separated by race, since this was the only way to compete with the African Methodist offerings and keep African Americans within the denomination while allowing them to have the freedom and equality to run their own ecclesiastical affairs. This need to keep pace with the African Methodist denominations became even more pronounced with the introduction of the freed slaves to the MEC following the Civil War. Describing the experience of the freed slaves in dealing with the MEC following emancipation, Hagood explained,

> In the North he found that the white people knew him only as a slave or a freedman. If the former, then he was considered a mendicant—ignorant, superstitious, and immoral, as a natural result of slavery. They could not think of taking him into their homes—cultured, refined, and religious homes—to be at once associated with the members of their families. As to their Churches, he was wholly unfitted for their mode of worship; for to him it appeared foolishness, fashion, and fastidiousness, void of "the true, heart-felt religion" of the plantation where "his sons and his daughters prophesied, his old men dreamed dreams, and his young men saw visions." As a result, he pretty soon began to feel uneasy, and sighted for "the seasons of the past." The white man of the North *could not possibly meet the social or religious demands of the slave.* If he put him in the parlor or school-room with the white children, or in the congregation of the Lord— though given a front seat, and in every conceivable way made welcome—he was uneasy . . . The white man of the North could not make the colored man from the South feel at home. If he had a separate building in which to allow him and his family to live, it would have appeared more like home to him.[98]

As a result, it was a gift of equality and hospitality for the MEC to offer racially segregated conferences for the bewildered and frustrated freed slaves.

At the same time Hagood supported separating annual conferences by race, he reserved harsh criticism for the expansion of the FAS's mission to include southern whites. His reason for this was not that he thought it was inappropriate for the denomination to aid illiterate whites ("No sane colored man within the MEC believes that it would benefit his race if the Church were to give up all its work in the South among whites,"[99]

98. Ibid., 199–200.
99. Ibid., 288.

he opined), but because the fundraising for the newly expanded society engendered prejudice. The FA&SES granted the donor the right to determine which race should benefit from his or her donation. As a result, Hagood reasoned, each race benefitted from encouraging prejudice in its favor in order to secure the largest number of donations.[100] Aside from this mistake, however, he complimented the work of the FA&SES and wished it well among whites and African Americans in the future.

Hagood's work seems shockingly supportive of the shifts in the MEC, which history has marked as the beginning of the end of that denonmination's concern for the freed slaves. What accounts for this? The first is Hagood's unswerving optimism. Taking the ways that the Methodists of the Revolutionary Period reached out to African slaves as normative, he was convinced "the MEC can never forsake the colored man, and be consistent."[101] It is because of this he absolutely rejected the argument that the desire for closer relations with the MECS was a driving force behind much of what the MEC did in how it restructured its race relations and evangelism among the freedmen. He wrote:

> Would it not be Christian-like and brotherly for the colored members to separate, so that organic union may take place between the "two great branches of Methodism in this country?" *Is that what keeps them apart?* We would, to the question as to separation, answer, No. If we understand the heart of the Church—and we think we do, having been born naturally and supernaturally in her lap—she does not ask as much. In 1844 the Church, by dropping her interests in and work for the colored man, could very easily and knowingly have preserved her union, power, and influence, kept back the rebellion for a time, received the encomiums instead of the vituperation and obloquy of every slaveholding nation in the world, and brought to her support the strong slave oligarchy of the South. She did not do it. She will never compromise with sin enough to accept even an organic union conceived in caste and born of a hate that excludes *one* the Lord said should be loved as herself.[102]

In making this argument, however, Hagood was sadly misinterpreting what he saw. The MEC *was* being consistent precisely by how it was separating out its African American members and neglecting the freedmen in favor of the white Southerners, especially the Southern Methodists.

100. Ibid., 285.
101. Ibid., 293.
102. Ibid., 314.

This is because its consistency was not found in how it related to African Americans, but how it related to WMCNB American civilization. Hagood believed the denomination distinguished itself by its prophetic actions on behalf of his race. In fact, it distinguished itself by its cultural ties to the United States, and in the decades after the Civil War when those ties were at their strongest, his race was becoming an increasingly diminished part of how that culture understood itself.

The other reason that Hagood maintained this support for the MEC is because he believed the church never wavered in its primary goal of carrying out revivalistic evangelism. To make this point, he concluded his book with the inclusion of an article from the *Northwestern Advocate,* which stated, "if we are in the South, as are other evangelical Churches, for the purpose of saving the souls of men, we deserve Godspeed. But if the only reason we can give for being there is to eradicate caste, social prejudice between races, the foundation for our errand will deservedly be alike unsubstantial with its completed results."[103]

While such rhetoric may have sat well with Methodists, harkening back to the heroic days of the Second Great Awakening in the United States, it was hardly accurate or helpful. As argued throughout this chapter, the evangelism engaged in by the MEC from the Civil War onward was pure American evangelism, and the very purpose of this evangelism in the South was to plant the Christian civilization of the North there. It was not a return to "purer" revivalism that led the MEC to cease its work of civilizing the South, but the fact that the armies of Christian civilization were recalled to the North to fight the battles with immigrants there. More than that, those armies sought white reinforcements from the South.

The South proved to be an ideal region for the MEC to develop its practice of pure American evangelism because the South contained a clear rival interpretation of what American civilization and its values should be. This forced the denomination to define precisely what values it wanted to propagate along with the gospel. The South was also home to a group of people who were disaffected from those rival values. This gave the Methodists an immediate field of people to evangelize, seeking to initiate them into their own view of what Christian American civilization should be. Based on this experience, Methodists were ready to move into other parts of the country with their perfected understanding and practice of evangelism as a means of propagating Christian American civilization. The most logical region to continue this work was in the West, where the Methodists had already begun work prior to the outbreak of the Civil War.

103. Quoted in ibid., 281.

4

The West

IN HIS ESSAY "THE Significance of the Frontier in American History" (1893) Frederick Jackson Turner penned: "In a recent bulletin of the superintendent of the census for 1890 appear these significant words: 'Up to and including 1880 the country had a frontier of settlement, but at present the unsettled area has been so broken into by isolated bodies of settlement that there can hardly be said to be a frontier line. In the discussion of its extent, its westward movement, etc., it cannot, therefore, any longer have a place in the census reports.' This brief official statement marks the closing of a great historic movement."[1]

In the essay, Turner defined the frontier as "the outer edge of the wave—the meeting point between savagery and civilization . . . it lies at the hither edge of free land."[2] He then argued that what made the citizens of the United States unique from their European forebears was the fact that they had to contend with the constant process of carrying civilization to the savagery of the frontier throughout the entirety of their history. As he explained it, "American development has exhibited not merely advance along a single line, but a return to primitive conditions on a continually advancing frontier line, and a new development for that area. American social development has been continually beginning over again on the frontier. This perennial rebirth, this fluidity of American life, this expansion westward with its new opportunities, its continuous touch with the simplicity of primitive society, furnish the forces dominating American character."[3]

1. Turner, *History, Frontier and Section*, 59.
2. Ibid., 60.
3. Ibid.

Specifically, he argued, the national character of the United States found its genesis in Americans carrying civilization constantly westward through establishing advanced economic practices and technology. These aspects of American civilization allowed them to move ever deeper in the American West, subdue its inhabitants, and capture the land for the most productive purposes.[4]

Turner acknowledged, however, that not all Americans saw the move west as occurring in a civilized, or even orderly, way. He quoted Lyman Beecher at length in describing how untamed the West was and how the mad dash of both Americans and immigrants to settle it did not guarantee that the purposes of civilization would be served. In recognizing this point, Turner noted how Northern civilization and religion joined forces to fret over the condition of the West: "The dread of western emancipation from New England's political and economic control was paralleled by fears lest the West cut loose from her religion."[5]

What Turner observed in Beecher was also true of how the Methodist Episcopal Church felt about the West. The MEC saw the West as having great promise, partly due to the denomination's historical successes in holding revivals along the frontier, but as also harboring potential danger. This was for two reasons. The first was due to the variegated population in the West.

There were the white American settlers from the East. These once had been civilized individuals, but they had lost their WMCNB values when they encountered the "savagery" of the West. The MEC home missionaries saw this group as one that needed to be reminded of its civilized nature and given the capacity to participate in Christian American civilization again.

One exception to the MEC's view of the white settlers in the West was the Mormons. The MEC viewed the Mormons as a tremendous danger to the life of the Republic for three reasons: (1) their polygamy, which stood in direct opposition to the Victorian home that Methodists understood to be the bedrock of a Christian civilization, (2) their un-Christian beliefs, and (3) their political aspirations.

In contrast to the settlers who were just coming into the West, there was another population that could claim to be native to the land: the Native Americans. This population was a vexing one for MEC home missionaries. While the missionaries were certain that the Native Americans

4. Ibid., 63.
5. Ibid., 86–87.

maintained a low level of civilization, most Methodists were aware of the strong-arm tactics the Federal Government had often used to strip Native Americans of their lands. As a result, Methodists saw the Native Americans as less a threat to Christian American civilization than as a group that deserved the best that civilization had to offer.

Added to these groups was a large number of Spanish-speakers who claimed the Southwest as home. Almost all of these were Mexicans who had become citizens of the United States as a result of the Treaty of Guadalupe-Hidalgo (1848) and the Gadsden Purchase (ratified by the Senate in 1854) annexing large tracts of land that had belonged to Mexico. This number increased as Mexicans crossed the Rio Grande searching for work in the cotton plantations of Texas after the Civil War. For the MEC, the Mexicans were a double threat to Christian American civilization. As Catholics they were a threat to democracy because of their allegiance to the pope. This threat was compounded by the serfdom Methodists believed the Mexicans lived in, thus stripping them of any notion of how to participate as citizens in a republican form of government.

A final group was the immigrants who were coming into the western cities, most of whom were from Asian descent. I will treat MEC home missionary work in the cities in the following chapter and so will not touch on it here.

The second reason the MEC was concerned about the West was the lack of infrastructure for Christian American civilization. WMCNB values and patterns of life both required a significant overhead of technology and material goods to be maintained. The West, however, had a paucity of these goods, making it easier for the various groups to remain in a comparatively savage state.

To create a proper environment to foster Christian American civilization in the West required three primary ingredients. The first was providing MEC pastors and/or missionaries who could inculcate WMCNB values into the various groups living in the West. The second was the construction of church buildings and other facilities where westerners could enact the patterns of life common to WMCNB Americans. The third was the female touch that would spread the civilizing influence of domesticity. This domesticity came both in the form of helping the girls and women in the West to understand WMCNB gender roles and in equipping them with the necessary goods to keep house as a good Victorian wife and mother should.

The MEC developed different mechanisms for exporting these various means of constructing Christian American civilization to the various groups inhabiting the West. Those who already knew what Christian American civilization was and simply lacked the accoutrements to participate in that civilization would receive what was necessary for them to reclaim their civilized patterns of life. Those who were unacquainted with WMCNB values and patterns of life because of their race and lack of education would have the necessary teachers and structures in which to learn how to participate in Christian American civilization's blessings. In the process, those who stubbornly hung on to an alternate understanding of civilization, particularly the Mormons, were either pressed to convert or suppressed.

As far as the Methodists of his day would have been concerned, when Turner famously declared that the frontier of the United States was closed, he did not use an apt metaphor. While Americans of European descent had successfully settled—if very sparsely in some areas—throughout the West, the region was still far from civilized. Virtually every demographic that called the West home was in need of having Christian American civilization bestowed upon it. As a result, the frontier remained very much open well into the early twentieth century as stalwart Methodist evangelists moved forward to carry pure American evangelism to the various populations in the West and so tame the savagery that continued to exist there.

RECLAIMING THE WAYWARD EASTERNER

The MEC exerted its greatest home missionary efforts in the West in evangelizing the white American settlers, deploying its preachers, the CES, and the WHMS in this task. Likely this is because this group, more than any of the other groups in the West, represented the greatest possibility of successfully being brought into the fold of Christian American civilization. Partly this optimism would have stemmed from the racial affinity this group had with the MEC membership. Partly it would have been because this population still had vestiges of the WMCNB values within them from when they had lived in the East. In effect, these were ready-made Methodists just waiting for Christian American civilization to catch up with them. However, this work would not be easy.

A great concern of many Methodists was that the lack of WMCNB patterns of life on the Western frontier caused white Americans to lose touch with their WMCNB values. In this way, the Methodists stood in full agreement with Turner's assessment,

> The wilderness masters the colonist. It finds him a European in dress, industries, tools, modes of travel, and thought. It takes him from the railroad car and puts him in the birch canoe. It strips off the garments of civilization, and arrays him in the hunting shirt and the moccasin. It puts him in the log cabin of the Cherokee and the Iroquois, and runs an Indian palisade around him. Before long he has gone to planting Indian corn and plowing with a sharp stick; he shouts the war cry and takes the scalp in orthodox Indian fashion. In short, at the frontier the environment is at first too strong for the man. He must accept the conditions which it furnishes, or perish, and so he fits himself into the Indian clearings and follows the Indian trails.[6]

Western Circuit Riders

A Circuit Rider in the West

To counteract this de-civilizing effect, the first order of business for the MEC was to send preachers to remind the westernized whites of the civilization they had left behind. However, work in the West was not for just any eastern preacher who was willing to make his way to the West. It required those who could hold onto the WMCNB values and patterns of life they knew while also adapting to the West.

Perhaps best known of these preachers was William Wesley Van Orsdel, who chose to be popularly known as "Brother Van" to fit better with the sensibilities of western settlers. Brother Van was the preacher credited

6. Ibid., 61.

with securing much of Montana for the Methodists beginning in 1872, and his exploits as part of the "Gospel Team" (comprised of himself and his pony) became legendary. His first sermon upon arriving in Montana was in a saloon. A year later, when he had become more acquainted with the territory, he rode a circuit that was over one hundred fifty miles and required him to cross the Rocky Mountains into Idaho. Several years after that the Conference called upon him to open Bitter Root Canyon for Methodist work in spite of constant warfare between settlers and Native American tribes in that area. Following this he attended a conference in Salt Lake City where Brigham Young personally and warmly greeted him. Throughout all this time he gained the respect and hearing of both cowboys and Native Americans. And, when he died, his last words were, "I haven't an enemy. Only friends. Tell the people of Montana that I love them all." This kind of life was surely made of the same stuff as were the lives of the early Methodist circuit riders, and MEC home missionary agencies publicized it as best they could.[7]

Van's biographers constantly remind their readers that he was originally from Gettysburg, Pennsylvania and that he was bringing the East to the West. Indeed, his earliest biographer cast his entire first sermon in the context of reintroducing Christian American civilization to the settlers in Montana: "He would talk for a while, and then, when the attention wavered, he would sing the songs that some of them had heard back East before they had come under the hardening influences of the rough western life."[8] His second sermon, given that evening, had the same civilizing effect. "Again he gave the message that many of them had been missing in a long period of separation from the church life, and again hearts were stirred, as for the first time in years the uncertain voices tried to follow the singing of the gospel songs which had been sung 'back home.'"[9] Using words and song, Van sought to woo the savage settlers to participate in Christian American civilization.

One of Van's compatriots was Rev. Thomas C. Iliff. Like Van, he learned how to negotiate his participation in Christian American civilization with ministry to settlers in the West. His arrival as the new Methodist preacher in Helena provides an excellent picture of this.

---

7. Brother Van inspired one biography before his death, another came later: Brummitt, *Brother Van* (1919); and Smith, *Brother Van* (1948).

8. Brummitt, *Brother Van*, 46.

9. Ibid.

He had stepped out of the stagecoach that had brought him from Salt Lake City arrayed for his debut on his new charge in immaculate linen frock coat, fancy vest, striped trousers, and a silk hat. Never was there a more tender tenderfoot. The new parson had walked up Last Chance Gulch to a chorus of uncouth noises from the miners . . . As he walked, he acquired a hilarious following, which seemed to take a dislike to his high silk hat. When a well-directed stone knocked the offending topper into the mud, young Iliff had the good sense to leave it there. Once he had reached the shelter of the "parsonage" next to the little church . . . he removed the "dude" garments, never to don them again.[10]

Fortunately, while the preachers may have taken to the external fashions peculiar to the West, they were able to resist the de-civilizing influence of the West on internal levels. Specifically, they retained their adherence to the gospel and to WMCNB values. They also strove to maintain the disciplines of living according to WMCNB patterns of life as best as they were able in the West.

In holding fast to their values and patterns of life, the preachers became the conduits through which these markers of civilization became available to the settlers. The preachers' whole lives, then, became the evangelistic work, as the settlers watched them and saw them enacting civilization. As one of Brother Van's biographers described Van and his companion, circuit rider Francis Asbury Riggin, "There was no one in all of the territory between the Salmon River in Idaho and Virginia City [in Montana] who did not know 'the Reverend' Riggin and 'Brother Van.' They were Christianity and civilization in the gold-mining wilderness of southwestern Montana."[11]

Based on the authenticity of their own lives, the preachers would then admonish the settlers to give up their savage and sinful ways in favor of this way of living. Revivals, as camp meetings of old, became the primary site for this sort of confrontation.

Dramatic stories of settlers repenting of their most barbaric sins and once again taking up the gospel and WMCNB values are common to this era. Once again, the work of Brother Van looms large in it. On one occasion, Van and Iliff held a revival over several days in Helena, MT. The last day, the brothel-keeper, his wife, and all his employees attended because the preachers had drawn such a crowd that he had no business over the

10. Smith, *Brother Van*, 128–29.

11. Ibid., 113.

previous two nights. Although the people in the congregation were prepared for violence to break out, the service ended with the brothel-keeper
and his wife becoming converts. He sold his brothel, started a legitimate
enterprise, and went on to become one of the first trustees of Montana
Wesleyan College. Another example is found when Van took on the challenge of engaging specifically with Billy Blay, a notorious town drunk who
led a dissolute life. Going to Blay's home, Van challenged Blay to come
to the revival service the next night. Blay did come and was converted.
After becoming sober, he shared that he had a wife and children back east.
He left to reconcile with them and later became a Methodist exhorter in
Wisconsin.[12]

Working alongside of these preachers were the Church Extension
Society and the Women's Home Missionary Society. Both organizations
sought to capitalize on the work of the preachers by providing the material
for settlers in the West to live according to the rhythms of life common to
WMCNB Americans who lived in the East.

A Place of Their Own

Old Methodist Episcopal Church (center building),
Oregon City, Ore. First Protestant Church Building
West of Rocky Mountains

12. Ibid., 132–33.

Dedication of Methodist Episcopal Church,
West Jordan, Utah

Concerned that the successful work of Van and others would come to
naught unless there was a way to keep the Methodist converts from re-
verting to their frontier savagery, the MEC sought for permanent means of
establishing WMCNB patterns of life in the West. Critical to this was the
construction of church buildings. These buildings provided a place where
converts could mark time and major life transitions by Christian rites, including weekly Sabbath worship, receiving the sacraments, and celebrating
Christian holy days like Christmas. As well, these buildings were a sym-
bol of human progress on the frontier. The power of these buildings was
considered so strong that it led William Taylor, a missionary to California
prior to the Civil War, to purchase and ship a fully constructed church
building around Cape Horn for his Methodist flock in San Francisco.[13]

The creation of the Church Extension Society (CES) by the General
Conference of 1864 greatly facilitated the erection of MEC church buildings in the West. In addition to helping the MEC occupy MECS church
buildings during the Civil War, the CES had a mandate "to secure suitable
houses of public worship and such other church property as may promote
the general design" through providing loans and grants for purchase or
construction of church buildings.[14] With the quickly subsiding interest in
evangelizing the South after the Civil War, the CES turned its attention
and resources to the home missionary work in the West to carry out this
work.

13. Buckley, *History of Methodism in the United States*, 2:145.

14. Ibid., 183.

The brief history of the CES's origins suggest that, in fact, it was the West that was the primary focus of the A. J. Kynett, the man who first envisioned the agency and served as its first Corresponding Secretary. Kynett, a Methodist preacher, in surveying the settlements throughout the Midwest, "saw that evangelism was not the sole need of the new communities that were springing up like magic, for the newcomers were nominally Christian and many of them genuinely so. For them the erection of a visible and suitable house of worship was the chief need in order to permanently establish Christianity in the new land. Accordingly, he evolved the plan of a Church-wide movement for Church Extension, and secured the adoption of his plan and measure by the General Conference of 1864."[15]

This "church-wide movement" included multiple local societies overseen by annual conferences and other groups of Methodists, usually those who lived in large metropolitan areas, who had a specific interest in constructing new church buildings in their localities. The chief work of the CES was to serve as a redistributor of funds, collecting an apportioned amount from each local society and then giving various amounts back to the societies as the agency determined each had need. This usually meant gathering more from the well-established conferences in the Northeast and contributing more to the frontier conferences, especially those in the West, in order to promote "aggressive" growth there.[16] Put another way, the regions of the United States where Christian American civilization was most ensconced sent funds to the places where it was most needed.

By all accounts, the CES was highly successful in its stated mission in the West, providing grants and loans to 10,083 societies for the construction or maintenance of church buildings during its first twenty years of existence.[17] It was also successful in its implicit goal of civilizing the West, as shown in an article the *Western Christian Advocate* ran in 1868. At the urging of CES's own board of directors, the paper published an approved loan request from a Methodist society in Lone Valley, California as an ideal example of the kind of work the CES was interested in supporting. The request was for a $3,000 loan to be repaid with no interest over the course of four or five years. The loan would pay off the mortgage of a Gothic church building that had come under significant financial distress

15. Kynett, "Our Church Extension Work," 117.

16. This point is reiterated in back-to-back General Conferences: Woodruff, *Journal of the General Conference of the Methodist Episcopal Church, Held in Baltimore, MD., 1876*, 600; and Woodruff, *Journal of the General Conference of the Methodist Episcopal Church, Held in Cincinnati, OH, 1880*, 588–89.

17. Buckley, *History of Methodism in the United States*, 2:404–5.

due to: 1) the high cost of labor and materials in California, 2) the fact a great number of church members had lost significant amounts of money because of copper mining speculation and because of agricultural failures caused by two seasons of drought, and 3) the fact that church members had to purchase for a second time land they thought they already owned due to irregularities in the original deeds. Not incidentally, Catholic Mexicans were the actual deed holders demanding payment from the Methodists in the valley.[18] Clearly, this was a mixture of reasons ripe for pure American evangelism—the rescuing of a grand, Gothic structure, the existence of which was a victory over both the oppressive Catholics and the vicissitudes of frontier life and economics!

Even after this initial burst of energy, the CES remained adamant that the work of the home missionaries would be lost apart from the construction of buildings. In 1900, it reported to the General Conference that the vast amount of money spent by the Missionary Society on home missions "can only be utilized for permanent results when accompanied by the work of Church Extension."[19]

In 1904 the General Conference declared the work of constructing church buildings and the work of the preachers in the West to be part and parcel of each other when it restructured the denomination's missions agencies, creating the Board of Home Missions and Church Extension by merging the CES with the home missions department of the Missions Society.[20] This new board oversaw all denominational missions within the United States, bringing together both the home missions concern with recruiting preachers and missionaries who would serve domestically and the church extension concern with constructing church buildings. The new board wasted no time in publicizing its work and seeking donations through widely distributing a series of essays and reports on the work it oversaw under the title *Methodism and the Republic* (1908). While this volume contained pieces on every part of the country, the Board's work in the West received heavy emphasis.

To write about the West, the Board engaged the editor of the Methodist newspaper *Pacific Christian Advocate*, Daniel L. Rader. Rader began his article by claiming that the West remained a frontier in many ways, and the lack of connection to the values of the East combined with the significant temptations before the settlers demanded that the church respond with its

18. "Church Extension," *Western Christian Advocate.*

19. Monroe, *Journal of the General Conference of the Methodist Episcopal Church, Held in Chicago, Illinois, 1900,* 723.

20. "Plan for Consolidating Church Benevolences," 6.

civilizing mission. He wrote, "the rapidity with which the people are filling the country, the sense of strangeness, the freedom which comes from the breaking of former affiliations, the daring connected with the fresh, warm blood in the young and adventurous, the rapid acquiring of wealth and the feverish restlessness associated with great success, all aggravate and emphasize the difficulties which confront the Church in Christianizing this land of boundless possibilities and incalculable future."[21]

The way to tame this adventurousness that caused people to throw off their ties to civilization too quickly was for "cultivated" clergy in the East to come west where they could construct church buildings and form Sunday Schools.[22] Kynett, serving as the Recording Secretary for the new Board, reiterated Rader's solution in his own article for *Methodism and the Republic*, which connected the evangelization of the settlers with the ability of the settlers to operate in a way reminiscent of the interdependent neighborhoods common among Americans in the early nineteenth century. Central to this interdependence was a place for the community to gather and sit under the influence of a Methodist preacher. To give white settlers a church building was to give them the capacity to be the epitome of American virtue. As Kynett declared:

> Our Home Mission work "sends out the living minister to preach the Gospel to the poor; but where shall he preach? Where garner the fruits of his preaching? Where organize his church and utilize the power of converted souls for further conquests? Where gather the Sunday school and nourish and train the Church of the future?" "These are questions fundamental to any true and permanent success, and Church Extension comes in with the answer. It says to the people, 'Do all you can, and we will help you.'" With this proffered aid the strength of the community is called out, the house of worship is erected, the Gospel is preached, souls saved, the church planted, the Sunday school organized; and this work, repeated all along the advancing lines of the Church militant, is Church Extension.

Specifically in reference to the West Kynett wrote:

> *The frontier States and Territories* are being rapidly penetrated by new lines of railroad, the country is filling up with marvelous rapidity, and towns and villages are springing up as if by magic. The people are comparatively poor and have everything to do.

21. Rader, "Pacific Northwest," 74.
22. Ibid., 75–76.

Churches are an imperative necessity to their religious welfare, and they must have aid to procure them. Builded [*sic*] in time they will prove garners of untold resources of Christian power for the future work of the Church. Never before were such vast opportunities presented. They cannot be neglected without great loss to the Church.

Kynett never explained what "in time" meant. It is likely that he feared the settlers would quickly lose touch with their Christian faith and WMCNB values apart from providing them the trappings of civilization, such as a church building.

In addition to the urgency of the work, the writers of other articles emphasized the tremendous possibilities the West held. Specifically, there were financial and social possibilities that the West held for the hard-working preacher. George C. King, who served as superintendent of the Nevada Mission, observed that, "investors are turning their attention to us from all over the world. Even Methodist preachers yonder in the East, some of them high in authority in the Church, with too much ready cash about them, are constantly writing to me to know if the investments of their 'friends' in such and such mining stock are safe investments." He ruefully commented that these same "Eastern preachers" were much stingier in their donations to the Western work than they were in their investments in the mines.[23]

Notwithstanding King's frustrations at the lack of donations he received from fellow preachers, the clear implication his article put forward was that the savvy Eastern preacher could not only bring civilization to the West, but could find easy access to the materials necessary to increase his social location within that civilization beyond what he could have in the East. So it was that both the white settlers and their preachers could enjoy the benefits of a better quality of life through the home missionary work of the MEC.

Housemaking in the West

While riches might ultimately await the Methodist preachers, the reality was that life in much of the West was hard-scrabble for preacher and white settlers alike. This was a danger to the Methodist attempt to reintroduce civilization to the white settlers. Even if the settlers converted under the ministrations of the Methodist preachers and erected a new church

23. Kynett, *Methodist Forward Movement in the United States*, 69.

building, the subsistence life of the West could quickly lure them back into savagery. Worse yet, if the preachers and their families were forced to endure a lower standard of living than the rest of the settlers because the preachers were dependent on the settlers for their salaries, the primary exemplars of civilization in the West would be lost. It is at this point that the women of the MEC stepped in to help.

First and foremost, the women helped by stepping up to the challenge of becoming home missionaries who, by virtue of their sex, were uniquely suited to breathing the civilizing air of domesticity into the rough-and-tumble life of the West. These female evangelists could be single, but more frequently they were the wives of the preachers. This married position demanded fortitude and spiritual maturity on the part of the women in it. Women's historian Cathy Luchetti (1989) explained, "her measure was taken, not in framed pictures or silver tea settings, but in the ability to support her husband's efforts with biblical good sense of her own. While the pastor handled sacraments, meetings, and prayers, his wife was expected to juggle children, donation parties, socials, and Sunday school. Calling and counseling duties were shared equally between pastors and their wives, who were often forthright women unashamed to sweep into a sickroom and query: 'Are you a sinner?'"[24]

For the majority of women, however, home mission work in the West took on the form of sending donations to the needy home missionaries. Believing that civilization required maintaining a standard of living made possible through industrial consumer goods, the WHMS undertook a massive program of equipping Methodist preachers and their families with the goods necessary to participate in the fullness of Christian American civilization. This activity was seen as so important that, as of their second annual meeting, the WHMS formed a "Department of Supplies" (later renamed the "Bureau of Supplies"), "believing that very much good can be accomplished by a judicious distribution of clothing, religious books and papers, and household articles in those portions of our country where they are very much needed."[25] This bureau quickly organized a process by which women in various locales across the East could receive lists of needed goods from Methodist clergy and home missionaries, fill barrels with the appropriate articles and ship those barrels at reduced or no cost by railroad to those in need. Within its first eleven months, the bureau

---

24. Luchetti, *Under God's Spell*, 36.

25. Women's Home Missionary Society, *Second Annual Report*, 53.

facilitated the sending of 236 parcels valued at $7,869.97.[26] Nearly twenty years later, the value of the parcels being shipped had increased nearly ten-fold to $72,989.66.[27]

The preachers and their families were in deep want because they expended all they had on bringing civilization in the form of church buildings and evangelistic services to the white settlers. This want was so great that the preachers and their families were forced to live in less-than-civilized conditions. J. L. Whetstone, first Superintendent of this bureau, described this situation:

> Could you enter the frontier parsonage, in some cases only a little sod house without a floor, in others a mere shell with the wind whistling through the scanty furniture, with few comforts, and often with but little food, you would realize the needs of these people . . . These self-sacrificing men and women seldom complain, but count it all joy if they may but win souls for Christ. So interested have we seen them in building churches and in building up Christ's kingdom, that their own absolute needs seem to be lost sight of, and money which should have gone for the support of their families has been by them turned over to the church building committee.[28]

The WHMS needed to support the preachers in order to secure the continuing advance of the Christian American civilization among the white settlers in the West. As Lucy Webb Hayes reminded the WHMS in her presidential address to the seventh annual meeting of the body, the advance of civilization in the West was especially important because:

> No part of the inhabitants of the United States are nearer to the hearts of the members of the Methodist Church than our own countrymen, the patriotic Americans who have crowded in such numbers to our Western frontier settlements from Mexico to British America. No one of the old States contains so large a proportion of the veterans of the Union Army and of their wives and children. Never before were so many American citizens braving the hardships and privation of pioneer life as may now be found on our widely extended frontiers. Our Church, with an instinctive foresight of the future of the West, has built a host of churches, and sent out her ministers to do and to suffer in the wilderness . . . Could all of our good friends read the grateful

---

26. Women's Home Missionary Society, *Third Annual Report*, 82–85.

27. Women's Home Missionary Society, *Nineteenth Annual Report*, 162.

28. Women's Home Missionary Society, *Fourth Annual Report*, 76.

letters coming from devoted clergymen when the box or barrel of the Woman's Home Mission is received, this part of the work of our Society would gain a much needed impetus, fruitful of beneficent results.[29]

It seems that the most appreciated item in the packages sent by the WHMS was the clothing. The reason for this was that the preachers often believed that they needed good clothing in order to carry out their evangelistic work in the West. May Leonard Well, Corresponding Secretary of the Bureau for 1891–1892, related this in a story about a young preacher: "In one instance, a young man attending the University and supplying a mission church told his Presiding Elder he must give up his work because he had not clothing fit to wear in his pulpit. The Presiding Elder applied to this Bureau; help was sent, and the young man remained in school and at work. His Elder wrote, 'In his new suit he looked as well as any minister in the land. His work is progressing gloriously and souls are being saved.'"[30]

This is, undoubtedly, precisely what the WHMS hoped would occur. The MEC would bring civilization to the West through conversion and construction which, in turn, would breed the need for civilized goods that could facilitate people following WMCNB patterns of life. The receipt of these goods would secure a person's capacity to continue participating in civilization and would create a clear line of demarcation between Christian American civilization and the savagery of an untamed West such that those who possessed these goods would be ashamed to cross back into the uncivilized ways of living.

In addition to preachers, the WHMS supported women and children with clothes for similar reasons. In the same report, Well wrote of several girls who had begun attending a WHMS industrial school, but who were in danger of being dismissed from the school because they did not have appropriate clothing to wear. Notified of the situation, the Bureau quickly stepped in to supply the needed raiment.[31] It is hard to miss the irony of the situation—that the WHMS both instigated and solved the girls' problem by first demanding and then supplying the appropriate garments. However, through this circular process the WHMS did successfully reinforce the importance of the girls remaining civilized. Indeed, the WHMS kept the girls trebly-bound to a civilized way of living. First, the WHMS provided the institution for their education, which was a critical step toward

29. Women's Home Missionary Society, *Seventh Annual Report*, 11.
30. Women's Home Missionary Society, *Eleventh Annual Report*, 79.
31. Ibid.

a higher standard of living. Second, the WHMS established standards as to what sort of apparel was appropriate for receiving an education. Third, the WHMS provided the goods necessary for the girls to meet those demands. The WHMS used industrial goods as a way of reinforcing its own Victorian notion of what a Christian American civilization looked like.

At the turn of the century, Mrs. James Dale, the Corresponding Secretary of the Bureau for Mission Supplies who succeeded Well, summarized the hopes of the Bureau by tying the goal of a fully realized Christian American civilization directly to the way these parcels enabled the women in eastern families to provide a civilized household in the rudest of Western conditions.

> Shall we cease our work? No, never; we will continue until we can claim America for Christ, a saved nation. Do you want a part in this? Help the brethren. Is this all? When the gates of heaven are opened, the Master will welcome those quiet, heroic wives to a larger place. We will have to wait for our welcome until they get in. Could you but see some of them, endurance written on their faces! We will stand by them always. Can you say what it means to keep a family on two hundred and ten dollars, and keep cheerful? To help all these "Is the old-time religion, and 'tis good enough for me; it will take us all to heaven, and 'tis good enough for me."[32]

If the circuit riders led the charge to reclaim the white settlers in the West, then the CES and its successor, the Board of Home Missions and Church Extension, served as their tactical command post and the WHMS as the supply lines. The preachers demonstrated the gospel and WMCNB values in their own lives and converted white settlers to adopt these, the CES provided the funds and functionality to organize the converts into congregations that could follow WMCNB patterns of life, and the WHMS raised the standard of living for the members and leaders of those congregations. The end result was a replicated Eastern civilization in the West composed of those prodigal Eastern whites who had lost their way in the distant Western lands. Through the grace of Methodism, they had come to themselves again and sought the fattened calf of Christian American civilization.

32. Women's Home Missionary Society, *Nineteenth Annual Report*, 161.

Dealing with the Irreconcilables

While the primary work of the MEC home missions in the West was geared toward the white settlers who were relatively easily reconnected to Christian American civilization, the church did not ignore the other populations. Methodist preachers, new buildings, educational missions, and WHMS domesticity appeared among the Mormons, the Native Americans, and Spanish-speakers. While each of these groups were disadvantaged from participating in Christian American civilization for various reasons, the home missions work nonetheless strove to create a situation in which the people in these groups could learn the values and patterns of life that would let them enjoy the blessings this civilization offered. Unfortunately, the fact that especially the Native Americans and the Spanish-speaking population were substantially different racially and culturally from WMCNB Methodists caused this work to bear very little fruit.

Mormons

MEC Map of Possible Mormon Expansion

During his ministry in Illinois Peter Cartwright met Joseph Smith, the founder of the Church of Jesus Christ of Latter-Day Saints, i.e., the Mormons, when the Mormons were settled in Nauvoo. At their meeting, Cartwright reported that Smith sought to hire him as a Mormon prophet, promising him high standing and a comfortable life among the Mormons if he accepted. Cartwright recorded in his autobiography that he rejected the offer, adding the editorial comment that he believed Smith to be "a very illiterate and impudent desperado in morals, but, at the same time, he had a vast fund of low cunning." At the end of this interview, Cartwright claimed Smith proclaimed angrily "I will show you, sir, that I will raise up a government in these United States which will overturn the present government, and I will raise up a new religion that will overturn every other form of religion in this country." Cartwright then concluded this account with a broad condemnation of the Mormons, claiming them to be thieves, con artists, arsonists, murderers, and scheming politicians who sought to rig elections in their favor. He opined, "They should be considered and treated as outlaws in every country and clime."[33]

Cartwright would be pleased to know that, nearly a half-century later, the MEC stood in full agreement with his condemnation of Joseph Smith and the Mormons. If anything, the stance against the Mormons had hardened because Methodists came to believe the Mormons were a clear and present threat to Christian American civilization. In Mormonism, the great triumvirate that Methodism championed as interrelated and necessary to Christian American civilization: the Christian faith, republicanism, and the home, all seemed to be under attack.

A writer for the *Western Christian Advocate* explicated how the Mormons carried out this attack by declaring that Mormonism was "a theocracy and false-religion, with polygamy as its cornerstone."[34] First, Mormonism was a "false-religion." It was not Protestant, nor was it even Christian. As a result, it was set against the fundamental truths of the universe established in Jesus Christ, as well as the basic moral fabric of WMCNB Americans. Second, the fact that the Mormons established themselves in Utah under their own "theocracy," which "dominates every social, religious, and political agency and influence"[35] demonstrated that the Mormons not only rejected the pure Christian faith of Protestantism, but they rejected the republican form of government that guarded Christian American civiliza-

---

33. Cartwright, *Autobiography*, 225–28.
34. Fisher, "Methodism in Utah," 172.
35. Ibid., 172.

tion. Worse than this, they seemed to have designs on trying to replace republicanism with their theocracy. Third, they practiced polygamy. Here was a rank practice that made a mockery of the Victorian home and the virtue of women. This poisoning of the women and their households ensured that the depraved forms of religion and governance the Mormons espoused would be perpetuated.

As a result of these perceived threats to the very roots of Christian American civilization, the Methodists gave no quarry in their evangelistic activities among the Mormons and in regions of the West where the Mormons held sway. Methodist missionaries in Utah particularly pressed the need to evangelize the Mormons, often depicting Methodism, and hence Christian American civilization itself, in a great struggle for survival against Mormonism that could only be won through the complete conversion of all Mormons to Methodism. H. J. Talbot, who oversaw the Methodist Utah mission in the early years of the twentieth century, laid out this view. In an article he wrote for *Methodism and the Republic*, he began by restating the theological, political, and social sins that beset the Mormons and the attendant dangers to the Republic fostered by these sins. He then presented a two-part plan for overcoming Mormonism. The first part of the plan was to reach the "Gentile" (i.e., non-Mormon) settlers in Utah through Methodist schools. These schools would inoculate the Gentiles to Mormon teaching and bind them securely to the Methodist Episcopal Church and the United States. Talbot explained: "The spirit of Mormonism is one of priestly absolutism; and the fruitage of its teachings, if unchecked, would inevitably issue in moral deterioration. No amount of sophistical reasoning can obscure this point. The Christian churches have steadily resisted this development, and not without creditable success. They have fostered respect for Federal authority. Wherever they have gone the flag has been unfurled, and they have emphasized loyalty to Federal institutions."[36]

Having made such a potent impact on the Gentiles, the Methodists would then implement the second part of the plan by moving to convert the Mormons themselves. Encircled by the loyal American Gentiles and the Methodist missionaries, the Mormons would eventually have to give way. Using militaristic language, Talbot declared this strategy would allow the MEC missionaries "to carry our banner to conquest over an unauthenticated religion."[37]

36. Talbot, "Methodist Episcopal Church in Utah," 87–88.
37. Ibid., 93.

The Methodist women were of like mind on this point, if not even more vitriolic in their denunciation of Mormonism. As early as 1866 the *Ladies' Repository*, a Methodist magazine for women, ran an editorial declaring, "Mormonism is the greatest abomination on the face of the earth, not excepting the lowest forms of heathenism. Every conceivable crime seems to be perpetrated among them. Blasphemy, murder, adultery, imposture, extortion seem to be integral elements in the system."[38]

With this sentiment among the Methodist women against the Mormons, it is not surprising that the WHMS, though it had its roots in southern work among the freedmen, quickly turned to combating Mormonism as one of its chief activities. At its inaugural meeting, it established a bureau for work among the Mormons and set 1/5 of its budget, the largest single line item, for "Mormon work."[39]

Like their male counterparts, a significant reason motivating this work is that women feared the political and religious errors of the Mormons. The Corresponding Secretary made this point clearly in her report to the WHMS in 1884: "Mormonism, in its relation to government, is a problem which perplexes the nation. Dispose of polygamy and a great ecclesiastical system remains . . . This system claims to be the *one true* Church." What made Mormonism even more dangerous was that it not only held these views, but was itself missionary in exporting them: "The teachers of this faith are gathering proselytes among all peoples. The literature of Zion is circulated to every quarter of the globe."[40] This raised the fearsome specter of the vast hordes of immigrants, already a threat because they were under the sway of Catholicism, becoming part of the even more sinister Mormon Church. This nightmare scenario was articulated in the very first meeting of the WHMS:

> Nearly two-thirds of the members of our Church are women, and it depends upon them to make and preserve homes of intelligence and purity where ignorance, Mormonism, and vice attempt to degrade them . . . Our country is the most inviting field of Christian effort in the world . . . The streams of immigration are pouring into it a million of people a year . . . These elements are fruitful of good if properly cared for, but if neglected they become the elements of danger and death, and a few generations

38. Literary Notices, *Ladies' Repository*, 573.
39. Women's Home Missionary Society, *First Annual Report*, 29.
40. Women's Home Missionary Society, *Third Annual Report*, 61.

will settle the question whether we shall be governed by Mormonism and infidelity or by morality and religion.[41]

Not only were the Mormons reaching the immigrants, they were seeking to gain political footholds throughout the western states. In response to this the WHMS tied the knot between Protestantism and the United States as tightly as possible as the starting point for finding a remedy from this growing threat, stating "The final solution of the Mormon problem is committed to the Christian Church of the Republic upon whose soil is perpetuated this holocaust of woe."[42]

Although unspoken in these reports, what likely most galled the members of the WHMS, and Methodists generally, was that the Mormons were directly challenging the primacy of the Methodist Episcopal Church, which stood at the vanguard of Christian American civilization. The Mormons desired this top position and, as the Methodists saw it, were willing to destroy the entire civilization and remake it in their own image in order to claim it. This smacked of nothing less than the bloody Civil War that the Methodists had recently emerged from victorious as ardent supporters of the Union. They were not about to allow an upstart sect with an alternative vision of American civilization to beat them after defeating the Confederacy over just such an issue.

Even with these deep religious and political concerns, it was polygamy and its attendant mistreatment of women and children that drew the greatest scorn from Methodist women. Casting this in charged biblical imagery, the Chairman of the Bureau for Mormon Work reported to the WHMS, "He who received the Magdalene only upon the departure of the seven devils, confers salvation upon the woman of the Church of Latter Day Saints only when she *surrenders* herself to the *possession* of the *Magdalene devils.*" To make this point, the Chairman offered the detailed account of a woman who had escaped from Mormon polygamy only to be branded an apostate by the Mormons and left with her children to fend for herself without food, adequate clothing or shelter on the outskirts of a Mormon settlement. Worse yet, her own daughters were being dragged back into the settlement to be part of polygamous marriages. Based on this the Chairman put forth an impassioned evangelistic call: "O, sisters of the Churches to whom this appeal is made, let us unite in one grand

41. Women's Home Missionary Society, *First Annual Report*, 43.
42. Women's Home Missionary Society, *Third Annual Report*, 61.

enterprise, which shall reassure and give relief to these long suffering women, and set at liberty many who shall come after them."[43]

The way the Bureau proposed to provide this help was through establishing an industrial home through which WHMS home missionaries could educate Mormon women. This education would teach the Mormon women how to participate as individual citizens in the Republic and as independent actors in an eastern economic structure. It would also teach the necessary skills to maintain a well-kept Victorian home.

As the Chairman of the Bureau explained it, the industrial home would be a place in which "the real *work* . . . should be to prepare young Mormon girls or mothers for independent support. There are scores who are held to the vile system because no way is open to which they can earn their daily bread. This made possible, their speedy escape is certain." Such independence would be provided through classes in both domestic work, including dress-making, plain sewing, and cooking, and in mechanical work, including training to become a telephone exchange operator, a telegraph operator, a stenographer, a typist, or a silk reeler. Finally, the Chairman made the civilizing intent of this education, with its clear anti-polygamy agenda, explicit in the appeal for funds to build the home:

> Sisters of the Churches, to *you*, upon whose souls the inertia of a false faith has never fallen; to you whose home has never been destroyed by the coming of "another," between you and your other self; to you whose lips have never sent forth that wildest wail which ever came from woman's heart when the strained ear catches the infant cry of your *husband's first-born not your* own; to you O *queens* upon an undivided throne this project appeals. Come, then, to rescue with the *might* of *right*. Build this industrial home. Set it upon some table-land overlooking the City of Destruction. From its loftiest turret run up the American flag, where its waving outlines may be visible far up the valley, far over the sea. There let them stand together—the Home and the flag—emblems of the Nation's heart and woman's place therein.[44]

In claiming this, she made an argument based on the very values that are central to pure American evangelism.

The Methodist women of the WHMS responded not only with the funds to build this home, but by 1889, when the WHMS was at the high

43. Ibid., 62.
44. Ibid., 62–64.

point of its missionary work among Mormons, the agency supported seven industrial homes, three schools, and several missionary women who visited Mormon women in their homes. This all was accomplished a scant nine years after the WHMS' inaugural meeting. Such was the importance of ending the Mormon threat.

For all of the money and rhetoric poured into Mormon work by the WHMS, by 1893 the WHMS briefly lost interest in the Mormons, supplanting the "Bureau for Mormon Work" with the more innocuously named "Bureau for Utah." The reason for this, as the Acting Secretary for the new Bureau for Utah explained, was

> the Territory has been opened to the settlement of Gentiles, and commerce and Christian education have been instrumental in producing great changes in the conditions requiring missionary aid. Polygamy is practiced only clandestinely. A good public-school system has been adopted and is well sustained, especially in the cities, which have grown into importance within this period. The small mission schools first established, and similar work provided for by other philanthropic organizations, are no longer needed in many places, and our Society has been advised to suspend these schools.[45]

The work of the WHMS, along with the work of all WMCNB Americans who had been concerned about the subversive nature of Mormonism seemingly achieved complete victory. The Mormon bugaboo, especially its polygamous activities, was beaten into such marginality that there was no longer any fear that it would overthrow the Protestant faith, the American Republic, or the Victorian home. In no small part, this was because the state had finally stepped in and mandated public education, which was the great federal carrier of Christian American civilization. With the work of teaching children safely in the government's hands, the WHMS could turn their attention to other things.

Methodist concern over Mormons abated further on 4 January 1896 when Utah joined the Union, thus avoiding the possibility of Utah becoming a break-away country. However, the joy over this momentary victory quickly vanished. Within a decade, Methodists again were sounding the battle-cry, angered by the growing contingent of Mormon-sympathizers, including professed polygamists, who were being elected to State and Federal Government by the citizens of Utah. The WHMS once again looked to the Federal Government to step in and quash this rebellion against

---

45. Women's Home Missionary Society, *Thirteenth Annual Report*, 82.

Christian American civilization, even as it had mandated public schools in Utah. To this end, at the 1901 Annual Meeting, the WHMS passed a resolution petitioning Congress to amend the Constitution "prohibiting the practice of polygamy, and granting the President and Congress power and authority to enforce the same."[46] The resolution also called on the various auxiliaries of the WHMS to hold study groups to learn about the abominations of Mormonism and to lobby their representatives in Washington for passage of this amendment.

Such calls to action became perennial parts of the WHMS meeting through the early twentieth century. In 1906, the Secretary for the WHMS Bureau for Utah sought to horrify the annual meeting participants by providing a "graphic description" of the funeral of one of the Mormon leaders, which was attended by the deceased's four wives and forty-five children. She also exhorted the women to lobby for the Senate to expel Reed Smoot, a Mormon leader and polygamist who was then completing his first term in office.[47] A year later, the Annual Address at the WHMS dedicated no less than four pages to the dangers of Mormonism, pointing to how polygamy "was neither condemned nor abrogated as a doctrine of the Mormon Church" in violation of Utah's promise to end the practice as a condition of becoming a State of the Union. Additionally, the address reminded its listeners that Mormonism continued as a political threat to the Republic. Gesturing toward Reed Smoot, the address declared: "This system, with all its demoralizing reign, its systematic violation of the laws of the land, its profound disregard for its own promises, has been indorsed, practiced, and taught by its adherents, and endured and tolerated by this Christian civilization . . . the country has been treated *ad nauseam* to the political aspirations and successes of this people, with their 'revelations' of unholy living, defiance to law and apologies for the same." It concluded, "Is it not time patience ceased to be a virtue?" and called the Federal Government to topple Mormonism through vigorously prosecuting anti-polygamy laws.[48]

Five years later, the Annual Address again took up the cause, with the WHMS president encouraging WHMS study groups be formed to study the book "Mormonism, the Islam of America," with the promise that the WHMS would not flag in its "fixed, implacable purpose to arrest the attention of the citizens of this Republic and concentrate it upon the evils of polygamous Mormonism . . . and its soul-stirring influence never

---

46. Women's Home Missionary Society, *Twentieth Annual Report*, 82.

47. Women's Home Missionary Society, *Twenty-Fifth Annual Report*, 37.

48. Women's Home Missionary Society, *Twenty-Sixth Annual Report*, 94–97.

cease until a new amendment shall be written into the Constitution of the United States that will destroy, root and branch, polygamous Mormonism in our great Republic."[49]

The ladies of the WHMS were not alone among the Methodists in decrying the Mormon presence in politics. The Methodist bishops entered the fray, pointing with alarm at the growing influence of Mormons in the regional politics of the West. They stated in their 1904 Episcopal Address:

> Mormonism has once more reared its hideous head in brazen defiance of the moral sense of the nation and in shameful violation of the pledge which secured statehood for Utah. It is vigorously pushing its propaganda in many parts of the country, especially in the States and Territories among and adjacent to the Rocky Mountains, where in a few years, there will be a population of many millions. No palliatives suffice to check the ravages of this cancer, much less to extirpate it by the roots. The only remedy in sight is the keen surgery of an amendment to the Constitution of the United States absolutely prohibiting polygamy on every acre of the national domain.[50]

Notably, the Committee on the State of the Church at the General Conference of 1904 took up this suggestion and voted unanimously to support a denominational petition to Congress for an anti-polygamy amendment to the Constitution.[51] This however, was the last pronouncement of the denomination as a whole on this issue.

While the denomination stayed silent on the matter, as late as 1920 the WHMS heard an address entitled "The Mormon Menace," which openly acknowledged that the chief battle with Mormonism was an evangelistic one. The presenter, Lulu Loveland Shepard, stated bluntly, "The strength of the Mormon Church lies, first, in its missionaries; it calls to the work every year 4,000 young men and women—1,000 of these are kept constantly in the field; they go out without purse or scrip, and must earn their own way."[52] These words more than anything else, point to the reason why Methodists needed to resist Mormonism. Its scrappy, evangelistic practice likely sounded all too familiar, echoing of the young Methodist circuit riders who went out with little or no support to share the good news of the gospel and to attract people into the Methodist Episcopal Church even as

49. Women's Home Missionary Society, *Thirty-First Annual Report*, 97.

50. Hingeley, *Journal of the Twenty-Fourth General Conference*, 148–49.

51. Ibid., 477.

52. Women's Home Missionary Society, *Thirty-Ninth Annual Report*, 51.

they adhered to the cultural values of their beloved Republic and helped forge good citizens for that Republic. To allow a new church the freedom to replicate the Methodist experience, especially a church that rejected the gospel of Jesus Christ, the value of family, and the politics of the Republic, was too much. The danger was too great, especially when Methodists recognized their own success in the past. The values that undergirded the idea of pure American evangelism in the West demanded that Mormonism be utterly and completely overthrown either by converting the Mormons or politically suppressing them.

Native American Indians

Original caption: Happy Indian School Children—
They are being Americanized

In 1816, John Stewart, an African American who became a Methodist at a camp meeting, took it upon himself to begin evangelizing the Wyandot Indians in Ohio. Word of his outreach, the first of its kind by anyone in the MEC, reached the ears of several prominent Methodist preachers who concluded they wanted to support him. More than that, they recognized the need to expand the work of the MEC to evangelize populations beyond those readily accessible to the conference-and-circuit system. The result was the formation of a Missionary Society in 1819, which the General Conference of 1820 formally recognized. Evangelizing the Native Americans was the initial prompt for the Methodists to begin the process of institutionally expanding its understanding and practice of evangelism. This work also was the primary focus of the new mission society during its first years.

Interior of a MEC Church Building for Members
of the Piegan Indian Tribe in American Garb

Despite this auspicious beginning, Native Americans received little formal attention from the MEC over the coming years. This is not to say that Methodists entirely ignored the Native American population, but that they tended to deal with them only when geographical necessity prompted it. Whenever a preacher found himself in a territory that included a Native American settlement, the preacher dutifully undertook ministry among the local tribes. However, this rarely bore much fruit. Frederick Norwood (1974), who researched the Methodist evangelistic missions to the Native Americans in some detail, concluded that "by 1921, the northern church had forty-one missions [among Native Americans] in operation, but many of these were weak or intermittent. As a matter of fact, Methodism, along with other religious bodies, had little to brag about. There were just too many difficulties in the way: lack of central program, geographical separation, lack of trained personnel, the cultural chasm, governmental policy, and a disregard for the Indians' own religious sensitivity."[53]

Norwood's assessment of Methodist outreach to the Native Americans was not entirely negative, however. He found that the MEC tended to be more sympathetic and supportive of the Native Americans than many WMCNB Americans. Curiously, this sympathy caused Methodist home missionaries to desire even more fervently to share the best of WMCNB values and patterns of life with the Native Americans. Norwood explained that "the best, perhaps, that can be said is that if the missionaries smuggled

53. Norwood, *Story of American Methodism*, 332.

in Western Civilization, they at least presented some of its better aspects, in contrast to the contributions of fur traders, mountain men, and pioneers generally. It was not missionaries who invented removal, repudiation, reservation, and rum."[54]

In light of Norwood's observation, two concurrent themes become evident in reference to how the MEC engaged in evangelizing Native Americans. The first was an acknowledgment of the deplorable state of Native American's quality of life because of the ways the white man, particularly through the Federal Government of the United States, betrayed and abused Native Americans. The second was the need to bring Native Americans to recognize and accept the superior cultural values and patterns of life held by WMCNB Americans. Added to this mix was the almost unshakable faith the MEC had in the federal government. This meant that, in spite of the terrible things the federal government had perpetrated against the Native Americans, the MEC placed its full support behind federal policies meant to encourage the civilization of Native Americans and encouraged the Native Americans to do the same.

What held these two seemingly contradictory themes together was the highly idealized vision the Methodists had of what the United States should be (the "pure" aspect of pure American evangelism). This ideal did not demand unquestioning loyalty to every action that white Americans undertook. As Bishop Simpson had explained, the foundation of the American civilization was the church and the faith that the church proclaimed. This meant that, while the church could exult in the great material blessings that the United States enjoyed as the result of the nation following the teachings of the church, it also had to remain ever vigilant lest the nation lose its purity and slip out of salvation. The whites-turned-savage by the frontier life of the West demonstrated how this could happen. Even the federal government was not above such a potential fall from grace.

The relationship of white Americans and the federal government to the Native Americans provided a situation in which the MEC found its vigilance requiring it to criticize and cheer the actions of the government simultaneously. They criticized the dishonorable actions in the past that led to the current poverty-stricken, dispossessed, uneducated, and uncivilized state of Native Americans. Chiefly, this criticism focused on the forced removal of the Native Americans from their traditional tribal lands. At the same time, sometimes even in the same breath, the Methodists

54. Ibid.

lauded the work of the federal government to uplift the Native Americans through setting aside reservations for them where they could live in peace, establish decent households, and secure an industrial education for their children from government schools.[55]

In approaching Native Americans this way, the Methodists demonstrated that pure American evangelism not only entailed helping those who were not WMCNB to share in the blessings of Christian American civilization, but holding WMCNB Americans accountable for living up to the values they claimed. In the case of Native Americans, Methodist evangelism was a combination of helping the Native Americans to participate in Christian American civilization while also atoning for uncivilized behavior of whites toward Native Americans. They did the latter by seeking to provide the advantages of WMCNB values and patterns of life to the Native Americans and by supporting the government's work toward educating the Native Americans.

As with other evangelistic work in the West, the WHMS and the Board of Home Missions and Church Extension spearheaded the Methodist outreach toward the Native Americans. The WHMS focused specifically on building industrial homes and schools in which it sought to acclimate Native American females to the values and patterns of life common among the WMCNB Americans, especially to the roles of women and girls in these household. As the WHMS "Bureau for Indians" reported, the purpose of a mission among the Native Americans was "to teach these women how to sew, to keep all these hands busy while the ears are hearing the Gospel."[56] The Board of Home Missions and Church Extension focused its work on a more direct approach of bringing Native Americans into WMCNB society by cooperating with government efforts to educate the Native Americans and by forming Methodist societies among them where possible.

In their third annual meeting, the members of the WHMS received their first report from the agency's newly minted Bureau for Indians. This report noted that there were no current activities by the WHMS among Native Americans, but that three possibilities were being explored toward establishing missions. In considering where these missions might be launched, the two themes prominent in the MEC approach to evangelizing Native Americans are apparent. The first is what the WHMS home

55. Harris, *Journal of the General Conference of the Methodist Episcopal Church, Held in Chicago, Ill., 1868*, 518.

56. Women's Home Missionary Society, *Fourth Annual Report*, 89.

missionaries perceived as the utter lack of civilization among the Native Americans largely because of harsh white treatment of the Native Americans. In quoting a pastor who dealt with Native Americans, the Bureau stated, "Many of them [the Native Americans] have no idea…of decency or virtue" and many Native Americans were desperately poor and struggling to survive.[57] The reason for this explanation was straightforward: "They say that the Great Spirit has taken the buffalo, the white man has taken his land, and nothing remains to the poor Indian." Indeed, whites were not only complicit in this initial act of dispossessing the Native Americans of their tribal lands, but continued in their acts of degradation. As the Bureau reported, "the presence of the United States soldiers only increases the abasement of these poor women."[58]

Even in this explicit condemnation of the ways that white Americans dealt with Native Americans, the WHMS refused to remain mired in the past. The same report that called out the terrible abuses of the Native American by whites assured its listeners "his [the Native American's] extremity is God's opportunity." Thus, for the WHMS, the savage state enforced on the Native American by the whites created a situation in which, "the Indians are now ready for the white man's God."[59] Put another way, the lack of civilization among the Native Americans caused by white mistreatment of Native Americans actually created the possibility of engaging in pure American evangelism. The fact that the Native Americans themselves might have been less open to receiving the white man's God after their experience with white men in the past did not seem to occur to the Bureau or to others in the WHMS.

The Bureau offered another reason for moving quickly to evangelize the Native Americans: the restoration of Christian American civilization's good name. By white women bringing to the Native Americans the quality of life that WMCNB values made possible, they could restore Christian American civilization and atone for the evil actions that whites had committed against the Native Americans in the past.

More was at stake than overcoming historical wrongs. The Bureau went so far as to argue that if Christian American civilization was not established properly, white Americans and Native Americans would continue to suffer for it. Indeed, it argued that the entire civilizing mission of the MEC was held in check:

57. Women's Home Missionary Society, *Third Annual Report*, 91.

58. Ibid.

59. Ibid.

The idea that advancing civilization [i.e., the advance of white American settlers to the West] will settle the Indian question is a quieting one to some consciences. If we had advanced, as William Penn advanced, with the open Bible and a just and brotherly contact, this would be a proper view. But the fact is wholly different. Greed, treachery and robbery have characterized the advanced corps of our civilization. When on our Western border the two races have met, it has been only to make both worse. Neglect of the Indians has been a hindrance to our own advancing civilization.[60]

Seeking to heed its own advice, the Bureau claimed in 1886, "Plant an Indian mission, and the influence is as potent among whites as Indians." To prove this point, the Bureau submitted a report that detailed the work of Mrs. Gaddis, a WHMS missionary who entered Pawnee Territory in July 1885. Upon arriving, she found that there was no practice of worship on the Sabbath within a forty-mile radius. Instead, the whites would gather to watch the Pawnee perform native "bear dances." She instituted observance of the Sabbath at her mission, with the result that both Native Americans and whites began to attend worship. "In this regard," the report concluded, "the mission has benefited both whites and Indians, and initiated a new and Christian civilization."[61] In 1911, the WHMS President again linked the fates of white civilization and the evangelization of Native Americans when she stated specifically in reference to the Navajo nation, "There are 28,000 of them. America will not be for Christ until these are redeemed."[62]

The WHMS was not alone in this assessment of the detrimental effect whites had on Native Americans. As early as 1868, the Committee on Temperance of the General Conference argued that the Native American (as well as the freed slave) was often held in a savage state because of alcohol provided to it by unscrupulous whites. Prohibition was not only necessary to end the supply of alcohol that led to this debauchment, but it was necessary to prove the exceptional morality of white American civilization. To make this point, the Committee specifically lambasted wealthy whites who thought that they were participating in the height of civilization by serving liquor as part of entertaining guests. Quite to the contrary, the Committee declared that such whites were even less participants in Christian American civilization than the Native Americans both

---

60. Women's Home Missionary Society, *Fifth Annual Report*, 89–90.

61. Ibid., 90.

62. Women's Home Missionary Society, *Thirtieth Annual Report*, 45.

because of their use of alcohol and because of their perpetuation of Native Americans in savagery by intimating that temperance was unnecessary to civilization.[63] Christian American civilization demanded pure WMCNB values, not simply the capacity to consume expensive goods, especially when those goods were at the heart of morally depraved activities.

Forty years later a missionary to the Yakima tribe supported by the Board of Home Missions and Church Extension bewailed the same problem of white Americans leading to the moral dissipation of Native Americans through alcohol. This was even more reprehensible because the Native Americans were beginning to show the capacity to participate in Christian American civilization materially.

> The general condition of the Indians morally, in all the reservations, is bad. Many of them have homes and some comfortable and quite prosperous; some of them are well-to-do in temporal things. But alas, alas! Whiskey, whiskey! Some Federal judge somewhere has rendered a decision that American Indians who have land holdings have the legal right to purchase and drink whiskey. So the drinking and drunkenness among the Indians of the Yakima Reservation are something terrible. The Indians are being demoralized and destroyed by whiskey. Horrible murders are committed among themselves, and it seems impossible to find out and bring the offenders to justice. But if the presence and efforts and influence of our Church, which has stood so long among them, should be taken away, indeed I do not know what would become of them.[64]

By 1900, the work of the WHMS had expanded to include six missions among distinct tribes of Native Americans as well as work among the Native Americans in Alaska. Even with this expansion and the interaction that the WHMS missionaries were having with the Native Americans, there was no change in the agency's goals for this work. The WHMS continued to strive atoning for the moral failure of whites in dealing with Native Americans and seeking to uplift the Native Americans to participate in Christian American civilization.

An example of this is the report on Indian missions included in the WHMS meeting of 1900. Seeking to reconcile the clear superiority of WMCNB civilization with the moral failures of white Americans toward the Native Americans, it stated, "God, in his providence, designed this rich

---

63. Harris, *Journal of the General Conference of the Methodist Episcopal Church, Held in Chicago, Ill., 1868*, 626.

64. Kynett, *Methodist Forward Movement in the United States*, 92.

continent for a great, Christian people. But it was not of God that his poor red children should be cruelly driven away, robbed of their beloved forests and homes, and then left in heathen darkness." The report proceeded to hold up the work of various WHMS missionaries as the solution to this incongruity. These missionaries were seeking to correct the wrongs done to the Native Americans by encouraging them to abandon the savage ways they had been forced to follow in favor of converting to Christianity and training at mission-sponsored schools.[65]

This same articulation of dual purposes for the WHMS engaging in missionary work with Native Americans was visible in the themes of back-to-back addresses to the group at its meeting in 1905. According to the minutes, the first address was given by the Secretary of the Bureau for Indians and was entitled "The Indian and Our Debt to Him." In it, "she stated that time after time the Indians had been driven back into savagery" as a result of white Americans' massacres and abuses. The secretary was followed by a speaker, who, after sharing about the various ministrations of the WHMS missionaries among the Native Americans in the Southwest, concluded, "The Indians are beginning to realize the superiority of the white man's religion, and wisely adopting it."[66]

Along with holding fast to the dual motivations of seeking to reclaim the purity of white American civilization and bettering the condition of the Native Americans, the WHMS also maintained the same blind spot in reference in relationship to the federal government vis-à-vis Native Americans. The organization remained committed to cooperating with the federal government's educational work, oblivious to the fact that it was the federal government that had been the chief instigator of white Americans' mistreatment of the Native American. As late as 1914 the WHMS minutes recorded that "the Indian children are sent to the public schools, thus using the most accepted method of making good American citizens."[67]

The Board of Home Missions and Church Extension expressed similar ideas as the WHMS. The article F. A. Riggin, Brother Van's sometimes revival partner who rose to become superintendent of a Methodist mission working with the Blackfeet tribe, is a good example of this. Writing in *Methodism and the Republic*, he began by trying to balance the favored status of WMCNB civilization with the various wrongs committed by white Americans against the Native Americans. He stated, "Every student

65. Women's Home Missionary Society, *Nineteenth Annual Report*, 108–14.

66. Women's Home Missionary Society, *Twenty-Fourth Annual Report*, 34.

67. Women's Home Missionary Society, *Thirty-Fourth Annual Report*, 36.

of American history knows what a terrible time we have had with Indians from the earliest settlement of our country down to the present. When the warlike spirit has been aroused by the encroachment of civilization upon their domain, conflicts have resulted and they have been driven along bloody trails until they have been 'corralled' in reservations in different places, widely separated."[68]

Seeking to ameliorate these wrongs, and especially to exculpate the federal government, Riggin explained "treaties have been made, and their development and civilization undertaken by the Government."[69] Particularly important to this work was the maintenance of the reservation system. While the Native Americans may have been "corralled" in these originally, the reservations proved to be a means of protecting the Native Americans from their old, savage, warlike tempers. Riggin opined: "This has been wisely planned. There are 250,000 Indians remaining of the various tribes. They could not be controlled in one body. The different tribes have been as antagonistic toward each other as to the white people. Thus each nation, or allied tribes, have separate reservations and different treaties, but all tending to the same end, viz., their Christian civilization."[70]

Riggin not only saw the suppression of intertribal antipathy as necessary, he suggested that Christian civilization did not allow for synchronization with any traditional values or practices of Native American civilization. As a result, the government was doing well to micromanage every part of Native American life, carefully removing the savagery that was there by nature and by white duplicity in favor of instilling WMCNB values and patterns of life. Particularly important was the government not giving Native Americans the ability to raise their own children.

> The beneficent spirit of our Government can be seen nowhere better than in its control of the Indian. Agents are appointed to personally supervise and direct, even in minutest affairs, and the employees of all kinds are under civil service regulation. The different trades are represented and a complete system of education carried on. Children of all ages are taken from the tepees and as much as possible of the Indian life is trained out of them. They have excellent industrial training. They are taught domestic science in all its branches. Cleanliness is impressed upon them. The Industrial Training School is a model of neatness. They are taught at the schools and missions of the churches the

68. Riggin, "Piegan Indian Mission: An Example of What Is Being Done," 300.
69. Ibid.
70. Ibid.

various phases of agriculture. By precept and example principles of Christianity are inculcated. All the advantages of the ideal home, industry, economy, thrift and the elements of the well-rounded character are kept constantly before them. The agent is father, governor, judge.[71]

In a later article in the same volume, a guest writer from the WHMS seconded the call for white education of Native American children. The author declared "if the Church of Christ felt its obligation in any adequate degree to win these young Indians to Christ, the day would not be far distant when there would be no heathen red men in our land, because, in the day of opportunity, the children were sought and won!"[72]

According to the missionaries, the Native Americans themselves accepted the need to reject their old patterns of life and values in favor of what the government and missionaries taught. To this end, Riggin ended his article by quoting from a speech that an old Native American gave to a group of mission-educated children. According to Riggin, the old man said: "The white man is so superior to the Indian, I am glad you are here at school to learn to do things like they do. The white man grows; he is like the tree, a thing of beauty; the Indian is like the rock, an immovable something. The white man builds fine houses, warms them and lights them and they are beautiful. He builds railroads and runs cars on them, he dresses well. How nicely they all look around you . . . You hear and follow the teaching of your teachers and missionaries and it will be well with you."[73]

Here is the American gospel on the lips of a Native American, evangelizing children of his own race to recognize the better quality of life made available by living according to the ways of the WMCNB Americans.

In 1920, there was an increased interest in evangelizing Native Americans by the MEC. The General Conference that year passed a report that directed the Board of Home Missions and Church Extension to allocate greater resources "for this needy and long neglected field, and to devise suitable measures for effective service and supervision of the same." The Presidential Address at the WHMS annual meeting of the same year trumpeted "a new study is being made, a stronger plan outlined, for the education and uplift of these many tribes."[74]

---

71. Ibid., 303.

72. Van Marter, "Woman's Home Missionary Society," 332.

73. Riggin, "Piegan Indian Mission: An Example of What Is Being Done," 307–8.

74. Women's Home Missionary Society, *Thirty-Ninth Annual Report*, 62–63.

Despite this brief flurry of activity, Methodist sentiments had changed very little concerning the strategy of these missions. The Presidential Address to the WHMS again recounted the wrongs done to Native Americans at the hands of whites and called on the Methodists to overcome this state of affairs through creating opportunities for Native Americans to participate in Christian American civilization. It also reaffirmed the faith of the WHMS in the federal government, even quoting the Federal Indian Commissioner who had said, "The solution of the Indian problem in this country is not to be found in merely increasing the material resources of the Indian people, giving them land and tools and cattle, but in and through Christian education, the upbuilding of initiative and character, the inspirations of faith and hope and fraternal good-will."[75]

Perhaps the inclusion of this quote was a quiet acknowledgment that the Methodists had seen little response to their missionary efforts. Despite decades of seeking to atone for the sins of the past, creating institutions to teach WMCNB values and patterns of life, and efforts to raise the next generation of Native American children to be Christians with the quality of life offered through adherence to the American gospel, little fruit had come from these missions. Although, as of the early twenty-first century, there are approximately 18,000 Native Americans who are part of the The United Methodist Church, this is far less than the transformative civilizing work of the entire people the WHMS and other MEC had hoped to encourage.

Part of this failure was likely the inability of the MEC to look beyond the government's work of creating reservations and state-run schools for the Native American population in the West. There was no vision for what the next steps would be. Did the MEC imagine the reservations eventually being abandoned as Native American children who became Christians and were inculcated with WMCNB values moved to the East where they could fully participate in Christian American civilization? Or, did the MEC believe that the Native Americans, like the white settlers, would develop a facsimile of eastern life on the reservations? None of this is clear. In spite of the desire to overcome the sins of whites toward Native Americans in the past, it seems the MEC never could overcome the fundamental assumption of the past that the Native Americans were a separate people from white Americans. This lack of ability to think of how whites could relate to Native Americans beyond being missionaries to those in desperate need of WMCNB faith and values seems to be what hindered the MEC

75. Ibid.

from achieving its goals in this home mission field. The MEC could only understand how to offer the building blocks to participate in Christian American civilization, not how to live in it with others who had such a different cultural background.

The Spanish-Speaking Population

Moises Garcia as he came out of the hills of Mexico to attend the Epworth League institute

Moises Garcia one year later, after a year in a mission school

A similar problem of not knowing how to relate effectively to a people with a different cultural background plagued the MEC home mission work among the Spanish-speaking populations in the United States.

Following the Civil War, the Methodist Episcopal Church began to undertake home mission work among the domestic Spanish-speaking population. It did so both within the United States, especially in the Southwest, and, following the Spanish-American War, in Puerto Rico. The approach in all settings was nearly identical, focusing on the construction of schools and seeking to convert the native populations of these areas from Catholicism to Methodism. The work of the New Mexico Spanish Mission under the superintendency of Thomas Harwood and the Spanish work undertaken by the WHMS in New Mexico both provide some of the best examples and documentation of this home mission.[76] Both ministries dealt with Mexicans who had become American citizens by the accident of the United States acquiring the land in which they resided.

The New Mexico Spanish Mission had its roots in the joint efforts of a Mexican Catholic priest who converted to Protestantism and a Spanish-speaking young man who had worked, strangely, among the Methodist Swedish mission in the East. Both felt called to preach in Spanish in New Mexico. The Methodist bishops supported this calling by providing a salary for these two men and sending them together with a superintendent to New Mexico in 1853. However, by the end of the year, the superintendent and young man had returned, leaving only the converted priest to the work. Over the next decade, a trickle of Methodist preachers found their way to New Mexico, though they made few inroads with the populace. It was not until 1864 when a delegate from the Kansas Conference submitted a resolution at General Conference directing the Committee on Missions to consider setting up a mission and mission school in both New Mexico and Arizona that the work began to revive.[77] This resolution paved the way for Bishop Ames to select Thomas Harwood to relocate from Wisconsin to New Mexico. Harwood made the journey with his wife, Emily, in 1869. In 1872 he was appointed as the superintendent of the newly formed New Mexico Mission. In 1884, at Harwood's request, the General Conference separated the Spanish work from the English work in New Mexico, and Harwood was appointed the superintendent of the New Mexico Spanish Mission. He served a total of thirty-eight years as a superintendent, concluding his service in 1910.

---

76. In addition to work among the Mexicans in the New Mexico, there was also Spanish-speaking mission work in other parts of the United States, especially in Puerto Rico when it became a territory of the United States following the Spanish-American War.

77. Harris, *Journal of the General Conference of the Methodist Episcopal Church Held in Philadelphia, PA, 1864*, 89.

The WHMS launched its Bureau for New Mexico and Arizona in 1886, which took in work among the Spanish-speaking population, the white settlers and the Native Americans. In 1890 the agency split the bureau, dedicating one to work among the Spanish-speaking people and one to work among the Native Americans.

As visible from the various fits, starts and recategorizations that the Methodists applied to their work with the Spanish-speaking population in New Mexico, this group of people presented the Methodists with some difficulty in determining what the group's relationship was to the United States.[78] Harriett S. Kellogg noted the difficulty in parsing the position of this demographic in her preface to Thomas Harwood's *History of New Mexico Spanish and English Missions.* She wrote, "It would be interesting in this connection to turn to New Mexico and ask the question, 'Aliens or Americans?' The answer might reverse the viewpoint from which we consider foreign immigration; for who, after all, have always been Americans? The Mexicans or their ancestors have, for untold centuries, occupied this strange corner of our country. Here is to be found the remnant of a civilization older than tradition."[79]

Kellogg's clear Americanism (even though the Mexicans lived on the land prior to the existence of the United States, they were still living on "our country," and the civilization of the Mexicans is dated by the existence of American tradition) does not eclipse the fact that she could not simply label the Mexican population as immigrants. This awkwardness, however, did not lessen the calling of the MEC to help this population participate in Christian American civilization.

Above all, WMCNB values demanded that Methodists overcome the Mexicans' adherence to Catholicism. Catholicism was seen by the Methodists, as well as by most Protestant whites, as a serious threat to the Republic because of how it turned individuals into lowly serfs rather than making them informed, active citizens. While the Mexican population was safely located in a remote part of the nation and, thus, did not present the immediate political threat that the Catholic immigrants from Europe settling in American cities did, Methodists still were wary of having too many Catholics active within the bounds or the United States. In its first report to the WHMS annual meeting, the Bureau for New Mexico and Arizona made this clear, fearing that if left unchecked Catholicism would

78. Since Mexicans were not clearly white or black, this snarled the binary race line many Americans otherwise used to interpret the world. Foley, *White Scourge,* 5.

79. Harwood, *History of New Mexico Spanish and English Missions,* vol. 1, preface.

merge with paganism and Mormonism to create a terrible, multi-headed, anti-civilization hydra. The report argued, "Now, American energy is pressing in upon those old Spanish lands, and it is high time. There is not an hour to spare. There are in them eighteen times as many Romanists as there are people of all other faiths counted together. If we do not push Evangelism resolutely, there will be in the South-west a group of Roman Catholics States tinctured with paganism, and Mormon polygamy."[80]

While the note of alarm raised in this passage did not persist in later WHMS writings about the Mexicans, the importance of severing the connection of Mexicans to Catholicism remained. As late as 1915, the Bureau for Spanish Work on the Pacific Coast (a bureau that the WHMS briefly created to work with Mexicans primarily in California, and later conflated into a single Bureau for Spanish Work in the South-West together with the bureau overseeing Spanish work in New Mexico and Arizona) declared with a grim tone of victory, "Some of the girls who came to us [at the WHMS industrial home in California] strong in the Roman Catholic faith found Christ as a personal Saviour and went out Protestant Christians determined to live for their master, even though it might mean persecution."[81]

In addition to the concern that Catholicism could taint the United States, those who worked among the Mexicans living in the Southwest gave another reason for seeking to release them from their loyalty to Rome: Catholicism hampered the capacity of the people to participate in Christian American civilization. Chiefly, according to Thomas Harwood, this was because Catholicism harkened back to another civilization—that of the medieval Spanish monarchy that sent its conquistadors to claim the land. He opined:

> What a golden opportunity was this for Romanism. The so-called infallible pope at their head, the crowned heads of Spain and her civil and military officials and soldiery, for the most part, at her feet; with no Protestant Bible, or Protestant press or Protestant preacher or public school in the way. The priests could sow the gospel seed, water it with their tears, bask in papal benedictions and reap the golden harvest! Ten generations of sowing and reaping and what is the harvest? What is New Mexico . . . in 1850 when my lesson begins? Intellectually, morally and religiously it was one of the darkest corners of Christendom. While the march of civilization had taken great strides almost everywhere else, New Mexico had fallen behind. Why?

80. Women's Home Missionary Society, *Sixth Annual Report*, 50.

81. Women's Home Missionary Society, *Thirty-Fourth Annual Report*, 189.

> For want of Bibles, schools, and proper instruction. These want-
> ing, there could be but little progress on any lines of material
> progress.[82]

According to Harwood the Catholic priests of his day enforced this connection with an ancient, decidedly anti-Republican civilization. A chief method of this enforcement was the priests keeping their parishioners poor by demanding exorbitant fees from their parishioners for Catholic rites. Harwood related an incident in which a priest came to consecrate the grave of a Mexican boy. The boy had attended the Methodist mission school Harwood oversaw, and when the boy died, the family requested Harwood perform the funeral service for him. Harwood obliged, charging the family nothing for the service and receiving no payment. However, a few days later, the priest in whose parish the family lived, learned of Harwood's actions. Unbidden, the priest came to expunge the Protestant pollution from the boy's grave and consecrate it properly through a funeral mass. At the end of the mass, Harwood, claiming the authority of the boy's father for the authenticity of the account, recorded the following exchange:

> The father knew it would cost something, and that he would
> have to pay it, so he secured . . . a number of silver dollars
> . . . so that he could pay the priest for his services. When it
> was all finished, he asked, "Father, how much do I owe?" The
> priest replied, "I ought to charge a hundred dollars, but as you
> didn't know any better, pay me nine dollars." The poor old man
> counted out the money and said, "Father, I can't look into your
> heart, nor into the heart of the other man [i.e., Harwood], but he
> did more than you have done, and he didn't charge me anything,
> and you charge me nine dollars, here it is, take it." The priest
> wheeled on his heel and left.[83]

The WHMS was even more pointed on this score. In the curriculum the WHMS used to educate children attending Sunday school about the people the WHMS helped, a passage stated, "The Roman Catholic priest comes to them once in a while, marries those who want to be married, christens the children, says funeral masses for those who have died since he was there before, and goes away with most of the money that the poor, *very* poor, people have saved against his coming—for the priest

82. Thomas Harwood, *History of New Mexico Spanish and English Missions*, 1:18.
83. Ibid., 1:140.

must be paid for everything he does, whether the people have enough to eat or not."[84]

Added to the destitution that Catholicism engendered among the people, it also bound them to superstition. Harwood, shifting to an almost gothic horror genre, described in detail an experience he had in witnessing the Good Friday observance of a group of especially zealous ascetic Roman Catholics called the *Penitentes*. Allowed to witness this practice by special invitation, Harwood was locked in a large room together with the *Penitentes*. Some bound themselves in a prostrate position before a life-size crucifix and picture of the Virgin Mary while others used cactus-whips to flagellate themselves for over an hour while singing mournful hymns.[85] In another passage, Harwood narrated how he watched a procession of Mexicans carrying an image of their village saint in order to secure rain for their crops. Mentioning that he thought the procession was "foolishness" to a Mexican friend of his, his friend replied, "You may curse their God . . . but don't speak a word against their saint or you will be likely to get hurt, if not killed."[86] Of course, Harwood took this very caution as witness to the perverse values and patterns of life Catholicism had fostered among its charges since it allowed superstitious saint-worship to take precedence over worship of God.

What is notable about Harwood is that, while he rejected the Catholic faith and the traditions it had engendered among the Mexicans, he he came to love the Mexican people. He observed, "that many of the poor Mexican people were really a burden-bearing people," and he desired to help them be free of that burden. Specifically in reference to the *Penitentes* he wrote, "I learned to sympathize with them very much. I had seen the *Penitentes* carrying their great wooden crosses on their bare shoulders, whipping themselves with cactus whips, as well as, paying large sums of money for baptisms, burials, marriages, confessions, etc., as well also as the tenth of their crops and herds and fleeces, and my heart had to be touched to sympathy rather than hardened to blame."[87]

Harwood's revelation of his feelings toward the Mexicans are a helpful reminder that the home missionaries of the MEC were not hard-hearted, imperialistic bigots. While most were guilty of the sins of racism and nativism, they were also compassionate toward those they evangelized,

---

84. Guernsey, *Lands of Sunshine*, 43.

85. Harwood, *History of New Mexico Spanish and English Missions*, 1:167–68.

86. Ibid., 1:135.

87. Ibid., 2:134.

genuinely desiring them to share in the blessings God offered. The best access to those blessings that they knew of came through sharing the American gospel so that people could have the best possible quality of life in this world and hope of life eternal.

The practical means of offering the American gospel to the Mexican population in the United States included supporting moral reform, particularly temperance, providing education, and seeking to establish Christian homes even in the midst of the grinding poverty in which they lived. Constructing church buildings and schoolhouses, holding preaching services, learning the Spanish language, and supporting the work of the federal government in parts of the country where Mexicans made up a significant portion of the population were all strategies connected to these activities. In its curriculum the WHMS described these efforts to help the Mexicans participate in Christian American civilization by stating: "Perhaps there is no better place in the country to show what America can do with 'raw material,' what 'made in America' may mean."[88]

Preaching and teaching moral behavior was critical to the work not only among the Mexican population, but also among the settlers in the Southwest generally. As with evangelism to the Native Americans, much of what the missionaries sought to do among the Mexicans they also hoped would bring white settlers back to WMCNB values and patterns of life. Harwood presented numerous stories of banditry, murder, and violence to underscore how the Southwest could easily corrupt white Americans and Mexicans alike. He even suggested that whites were often the instigators of that corruption. In one instance he recorded the address of a Methodist Mexican preacher to his congregation in which the preacher said to "look out for the railroad for it was bringing whiskey, gamblers, horse racers—and the country would go wild."[89] In another instance, he described how an American soldier, after participating in a service conducted by Harwood and his wife, felt convicted about the fact that he was living with a Mexican woman without being married to her. The soldier requested a Methodist wedding, explaining that his bride-to-be was Catholic, but that she was "real nice, and she will not object to a Protestant marriage."[90]

Temperance was especially important to Harwood because New Mexico was a wine-growing region, a point that he specifically connected

88. Guernsey, *Lands of Sunshine*, 52.

89. Harwood, *History of New Mexico Spanish and English Missions*, 1:307.

90. Ibid., 1:73.

to the presence of Catholicism among the Mexican people.[91] After becoming superintendent of the mission, he often supported temperance lectures during his quarterly conference visits to the societies with the dual goals of ending the practice of drinking wine and driving a wedge between the Mexicans and the Catholic Church. He happily declared that after one such lecture a woman who owned a vineyard came forward to foreswear her complicity in wine-making and promised to cut down all her vines. This led him to conclude, "There is a better day coming for this oppressed and priest-ridden country."[92] Along these same lines, he responded in *El Abogado Cristiano*, the Spanish-language newspaper the New Mexico Mission published, to an article in the Catholic *Review* that chided the Methodists for destroying the faith of the Mexicans: "We took these people as we found them, except those who were drinking or selling liquors, gambling, Sabbath-breaking, etc. These promised to quit their vices, and we are glad to say the most of them did. Does the Review blame us for that? Does it blame us for making better Christians of them? Why then did his church not furnish better material for us to work upon?"[93]

Methodists saw founding schools as another essential element of this work among the Mexican population. As with the Native Americans, Methodists often believed that the older generation would be very difficult to bring into Christian American civilization. However, if the children could be indoctrinated with WMCNB values and patterns of life, then there was hope for the future. As the President of the WHMS opined in her annual address in 1901, "The childish prattle and trembling utterances of the aged all join in their foolish forms and ceremonies . . . One month in our 'Harwood Home' [a WHMS-sponsored school in New Mexico named in honor of Harwood and his wife] means more for the young woman than a year in a day-school."[94] To this end, the WHMS supported at least three schools in the Southwest, with some opening and some closing, from the period of 1900-1920. In 1920, the three schools, located in Albuquerque, Tucson and El Paso, totaled 49 teachers, 133 resident students, 497 day students, and a combined budget of $26,020. In addition to this, the New Mexico Mission supported several day schools and a boys' industrial school, which later became Albuquerque College. Of these, Harwood

---

91. Ibid., 1:19.

92. Ibid., 1:294.

93. Ibid., 2:173.

94. Women's Home Missionary Society, *Twentieth Annual Report*, 90.

wrote, "Our school work has always been an important factor in our Mission. It has served as an entering wedge in our Mission."[95]

The Methodists greatly anticipated the arrival of the public schools in the Southwest to support them in their work with the Mexican population there. However, it was soon disappointed when Catholics quickly moved, as the Methodists saw it, to forestall the work of these schools. Harwood explained that in New Mexico the schools were to be administered by four commissioners who were elected annually in each county. To Harwood's dismay, the preponderance of Catholics living in these counties made the majority of these commissioners Catholic. As a result, the "public schools are nothing more nor less than Jesuit schools, where the priests have entire supervision . . . little is taught in these schools except prayers, and the superstition of the Romish Church." Also condemnable, according to Harwood, was the fact that the priests refused to teach English because they "are opposed to the Mexican children learning the language of Protestantism."[96] As a result, from Harwood's perspective, the mission schools overseen by the various Protestant denominations were the only real possibility for offering the Mexican people in the Southwest the tools for participating in Christian American civilization.

Integrally related to its educational mission was the Methodist effort to develop proper domesticity among Mexican families, especially by training the Mexican girls and women. Harwood explained the necessity of focusing on the women in New Mexico: "The Mexican women have great influence . . . so in order to accomplish much for Christianity here, something must be done for the girls."[97] In part this work among the women was evangelistic, calling them to leave their Catholicism in favor of Methodist and American values. Another part of this work was bringing Mexican women "up" to American standards. Harwood presented this idea almost in passing when he described his delight at having an American woman serve as the hostess for him one night during his circuit travels. He wrote, "She is the only American woman in the place. Mexican women for house-help are of not much account. Many of them can't cook to suit Americans."[98] Harwood did believe that the Mexican women could be brought along to these more exacting standards, and he knew just who

---

95. Harwood, *History of New Mexico Spanish and English Missions*, 2:431–32.

96. Ibid., 1:253.

97. Ibid., 1:254.

98. Ibid., 1:215.

should take on this work: "it seems to me it belongs to the ladies of our churches to do it."[99]

The ladies of the WHMS were only too happy to oblige. Like Harwood, they were deeply concerned with the lack of Christian womanhood that existed among the Spanish-speaking peoples. In an address entitled "Children of Our Mexican Neighbors" given to the WHMS annual meeting in 1905 as an appeal for greater funds for work in Arizona and New Mexico, the women heard, "The condition of the people is deplorable. They are so apathetic and indifferent that the work is discouraging. The father is the lord. The mother, for her comfort, sits sometimes on the sunny side of the house and smokes her cigarettes."[100] Beyond these decidedly poor family-conditions, the deprivations of poverty also challenged women in being able to establish a Christian home. The women of the WHMS were especially schocked by the lack of cleanliness their missionaries discovered. In 1897 attendees at the WHMS annual meeting heard that one of the most remarkable changes girls who came to their Albuquerque home experienced was that they were no longer "unkempt and unwashed." Nearly twenty years later this was still a concern of the WHMS, especially when the missionaries had to deal with an outbreak of typhus. The missionaries hoped the "epidemic taught the Mexicans the value of cleanliness," noting that an increased number of people from the neighborhood had come to the WHMS homes to bathe there.[101]

To combat the decidedly un-American households the Mexican women kept, the WHMS engaged in their usual process of seeking to uplift the women by teaching them the value of domestic work. They especially focused on sewing, cooking and other practical skills that women might need to provide for their families. The WHMS Sunday School materials, using the metaphor of "developing" from photography, offered a way of understanding how the curriculum sought to uplift the girls who came to the WHMS schools:

> This is what you see, coming out little by little, as a real photograph does in the artist's dark room; tiny adobe houses, in the midst of desert sands; mothers and fathers who have never had the chance to learn how to read and write; no cooking except that of the desert, the principal food being *tomales* and *frijoles*; no sewing but the crudest; few clothes, no shoes; not the

99. Ibid., 1:255.

100. Women's Home Missionary Society, *Twenty-Fourth Annual Report*, 29.

101. Women's Home Missionary Society, *Thirty-fifth Annual Report*, 145.

slightest idea of study; no table manners, for they have never seen a table set for a meal, much less a tablecloth; beds and night-dresses entirely unknown; and, with all of this, they are shy and wild as young birds. Open your eyes now to what we see to-day; brown-skinned and rosy cheeked girls in neat brown uniforms, with red ties and hair ribbons, bright eyes and clear heads, learning lessons as well and as quickly as you do; deft hands that can make beds, wash dishes, sweep and scrub, as thoroughly as anybody; that can make dresses, too, and crochet and embroider, as well; girls who can make good bread, more than a hundred and fifty loaves a week, and get good meals, in American style, and set the tables and wait on them properly. Which pictures do you like best?[102]

The class of 1922, Harwood Industrial School (W. H. M. S.),
Albuquerque, New Mexico

102. Guernsey, *Lands of Sunshine*, 42.

Original caption: Cooking class in a Methodist school
which exists simply for girls who need another chance

While the race of the girls could not be completely eradicated—they were still "brown-skinned"—the WHMS hoped to domesticate the girls. Certainly the WHMS lifted the girls' standard of living by doing this. It also imposed a clearly WMCNB set of values on the girls. In doing this, the WHMS sought to uplift not only these girls, but the families connected to them. This uplift took the form of everything from helping Mexican men and boys acquire a taste for American pies[103] to having girls take over the care of their families from their less-capable mothers[104] to sending the girls out as missionaries, either as employees of the WHMS or as those who will get married and establish good homes among their own people. It is the latter kind of missionary that the WHMS took most pride in, as shown by descriptions of weddings dotting the WHMS publications. The most telling in terms of pure American evangelism was the one presented in the Sunday school curriculum: "the dresses, the flowers, the presents and the refreshments told the story that another home was begun, a home whose mistress would be one of our trained girls who knew how to keep it neat and clean, to cook well, and, we believe, to set a good and helpful example to her neighbors who, perhaps, had not had a chance to learn better ways."[105]

Here was the epitome of success for the WHMS—a Mexican girl taken from the deep poverty, superstition, and ignorance that was hers by virtue of being born into a Catholic setting and transformed into a

103. Ibid., 60.

104. Women's Home Missionary Society, *Fourteenth Annual Report*, 100.

105. Guernsey, *Lands of Sunshine*, 30–31.

paragon of Victorian virtue. Through her training in the school, she gained the values and skills necessary to create a proper household to propagate Christian American civilization, and the wedding presents she received gave her the material goods necessary to enjoy the full quality of life this civilization offered. In effect, she was transfigured from brown-skinned Mexican to white-wearing American bride and her glory was meant for the Mexican masses to see.

The perceptions that the MEC missionaries had of the Mexican population changed little over the course of time from 1864 until 1920. The problems of deeply entrenched Catholicism, poor education, and widespread poverty among the people remained in spite of the MEC's best efforts at instilling the values, education, and patterns of life shared by WMCNB Americans. The MEC did seek to supplement its missionary work in the Southwest by ordaining Mexican men. Still for all the individual success stories of men who became Methodist preachers and girls who graduated from the WHMS industrial schools to become Victorian matrons of their own households among the Mexican people, the overall impact Methodist missionaries had was negligible.

As with the Native Americans, it is likely that a significant reason for this failure came from the lack of the MEC imagining itself in any relationship with the Mexicans outside of a missionary one. While the Methodists lauded the few Mexicans who adopted the values and patterns of life that they taught, they were not ready to invite these protégés to come live in the Northeast where they could participate in Christian American civilization within its heartland. Even Harwood, in his efforts to relate to the Mexicans, could never see them as anything more than a hard-pressed people in need of the compassion and pity of the superior whites. With no capacity to integrate the Mexicans into the fellowship of WMCNB Americans, the MEC could only hope to set up a facsimile of Christian American civilization in the Southwest and leave it to its own devices. It is hardly surprising that this endeavor failed, especially in the face of the centuries-old values and patterns of life that already held sway there.

A DISAPPOINTING SUCCESS

With all of the ways that the western home missionary work fit with pure American evangelism, and with the commitment of the CES and the WHMS to see this work accomplished, it is puzzling the extent to which the MEC as a whole often left its missionaries in the West destitute and struggling.[106] Lucy Webb Hayes noted this in her presidential address to the WHMS in 1888. She stated, "The story of the Methodist preacher on his circuit in the forest, on the plains, and in the mountains, is rarely heard and little known in the old and prosperous States. One hundred dollars a year for the minister, his wife, and the little ones, often in a cold climate, where almost everything is lacking and where all things are costly, it has been truly said, is barely enough, not to live upon, but to starve upon."[107]

While the preachers may have reminded the denomination of its antebellum heroes, and might have some fortune awaiting them in the mines of the West, many eastern Methodists seemed ambivalent at best about the actual lot of these preachers. This can best be seen in the cries for attention that the preachers themselves and the agencies that recruited them registered. The 1908 annual report of the Board of Home Missions and Church Extension declared that in Montana seminary trained men who could earn $2,000 in the North or East must subsist on only $800 and a parsonage. In New Mexico, the salaries ranged from $200–$300 per year depending on the charge. In both missions, missionary money was desperately sought to bring new, well-trained preachers to the people, especially to Methodists who had moved west and wanted to maintain their Methodist practices.[108] Allowances for single women and home missionaries working among the non-white populations were significantly less.

The likely reason for this seeming ambivalence of the MEC is twofold. First, while tales of "Brother Van" and his compatriots in the West might make for romantic reading, it was hardly the stuff for which Methodists wanted to be known in this era. The MEC was self-consciously claiming its position as the lead church representing Christian American civilization. A silver-tongued and politically-connected Bishop Simpson was far preferable to a rough-talking cowboy circuit rider holding preaching services in brothels and saloons. The latter might be necessary to spreading the civilization epitomized by the former, but the denomination did not need to provide the same resources to the latter as to the former. Norwood explained the Methodist desire to overcome its revivalistic heritage by stating, "The pioneer circuit rider came more and more to look like a home missionary."[109] The more the home missionary still looked like a circuit rider, the less the denomination valued what the home missionary did.

106. Barclay, *History of Methodist Missions: Part Two*, 42.

107. Women's Home Missionary Society, *Seventh Annual Report*, 11.

108. Kynett, *Methodist Forward Movement in the United States*, 61, 66.

109. Norwood, *Story of American Methodism*, 261.

The second reason for the MEC's ambivalence toward the West was the inability of the church to determine what the ultimate result of evangelizing and civilizing many of the populations in the West would be. The white settlers could be absorbed into the standard conference-and-circuit system of the MEC as they formed congregations. Likewise, Mormons could either be converted and brought into these congregations or legally suppressed so that their ideas did not pollute the larger Republic. What, however, of the Native Americans and the Mexicans? Here were populations that had an honest claim on living in the United States, but were worlds apart racially and culturally from the civilization that the MEC brought with them. The cultural divide was hard enough to cross in doing the home missionary work. The racial divide presented a nearly insurmountable obstacle.

This was unlike the racial struggles WMCNB Americans had in relating to African Americans. Although racist, the WMCNB Americans from the North had spent years and great effort thinking about how they would live together with African Americans. They had fought a war and expended vast political energy to amend the Constitution over this issue. While many would argue that even today this work is unfinished, it was (and is) a visible issue that laid the groundwork for battles to end segregation and uphold civil rights. None of this happened in relation to the Native Americans and Mexicans. Beyond the paternalistic desire to offer them Jesus and a better quality of life, there was no sense of how to live together with these groups in the Christian American civilization if they ever desired to take the Methodists up on this offer.

Given how racially, technologically, politically, and economically inferior these groups would have seemed to the WMCNB Methodists, it is perhaps not surprising that the MEC had no real thought about how they would all share in Christian American civilization together. It also is understandable why the MEC may have desired, if unconsciously, to hold its home missionary work with these peoples at arm's length. The church desired these groups to participate in Christian American civilization, but not in a way that would introduce them into the life of WMCNB. After all, this introduction, even if of converts who fully desired the better life offered in the American gospel, could disrupt the patterns of life so prized by the Methodists.

Regardless of the MEC's relative lack of support for the home mission work in the West, it is likely that the home missionaries and the agencies that did back them would have reason to celebrate the outcome of their work. To the extent that they saw the vast wilderness of the West dotted with new Methodist church buildings and schoolhouses, each attended to by committed preachers and missionaries, and to the extent that these buildings were filled with the variegated populations of the West—Eastern settlers, refugees from Mormonism, Native Americans, and Mexicans—and to the extent that each building saw some of those within it go forth and help instill the WMCNB values and patterns of life they learned in those buildings in yet others of their own groups, the Methodists could claim that they had succeeded. Christian American civilization had indeed been spread into the frontier and, while more work needed to be done, the beachhead for continuing that work was well-established. In the West, pure American evangelism had accomplished its purpose.

5

The Cities

THE CITY WAS THE most enigmatic of all home mission fronts for the Methodists. On the one hand, their existence was a monument to the greatness of Christian American civilization. The vast number of people who streamed to the United States because of the opportunities for personal betterment that it offered, the burgeoning industries that brought wealth to the nation, the increasing technological innovation that helped raise the standard of living—all of these found their seats in the American city. Yet, the city inhabitants participated in a culture that permitted people to hold values counter to the values of Christian American civilization. From the MEC's perspective, a central reason for this permissiveness was that the city was full of immigrants who imported their inferior values with them. The result of all this was to make the city simultaneously a place of great anticipation for the Methodists as they looked for the final establishment of Christian American civilization, as well as an alien, if not hostile, environment for the Methodists.

The competing natures of the city made it perhaps the most critical of all locations for engaging in the Methodists' task of evangelizing and civilizing others. To succeed in uplifting the peoples of the city was to succeed in the final goal of securing all peoples within the United States to a Christian American civilization. To fail was to cede the nation to the greatest evil powers that the Methodists knew. It was in how the Methodists worked out their evangelistic strategies to bring this civilization to the city that my idea of pure American evangelism becomes evident. A passage in the second to last chapter of *Methodism and the Republic* (1908) epitomized this tension: "In all efforts proposed for the evangelization of America the city must be given an important place; for, since it is becoming an acknowledged fact that the Stars and Stripes cover the most valuable missionary field in the world, it must be conceded that our greatest municipalities are the battle grounds upon which the campaign is largely to be fought and the ultimate victory gained."[1]

Referring to the cities as "the new frontier," the MEC initially sought to evangelize the peoples in the cities by engaging in their traditional practices of pure American evangelism used in the South and West. Such organizations as the Board of Home Mission and Church Extension (BHM&CE) and the Women's Home Missionary Society (WHMS) took on their standard roles of recruiting funds and personnel from the prosperous churches in the East to promote conversion, education, and domestic training among the cities' inhabitants.

However, as the denomination became more familiar with the nature of the city, which was evolving through the late nineteenth century and early twentieth century, it began to recognize that its traditional practices of evangelism would not be sufficient. The complexity of the city, its changing demographics, and the powerful allure of various immoral activities forced the Methodists to consider what new forms of evangelism might be necessary. These new forms of evangelism were necessary not only to connect the peoples of the city to Christian American civilization, but to forestall what the MEC saw as the deleterious influence the city was beginning to have on the culture of the United States more broadly. For this reason, even as the denomination cast about for new ways to convert the people of the city, it also sought to establish a defense perimeter around the rural areas of the United States, which it deemed the stronghold of WMCNB values and patterns of life.

More subtly, the cities forced the MEC to begin to redefine how it understood evangelism. Historically, Methodist evangelism focused on the individual. From the end of the Civil War, this focus shifted to entire groups of people (e.g., the Native Americans, the freedmen). The cities, however, served as the home for so many disparate peoples, that this focus on individual groups of people was not always helpful. Moreover, the political economy of the city radically impacted the lives of people, causing them to find their identity in terms of their socio-economic location as well as by their race or nationality. As the Methodists came to see this, they began to recognize that evangelism also needed to include work meant to manifest Christian American civilization in the political, economic, and social systems of the city. Methodist Social Gospelers, especially Frank

1. Boswell, "Methodism and the Cities," 309.

Mason North, who served as the corresponding secretary for the New York City Missionary Society of the Methodist Episcopal Church, led the charge on this work by creating innovative vehicles for humanitarian aid that would both care for the needy and propagate the gospel.

In developing these new practices and understandings of evangelism, the rhetoric of civilization waned among the Methodists in favor of eschatological imagery. Even if the more nationalistic allusions ended, however, the importance of establishing WMCNB values and patterns of life that Methodists had always associated with Christian American civilization remained steadfast. Indeed, the increased use of eschatological verbiage in place of discussing nations or civilizations signaled a more strident form of pure American evangelism. It argued that to transform American cities so that they operated according to WMCNB values was not only a means of spreading Christian American civilization to all regions of the United States, but to bring the Kingdom of God to earth.

Organizing for Evangelism in the Cities

The MEC bishops acknowledged the complexity of the city the first time they broached the topic in their address to the General Conference of 1880. In doing so, they acknowledged that the MEC did not have the capacity to engage in city evangelism effectively. The existing forms of home mission, used in the South and West, proved to be of only marginal success in the cities. This was because each city differed from the other. What worked in New York might not work in Philadelphia or Chicago. Likewise, the demographics of the various cities made each one a unique mission field, or, more accurately, a complex of mission fields, in its own right.

This does not mean that the denomination did not attempt to use its tools of sending missionaries, constructing church buildings, and offering education to urban dwellers. It did all this, but it sought new mechanisms for delivering this mission. Rather than trying to force the existing denominational structures into the city, Methodist leaders came to realize that they needed to baptize effective outreach work that came up from the grassroots level of Methodists who had already organized to reach the city on the local level. As a result, General Conferences began to give official denominational sanction to ministries that were already underway in the cities and showing promise for good results. Two examples of this are salient: deaconess work and the National City Evangelization Union.

Deaconesses

Deaconess Training School

In 1883, the WHMS received thirty applications from women who sought to be full-time home missionaries in a variety of settings and roles: "Mission Chapels, Mission Sunday-schools, Missionary visitor, teacher, or Bible reader, distribution of Bibles, tracts, etc., the relief of the poor, the sick, the friendless, and the rescue of the depraved; or, in a few words, all the work in our cities, towns, villages, and country neighborhoods, which is similar to the work done in our mission fields, whether to white or black, native-born or foreign people."[2]

During the same year the WHMS, led by the efforts of Lucy Rider Meyer, raised money for the purchase of a house where women chosen for this work could come, reside, and gain instruction on how to carry out their duties.

In 1884, the WHMS organized those women who specifically desired to serve as home missionaries in cities under the Bureau for Local Work. This bureau deployed missionaries to local auxiliaries of the WHMS located in major urban centers. It was with this infrastructure, training, and personnel already in place that the General Conference of 1888 voted to create the order of deaconess in the MEC. The conference handed the new order over to the WHMS for oversight. The WHMS agreed to this and promptly created the Bureau for Deaconess Work.[3]

2. Women's Home Missionary Society, *Third Annual Report*, 81.
3. Women's Home Missionary Society, *Ninth Annual Report*, 56-60, 88.

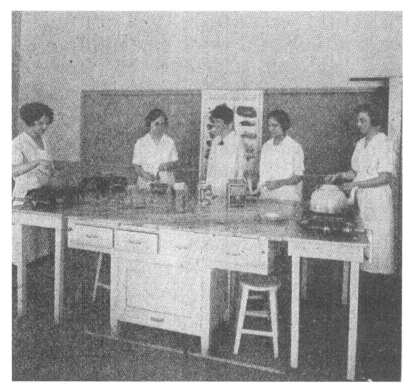

Cooking class in a deaconess seminary

A deaconess, as the General Conference defined it, was essentially a Methodist version of a Catholic nun. She was:

> a woman who has been led by the Spirit and the Providence of God to forego all other pursuits in life that she may devote herself wholly to the Christ-like service of doing good; and, having received this Divine call, has been tested and trained during a probation of at least two years; and, after such preparation, has been approved by the Church and solemnly set apart to this vocation in the Church . . . The single aim and controlling purpose of the Deaconess is to minister, as Jesus did, to the wants of a suffering, sorrowing and sin-laden world . . . Her work is to visit the sick, pray with the dying, comfort the sorrowing, seek the wandering, save the sinning, relieve the poor, care for the orphan, and to take up other Christlike service.[4]

4. Hingeley, *Journal of the Twenty-Fifth General Conference*, 907.

To show her special vocation, she wore specific garb, remained chaste, and lived together with other deaconesses in special deaconess homes under the authority of a matron.

However, there were some distinct differences the Methodists were insistent on drawing between their deaconesses and Catholic nuns. Specifically, "No vow of perpetual service is required of the Deaconess. She renders a free-will service and, so long as she is in good standing as a Deaconess, is entitled to a suitable support. Her relation as Deaconess being voluntary, she may withdraw from it at any time, but she shall give reasonable notice of her intention."[5]

There was disagreement within the WHMS as to whether the deaconesses optimally would remain single missionaries for life or would serve only when they were young, with the expectation that they would leave the order after a few years to be married. Both perspectives, though, were fueled by the notion of Victorian motherhood. The former saw the deaconesses exercising their maternal instincts by perpetually caring for those in need, the latter by establishing a family. In this way, deaconesses upheld the Victorian virtue of the home as paramount by seeing their ultimate goal in life wrapped up in motherhood. Catholic nuns, however, denied their call to Victorian womanhood by surrendering their divine call to motherhood permanently to the Church.

Once the doors were open for women to receive a license as deaconesses, the MEC saw amazing growth in this ministry. Within only two years, the WHMS planted eleven deaconess homes in major cities throughout the United States. The majority of the women residing in these worked as nurses in Methodist hospitals, as well as visiting sick and enfeebled individuals throughout the city. While performing these duties the deaconesses never lost sight of their evangelistic mandate. The secretary for the Bureau for Deaconess Work made this clear in her report to the WHMS annual meeting of 1898, "There is no better way to preach the gospel among the children of toil and sorrow in any large city; no better way to arrest the attention of careless and Christless people of all classes; no better way to come close home to the heart of humankind, than through the loving ministerings given in the sick-room. Here the deaconess can minister to the poor and rich, and lead them also to see that there are no riches like those that are invested in the bank of heaven; that there is no object so important as preparing for the great eternity beyond."[6]

5. Ibid., 907.
6. Women's Home Missionary Society, *Seventeenth Annual Report*, 123.

The deaconesses took this message to heart, sharing the gospel with gusto in the midst of their other ministrations. For example, the Lucy Webb Hayes Training School and Deaconess Home in Washington, DC reported that, in addition to spending a total of 679 total hours working in the hospital during a seven-and-a-half month period, the deaconesses also made 4,639 visits during which they had 1,007 opportunities for prayer, "secured" 395 scholars for Sunday school, "induced" 28 people to attend church, and celebrated 79 people who professed conversion.[7]

As with other WHMS home missions, the greatest joy was found in those being evangelized becoming advocates of the missionary work themselves. The deaconess home in San Francisco, for example, reported exultantly that one of the new deaconesses there was "a Japanese girl who, having been converted, is now receiving training, and performing deaconess work among her own people."[8]

In the midst of this evangelistic work, the WHMS impressed on deaconesses the importance of helping their urban charges participate in Christian American civilization. In 1901, for example, the corresponding secretary of the WHMS spent most of her report bewailing the deteriorating moral state of the nation. Noting specifically the assassination of the President McKinley (who had been an active member of the MEC), she focused on the dangers of anarchism combined with an illiterate set of "steerage immigration" finding a home in American cities. Pulling all of this together, she grandly declared, "The spirit that would strike down the head of this Nation with the hope of gain by introducing confusion into society by the destruction of law, order, and government, would, if it had the power, pluck God from the throne of the universe, destroy all physical and moral law, and plunge all things into chaos and black night."[9]

After this cosmic pronouncement, she turned to the deaconess as the God-ordained means of setting all this right: "[T]he deaconess . . . moves as an angel of light among these dark masses, bearing the banner of Christ . . . Legal enactments can not save us from the boastful Goliath of Anarchism, or make law-abiding and reliable citizens; but the Gospel of Christ can . . . May God inspire earnest, consecrated women with a zeal to help save the Nation by giving themselves to the saving of individual men and women who are blindly groping for rest to their perturbed souls."[10]

---

7. Women's Home Missionary Society, *Fourteenth Annual Report*, 118.

8. Women's Home Missionary Society, *Eleventh Annual Report*, 91.

9. Women's Home Missionary Society, *Twentieth Annual Report*, 76.

10. Ibid., 76–77.

It was not only the poverty-stricken, anarchic immigrant that needed the deaconess, though. In her Annual Address in 1910 the President of the WHMS stated, "our deaconesses go to the poor rich women and inspire them to higher motives and to unselfish lives."[11] This, too, was pure American evangelism. The wealthy women whose taste for luxury caused them to cease living according to the values of Christian American civilization, particularly the value of sharing the abundance God had given Christian Americans with those who were not as blessed with material goods (thus making them "poor rich women"), were as much in need of conversion as were the poor laborers. If the latter group threatened society because of its activism against the Republic, the former group threatened society with its apathy toward its fellow human beings. To emphasize this point, the president followed this comment by inviting all women, regardless of class or education level, to become deaconesses.

It was because deaconesses dealt with fundamentally existential issues, such as sickness, life and death, that they were able to flatten their evangelism sufficiently to recognize the failures and needs of all groups of people. No one class stood in perfect relationship to God, nor did any one group of people stand less in need of being instructed in the values of Christian American civilization. In the midst of the variegated work they did, they were agents of pure American evangelism, helping hold the nation together by drawing those of every rank and station into a civilized life.

National City Evangelization Union

The National City Evangelization Union (NCEU) was a conglomerate of local Protestants—Methodists and otherwise—who began coming together in 1888 for the purpose of doing ministry in the cities. Each city had its own NCEU, which operated how it saw best to bring about the evangelization of the residents there.

As with the deaconess ministry, the General Conference of 1896 formally sanctioned the NCEU as an organization of the MEC based on the work that was already in existence. In no small part, the conference did this because of the continuing danger the cities presented to Christian American civilization. This was made clear in the episcopal address to the General Conference of 1896. In these remarks, the bishops described the NCEU as performing the work of God in the cities that was necessary

11. Women's Home Missionary Society, *Twenty-Ninth Annual Report*, 95.

to save the nation, stating "They reinvigorate churches from which the former members have moved away, select new sites, open Sunday schools and missions, and give to undeveloped Christian forces an ample field of work. They have spiritual life enough to attack the worst places and attempt the most difficult things for Christ . . . The problem of our cities is the problem of our national existence. To deal successfully with this is to save our national life. There is no power but the power of God unto salvation that can do it."[12]

In 1904, after the appropriate denominational apparatus was in place to sustain the NCEU as a uniquely MEC venture, the General Conference articulated a job description for local NCEUs:

> The scope of the work of the local union may, among other objects, properly include the planting of churches, and Sunday schools, the aid of weak churches, missions to foreign populations, the transforming of downtown churches into new centers with modern methods of service, the institution of kindergartens and industrial schools, evangelistic, social, and Christian settlement work, conducting rescue missions and institutions for the relief of the destitute and the outcast. A local union may also combine with its plans for evangelization methods for promoting the connectional social life of the several churches.[13]

Like the deaconess job description, what is most striking about this passage is the wide variety of activities it takes into account. It spans the gamut from sustaining struggling congregations in downtown locations to caring for the poor in hands-on ways. This is a testimony to the complicated nature of city evangelism.

In 1908, the NCEU reported to the General Conference that it enjoyed significant success in its various ventures, boasting a total of seventy active local unions, which together had purchased $10 million worth of property and expended another $4.7 million toward urban ministry since the inception of the NCEU in 1888. Perhaps because of its success in this realm, this report also proved to be the NCEU's swan song. During the same conference the Board of Home Missions and Church Extension (BHM&CE) demanded that the NCEU become a subsidiary agency to it. The General Conference acquiesced to this, and by 1912, the NCEU was

---

12. "General Conference of the Methodist Episcopal Church: The Episcopal Address, 1896," 12.

13. Hingeley, *Journal of the Twenty-Fourth General Conference*, 508.

no more. In its stead, the BHM&CE stood over the MEC's city evangelism efforts, having renamed all the local unions "city societies."

In one way, the BHM&CE's desire to have sole administration of the city unions made sense. Both it and its predecessor organizations, the Missionary Society of the Methodist Episcopal Church and the Church Extension Society, also operated through local organizations. Some of these organizations dated back to the 1870s and focused entirely on work in the cities, such as the New York City Missionary Society and the Chicago Home Missionary and Church Extension Society. These organizations served both as fundraisers for the denominational agencies as well as points of distribution for denominational funds as they enacted practices of city evangelism on behalf of the Methodist Episcopal Church. Since it is on this local level where the majority of evangelistic activity occurred, it is to this we now turn with a specific focus on the work of the societies in Chicago and New York City.

LOCAL CITY EVANGELISM

Both the Chicago and New York Missionary Societies recognized the enormity and multifaceted nature of their expressed goal of evangelizing their respective cities. Perhaps because of the daunting size of this task, both societies used the word "evangelization" often, reminding themselves in their annual reports of the soteriological goal of their work. The New York society was especially explicit on this point, as demonstrated in the keynote address offered to the society in 1874, "O, brethren, we must never forget that the great business of the Church is to save men, that the one great work of a minister is to lead his people in saving souls."[14] Perhaps because of this reminder, the society annually reported the aggregate number of "conversions" attributed to the congregations and missionaries it supported. At its fortieth anniversary in 1906, the society boasted 22,849 conversions over the life of its work.

Initially, the city societies used the tried-and-true practices of evangelism the Methodists had deployed in other home missions, *viz.* funding missionaries and church construction. Since the city was the new frontier, the Methodists reasoned that the methods used on the western and southern frontiers would be just as effective.

---

14. *Report of the New York City Church Extension and Missionary Society of the Methodist Episcopal Church for the Year Ending March, 1874*, 11.

The City Pastor

A Chinese Immigrant Pastor and His Family
in American Garb, Portland, Ore.

Original caption: It is high strategy to train the leaders of foreign-speaking
groups in a Christian college—Foreign-speaking students
at Boston University

Much as Methodists lionized the circuit rider, so the city societies held
up the urban pastors as heroes facing the travails of a new, urban frontier.
During its tenth anniversary, for example, the New York society described
how their pastors canvassed every nook and cranny of the city, braving
the worst and most wretched locations in order to share the gospel, distribute gospel tracts, and invite people to Methodist services. It summed

up these activities in words that could have fit the Western circuit riders just as aptly: "The pastors . . . have toiled with a zeal becoming their calling to reach and attract the masses and to build up the kingdom of Jesus Christ."[15] Nine years later, it reiterated this point, declaring, "only the best men can succeed in this work . . . No man who is not able and willing to work hard, who has not a passion for saving souls, who is unwilling to give his time and energy to the work of pastoral visiting, ought to seek these places as fields of ministerial labor. They are very hard and thankless places for the man who does not love such work, while for those who do really love it there are no fields of toil in the Conference where a man can be more happy and useful than in these."[16]

In 1906, Frank Mason North, who served as the corresponding secretary of the New York society starting in 1892, penned his own panegyric to the urban pastor. In doing this, he remembered to include women, since their work as deaconesses had long been established by this point.

> Tact, patience, invention, aptness of speech and method, discernment, optimism, confidence in God and assurance of victory—these qualities penetrated ever by the life of the Spirit and adorned these by the gentleness of Christ—keep heroic men and women in the dark places of need, and at the very front line of the conflict, without a murmur and without fear. No braver sons and daughters of the church ever bore her banners than they who have gone forward on this crusade, no friends of Christ, more living or more pure, ever told by word and life that story for which a weary world is ever waiting.[17]

For all of the loquaciousness of the New York society concerning the heroism of urban pastors, the more taciturn Chicago society took an even more expansive view, suggesting that not only the city, but the entire nation hung on the faithfulness of the preacher:

> The preacher has invested his life for the Church . . . If we could eliminate out of our modern life all the fine inspirations, noble impulses, and redeeming influences in this great land that have emanated from the life of the ministry, there is not a state in the Union that would be fit to live in. All the best in our public

15. *Report of the New York City Church Extension and Missionary Society of the Methodist Episcopal Church for the Year Ending December 31st, 1876*, 13.

16. *Report of the New York City Church Extension and Missionary Society of the Methodist Episcopal Church for the Year Ending December 31st, 1884*, 13.

17. *Year Book for the Year Ending April 30th, 1906 Containing the Fortieth Annual Report of the New York City Church Extension and Missionary Society*, 50.

institutions, all the purest in our social life, all the strongest bul-
warks of our civilization, have directly or indirectly come from
the Christian ministry through the Christian Church . . . [T]he
hope of the race is in the Church and in her Christian ministry.[18]

In making this claim, the Chicago society attributed Methodist
preachers as the source of all things good in America. Who better to help
shape the cities in their wildness and immorality than the preachers who
had shaped a nation that had begun as nothing more than a wild frontier?

Church Extension in the Cities

Proposed First Italian Methodist Episcopal Church
and Community House, Chicago

Supporting the construction and repair of church buildings was likewise a
critical activity of both the Chicago and New York societies. Most of their
respective annual reports discuss purchasing new plots of land, erecting
new church buildings, helping congregations who were struggling under
significant debt loads because of their buildings, and following the progress of the congregations or other ministries inhabiting the buildings the
societies aided.[19] These societies understood that it took substantial sums
to provide and maintain church buildings, and worked hard to raise the
money to care for these issues. They also expected substantial returns for
their troubles on behalf of local congregations.

18. *City Foursquare*, 6.

19. *Report of the New York City Church Extension and Missionary Society of the
Methodist Episcopal Church for the Year Ending December 31st, 1883*, 10–13.

Original caption: Our Polish church in Detroit

Bishop C. B. Galloway of the Methodist Episcopal Church, South, who the New York society invited to be its guest speaker at its 1895 annual meeting, summed up the importance of construction to Methodist ministry in the cities. He explained, "church buildings are the essential condition of denominational stability and progress," claiming that the strength of a religious organization was visible through the number of new buildings it erected. On this score, he happily pointed to the large number of new Methodist buildings in the United States contrasted to the ever-decreasing number of pagan temples being built in other nations. Beyond providing evidence of vitality, he argued that by securing places where a denomination's unique doctrines and forms of polity could be practiced without interference, buildings guaranteed more faithful adherents to the denomination in the future. As he put it, "We must have our own buildings in which we can minister according to our own usages, and train our children according out own rules of family life."[20]

20. *Report of the New York City Church Extension and Missionary Society of the Methodist Episcopal Church for the Year Ending March 31, 1895,* 21–26.

Swedish Methodist Episcopal Church, Rockford, Illinois

That the city societies took seriously the idea of stamping the Methodist and, therefore, the Christian American, character onto people is clear in who they sought to bring under the influence of their urban pastors and into the hallowed halls of the buildings they constructed. Certainly, as Bishop Galloway suggested, they wanted to provide leadership and places for their own children. However, mirroring the discomfort of WMCNB Americans, they also wanted to reach those who were not in line with, and thus were a potential threat to, Christian American civilization. These groups included the immigrants, the poor, the rich, and the children of immigrants.

Evangelizing the Urban Dwellers

City Evangelism and Immigrants

Original caption: Pouring in at the Nation's Gateway

As with the larger denomination, one of the initial concerns of the city societies was with the immigrant. Just as the Freedmen's Aid Society and WHMS turned their attention to the influx of immigrants into northern cities during the late nineteenth century, so the local urban societies emphasized the importance of evangelizing the immigrants that were on their own doorsteps. In their episcopal address in 1880, the MEC bishops gave two reasons why the MEC needed to focus on the immigrants: their uncivilized background and denominational competition.

> The growth of those cities has been very largely from foreign immigration . . . This entire foreign population has been brought up, not only without Methodist influence, but generally in hostility to it. A large proportion of the immigration from Europe is Roman Catholic . . . The Protestant element on the Continent is divided between the Episcopal Churches . . . and the Lutheran or Reformed Churches . . . Thus the Presbyterian and Protestant Episcopal Churches have received large additions, both in number and means, from the immigration to our cities, while Methodism has received but few, and those as a general rule of the working classes . . . Another consideration is, that the other leading Protestant Churches were, in the older cities, a century or so in advance of the commencement of our own Church. They had secured sites for their churches, their friends had possession of large portions of the real estate of the country.[21]

21. Woodruff, *Journal of the General Conference of the Methodist Episcopal Church, Held in Cincinnati, OH, 1880*, 415–16.

MEC Instructional Material in Multiple Languages

The immigrants coming to the United States were not only unfamiliar with Methodism, but often held to values that were contrary to the WMCNB values the MEC championed. Compounding this was the presence of older denominations with the twin advantages of deeper ties to European countries and established real estate holdings in the American cities. These denominations were primed to claim the various immigrants as members.

The fact that many of the European immigrants were Catholic was of particular concern to the MEC. Methodists believed that immigrants coming from a Catholic background not only were resistant to Methodist overtures, but were partisans for a monarchical civilization over which the pope reigned. This belief led to fears of possible attempts by the pope to upend the Republic through sending masses of Catholics into the United States.

Such a fear was not new to Methodists. An article written before the Civil War entitled "The Conversion of Immigrants" in the *Western Christian Advocate* described Catholics thusly:

> They know little of the Gospel of Christ, and have less sympathy with our civil and sacred institutions. This heterogeneous mass are to be approached with . . . the thorough conviction that if they cannot be woven, and fused into our system, and made with us one people, they will constitute a most malignant

element for our utter destruction . . . If they get the mastery at our elections, retaining their European habits and vices, we might as well at once give in our allegiance to the old man at Rome, and receive as our protector some blood-thirsty Spanish-American wretch.[22]

Original caption: This lass is an Italian migrant worker in a string-bean field, Central New York state

The author declared that it was only sharing Christ with the immigrants that would provide Americans a sure protection from such a fate: "Our only safety is in their conversion." Nothing less than the survival of Christian American civilization hung in the balance, for "there never was, and there never will be, any national civilization without the inculcation of inspired truth from the living lips and the burning heart."[23] This sort of logic, which tied the need to inculcate specific values into immigrants

22. Edwards, "Conversion of Immigrants."
23. Ibid.

through evangelism for the sake of Christian American civilization, set the stage for pure American evangelism following the Civil War.

Several decades later, the Methodist rhetoric against Catholicism was no less strident. In the episcopal address of 1900 the bishops decried, "the presence among us in great force of a foreign hierarchy which, whatever disguise it may assume or however liberal many of its adherents may be, is by its fundamental principles the unchanging foe of civil and religious liberty."[24]

In addition to the clear and present danger of Catholics streaming into the United States, the bishops of the MEC began to recognize other variables that made the city a difficult place for the Methodists to evangelize. Specifically, there was the unique political economy of the city. Defined by industrial capitalism, the cities, more than anywhere else in the United States, demonstrated the discrepancies between the socio-economic classes, with the wealth of those who owned the capital standing in stark contrast to the poverty of those they employed. The result of this was to make the cities a potential seedbed for unrest and corruption. The bishops dealt with this in their address to the General Conference in 1888.

> An evil which has long existed in the countries beyond the seas, but which is comparatively new with us, has begun to show itself in our land, presenting problems to the Church, as well as to the nation, which are not of easy solution . . . That millions of laborers compactly organized under leaderships liable to become unscrupulous, chafing under real or fancied grievances, are an element of great power and no little danger is a fact too palpable to be concealed or overlooked. The entrance of this element into the political party strifes of this country adds to the perplexity and the peril of the situation.[25]

The "danger" the bishops cited may be an oblique reference to the Haymarket Square bombing, which occurred in 1886. The bombing deeply troubled WMCNB Americans, as it pointed to the increasing class conflict within the United States, the violence endemic to that conflict, and—most unsettlingly—the ability of foreign anarchists to insinuate themselves into the conflict.[26] The potential for European radicals to cause

---

24. Monroe, *Journal of the General Conference of the Methodist Episcopal Church, Held in Chicago, Illinois, 1900*, 76–77.

25. Monroe, *Journal of the General Conference of the Methodist Episcopal Church, Held in New York, 1888*, 57–58.

26. Jacobson, *Barbarian Virtues*, 88–95.

damage on American soil only compounded the fear Methodists, along with numerous WMCNB Americans, already had about the danger of providing immigrants access to the political system in the United States.

Putting all of this together, in entering the city Methodists faced a mass of people who were immigrants, often Catholic, participants in an increasingly tense class conflict, and possibly in favor of rebellious or anarchist activity against the government. Worst of all, these people were settled in the places that were becoming the heart of American political and economic power, giving them disproportionate cultural influence in spite of their inferior races and lack of technological, political, or economic acumen. This combination made these people dangerous to Christian American civilization, a possible fifth column ready to bring the entire civilization down from the inside.

This stark reality presented the Methodists with a clear need for their work of bringing Christian American civilization to the cities. This evangelism was quickly identified with Americanizing the immigrant in order to make them participants in Christian American civilization. In the immediate aftermath of the Haymarket riot, for example, the Chicago society's corresponding secretary declared ominously:

> The rapid increase of the population of our large cities is a cause of great anxiety, especially in view of the class of foreigners that annually crowd into them . . . [F]oreigners who are unacquainted and in many cases out of harmony with our American institutions . . . These must be Americanized if we would preserve the civilization of our country. If left to themselves they will largely increase the number who sympathize with and aid the anarchists in our midst . . . [who will cause, in turn,] greater destruction of life and property in the near future than we have yet seen.[27]

A few years later, though not striking as strident a note, the corresponding secretary still acknowledged the intimate connection between Americanizing immigrants and evangelizing them. He explained that coming into Chicago there was a "constant influx of foreign population bringing with them their peculiar ideas of social, religious, and governmental

---

27. *Annual Report of the Chicago Home Missionary and Church Extension Society for 1888*, 5–6.

life, massing in neighborhoods by themselves, thereby rendering the task of Americanizing, educating and Christianizing them more difficult."[28]

This idea of connecting the Americanization and the evangelization of the immigrant was widespread, as was the observation of how difficult it was to accomplish these twin goals. G. W. Miller of Philadelphia asserted this point in a rather unflattering metaphor when addressing the New York society: "Still another feature of your great problem of city evangelization is the great preponderance of foreign population. Four out of every five of your people are of foreign origin. Your population has drifted to you from every whither. Your city, like the elephant in a menagerie, which disposes of hat, branches, peanuts, orange peel, cakes, and candy, is expected to take in all this raw material of various nationalities, and turn out in due time American citizens."[29] Given the imagery he employed, it seems likely that Miller did not consider the logical analogy for what American citizens would be if the immigrants were symbolic of the elephant's food!

At the same time that the urban societies heard such sweeping comments, they also developed a capacity to nuance their understanding of immigrants in a way that was not common among their fellow Methodists. Perhaps because the men and women involved with the work of these societies lived in the same cities as the immigrants, it allowed them to recognize that not all immigrants were dangerous or even undesirable in a Christian American civilization. Indeed, some immigrants might make welcome additions to such a civilization. The New York society delineated the groups in the following way in its annual report of 1890:

> It must not be understood that all these people who are foreign-born or the children of parents foreign-born are worthless, or their influence antagonistic to our American civilization. On the contrary, very many of the brightest lights in all the professions, many of the most successful among the merchants, and certainly multitudes among the most astute politicians, must be included in this number. Nor is there any evidence that this influx of foreigners has either physically or mentally debased our population. Neither in blood nor in brain has there been any deterioration. There is, however, a darker side to this subject. A considerable class of those who come to us from other countries are morally worthless, and some of them worse than worthless.

28. *Annual Report of the Chicago Home Missionary and Church Extension Society for 1893*, 7.

29. *Report of the New York City Church Extension and Missionary Society of the Methodist Episcopal Church for the Year Ending March 31, 1884*, 37.

They are a menace to our Christian civilization. They care but little for law, and nothing for the Sabbath or other institutions of the Church. They are clannish, and so concentrated in certain localities as to render inoperative ordinary evangelizing agencies . . . No greater problem can possibly engage the attention of the Christian people of New York than how to Christianize the unchristianized portions of the community. Patriotism and philanthropy and personal safety all harmonize with the highest Christian motives in the prosecution of this work.[30]

The same year, the Chicago society explained that the better class of immigrants came from those parts of the world where a Christian civilization, if not an American Christian civilization, was already well-entrenched:

[M]any of these are from England, and come to us with a thorough knowledge of our language, and well-established habits of economy and industry, and with abundant means to conduct a profitable business. Many come with fixed principles and habits in harmony with our established Protestant churches. The same may be said of many of the Irish and other nationalities. It should be borne in mind that many of our best Christian workers, both men and women, ministers and laymen, in our English-speaking churches, are of that class of people. These at once form an important part of that great army to which we look for the spiritual enlightenment and evangelization of our rapidly increasing population.[31]

Two years later, the corresponding secretary of the New York society even argued that it was un-American to deny hospitality to the better class of immigrants.

I have no sympathy with those who assail the thoroughly American sentiment that this country is to be for all time "the home of the free" and an asylum for the oppressed of all nations. The tide of immigration which has set toward this country for many years has undeniably greatly enriched it. Without it we never would have attained the greatness which has made us the wonder and admiration of all the world . . . Who can doubt that their coming will continue to add to our national wealth and welfare

---

30. *Report of the New York City Church Extension and Missionary Society of the Methodist Episcopal Church for the Year Ending March 31, 1889*, 17–19.

31. *Annual Report of the Chicago Home Missionary and Church Extension Society for 1889*, 5.

if we are wise in our generation? It would be supreme folly to close our ports against immigrants, even if we could do so.[32]

Even recognizing the good attributes of some immigrants, these immigrants still needed to be Americanized. The report from the corresponding secretary went on to make this point, advancing the well-healed arguments of protecting the Republic as the reason for this.

> But to all able-bodied and well-disposed people from every clime we must extend a friendly hand and manifest a deeply fraternal feeling. We must welcome them to the same privileges which we and our children enjoy. Only this remember, they must be Christianized and Americanized. Our legislators and rulers must be aroused to the importance of safeguarding the elective franchise. Our public schools must be nurseries of patriotism. Our Christian Churches must blaze with evangelistic fervor. American Christian citizenship affords the highest advantages and opportunities known to mankind; and it involves also the gravest duties and responsibilities. We cannot and are not worthy to enjoy the former if we repudiate or neglect the latter.[33]

Turning these words into actions, both these societies funded several missions to foreign populations. The Chicago society supported work among Bohemians, Croatians, Poles, Chinese, Italians, Germans, and Scandinavians. The New York society supported Italian, German, Swedish, Norwegian, Japanese, Chinese, and Jewish missions. (The latter was an outreach to Jews for their conversion to Christianity, but was classified as a work among foreigners. Both societies also supported missions to African Americans. While the societies realized that the African Americans were not immigrants to the United States, they continued to categorize these missions in the sections of their reports that dealt with outreach to foreigners.) All these missions employed pastors who spoke in the native tongue of the population the societies sought to evangelize. These missions also constructed church buildings that looked remarkably like other Methodist Episcopal Church buildings. By doing this, the urban societies advanced what we can describe as pure American evangelism on two levels: by upholding the uniquely American idea of welcoming the stranger and by providing the means for the stranger to be inculcated

---

32. *Report of the New York City Church Extension and Missionary Society of the Methodist Episcopal Church for the Year Ending March 31, 1892*, 16.

33. Ibid., 16–17.

with WMCNB values. The similarities of the church architecture further helped both the immigrants and the WMCNB Americans who traveled past the buildings, suggesting that the immigrants were seeking to conform materially with Christian American civilization.

City Evangelism and the Poor

Original caption: While they make over old shoes, they are themselves remade by productive employment—Goodwill Industries,
Morgan Memorial, Boston

In addition to having a more nuanced understanding of immigration than others in the denomination, the urban societies also had a greater appreciation for the implications of economic class on social life in the United States. This is not to suggest that the Methodist leadership on a national level was insensible to this. As early as 1876 they declared in their episcopal address:

> The true Church has always preached the gospel to the poor. This has been characteristic of Methodism throughout its

history. It is not only Christ-like, but it is expedient. The Church which preaches to most of the poor of this generation, other things being equal, will preach to most of the rich in the next generation. While we have not been inattentive to the pastoral and spiritual interests of the more wealthy of our congregations, we have been especially desirous to provide for the religious necessities of the poor; hence the new and more needy parts of the work have received our special attention and care.[34]

Original caption: It carries its own sign, and is located in San Francisco

In 1888 the bishops became more pointed in their episcopal address to the General Conference, questioning the evangelistic strategies often deployed by the MEC and their effectiveness among the poor:

> But there is a spiritual side to this question which we cannot disregard. It is primarily the old question of the relation of the Church to the masses, especially to the poor. Are they drifting away from us? Have we lost our love for them, or the aggressive spirit which carries the Gospel to their homes and hearts? Have we forgotten our mission as we have increased in wealth? Nothing is more alarming to the philanthropist and the patriot

34. Woodruff, *Journal of the General Conference of the Methodist Episcopal Church, Held in Baltimore, MD., 1876,* 404.

than the alienation of the laboring people from the evangelical churches. Is this alienation a fact? If so, what is its cause? If we have given too much attention to the rich, or cherished too much regard for social position, or have in any wise neglected the poor, we have departed from the spirit of our calling. In the sanctuary of God, if nowhere on earth, 'the rich and the poor meet together' in brotherly fellowship, and the gracious God who becomes the Father of all that believe in Jesus Christ receives alike their prayers and services. If fine churches are in the way they do not honor us, and it were better never to have them than that they should stand as monuments of unchurchly pride, or as barriers between the Gospel of Christ and the poor for whom he gave his life. Of course our finest churches were not intended to exclude the poor, nor do our wealthiest people desire the exclusion of any; but good intentions weigh little against the fact that many of the poor do not feel the welcome so kindly intended for them, and do not come into churches which appear to them intended for other classes. This fact reveals a portentous evil, and demands a remedy at whatever cost.[35]

They made the argument even more baldly at the turn of the century when they put forth the following charge to the General Conference of 1900:

It is to be borne in mind that the poor abound; that, therefore, in lowly conditions for the most part the aim of the Gospel is to be wrought out; and that the salvation of the common people is therefore, preeminently the salvation of the race . . . It is often alleged that there is a wide alienation of the working classes from the Church, that churches tend to become rich men's clubs, that many ministers lack brave faithfulness toward the wealthy and tender sympathy toward the poor; and the gospel of the Nazarene often fails of effect among the classes with whom his lowly life was identified. There is enough of truth in these allegations to set us upon serious inquiry.[36]

These excerpts over two decades demonstrate that the MEC's leaders were very much conscious of the impact their growing wealth and respectability had on their capacity to engage in effective evangelism among the poor. Contrary to oft-repeated themes in American Methodist

35. Monroe, ed., *Journal of the General Conference of the Methodist Episcopal Church Held in New York, 1888*, 58–59.

36. Monroe, ed., *Journal of the General Conference of the Methodist Episcopal Church Held in Chicago, Illinois, 1900*, 71.

historiography, the Methodists did not forget about the poor as they advanced in their own social location. The evangelization of the poor remained a critical activity for the Methodists, and one that they genuinely desired to continue.

However, as the nineteenth century wore on and turned to the twentieth century, the Methodists struggled more and more with understanding how to evangelize the poor effectively. Again, the bishops demonstrated this. In their 1888 address, they laid out a three-part strategy for evangelizing the poor. The level of equivocation this strategy included is notable, particularly in reference to traditional evangelistic efforts that the denomination once had regularly engaged to reach the poor.

> 1. Chief among the agencies to meet this demand are local missionary organizations. In New York, Chicago, and other cities these are doing royal service. 2. The use of evangelists with methods of work not usual in our churches has sometimes met with encouragement and done good, but we have declined appointing traveling ministers to such services. Their sphere of operation is largely within the bounds of organized churches where the pastors are in full authority, and the appointment of evangelists to work in such fields under official sanction might introduce confusion if not unseemly conflicts of jurisdiction. We do not feel ourselves authorized to make such appointments, and are unable to see any way of giving them a place in our system without embarrassment. 3. The organization of voluntary societies in our churches in the form of alliances, leagues, unions, and associations, to a limited extent, is useful in promoting evangelical work and in reaching classes of people not otherwise easily accessible, as well as in cultivating the social life of communities in a Christian way and in encouraging the young.[37]

As the denomination moved into the twentieth century, the bishops increasingly tied their concern for the poor to the "labor problem." In doing this, they moved further from the kind of personal evangelism they at least qualifiedly endorsed in the above passage. The result of this was to position the denomination to evangelize the poor largely through dealing with systemic issues of economics and politics rather than by calling individuals to participate in Christian American civilization through conversion and the appropriation of WMCNB values.

37. Monroe, ed., *Journal of the General Conference of the Methodist Episcopal Church Held in New York, 1888*, 59.

Even as this drift toward systemic work took place, the local city societies continued to engage with the poor. The New York society seemed to relish the relatively inconspicuous nature of this work. In its 1884 annual meeting, the corresponding secretary recorded:

> Many of these fields of labor are so situated that the largest amount of hard, thorough work makes but little show. It is work among the poor and sick and unfortunate, who need every thing from the church, and who can give nothing in return but their prayers and good-will. The very poor are constantly changing their residences, and this class comes and soon departs. There are many who need pastoral work who are unable to come to the church because of their work and their lack of suitable clothing . . . They do not appear to swell the number of members or of the congregation, but they do greatly increase the burden of the pastor's work. This is grand Christian work, done in secret, having only a nominal record in our reports, but known of God.[38]

By 1893, Frank Mason North sketched out a plan for how the New York society could centralize and vitalize a mission to the poor. He envisioned "a great center on the bowery, ample in accommodations for every kind of helpful work for every kind of needful people—a veritable 'House of all Help.' Here would center Methodist mission work, evangelistic, humanitarian, educational."[39] North went on to explain how this center would provide the best resources and expertise to the Methodist societies and missions throughout the city as they sought to minister to the poor. It would employ students from Drew Seminary and Union Theological Seminary, giving the church the benefit of their formal education and giving the students the benefit of hands-on experience with the neediest people of the city. North had the pleasure of seeing his plans quickly realized. The society moved within the next year to purchase property to create the Bowery Village Church and establish the center.

In opening this new "Center on the Bowery," the New York society brought its members, as well as the local Methodist societies throughout New York, into closer contact with the poor. It is not surprising, then, that the following year one of the addresses given to the society challenged some of the basic Victorian assumptions about the poor. The address, offered by clergyman Louis Albert Banks, suggested there were three

38. *Report of the New York City Church Extension and Missionary Society of the Methodist Episcopal Church for the Year Ending December 31, 1884*, 15.

39. *Report of the New York City Church Extension and Missionary Society of the Methodist Episcopal Church for the Year Ending March 31, 1893*, 19.

categories of poor people: the Lord's poor, the devil's poor, and the poor devils. The first were those poor people who could "show an orthodox pedigree for three or four generations." The second were those who were poor and involved with immoral and criminal activities. They were often in jail and frequently returned to sinful behavior when they had opportunity to do so. The final group was composed of those who simply found themselves on the losing end of a series of unfortunate circumstances, but who had no Christian faith.[40]

Categorizing the poor was nothing new to the Victorian mind. Many Victorians believed that the "deserving poor" needed to be winnowed out from the "undeserving poor," so that aid would be given only to the former. To this end, many charity organizers in the late nineteenth century ended indiscriminate handouts and soup kitchens for fear of enabling sloth on the part of the undeserving poor who refused to engage in honest labor.[41] However, Banks broke with this convention. He claimed that Christians were just as beholden to care for the undeserving poor, i.e., the devil's poor and the poor devils, as for the Lord's poor. In somewhat romantic language, Banks exposited, "we need that the great heart of the Church shall be anxious about this, shall be full of pleading for it, shall be full of heartbreaking sobs and tears for it, that the *whole* Church shall be aroused to the fact that the one thing that Christ values in the world is to rescue these lost ones."[42] In laying this charge on the church, Banks demonstrated how interaction with the poor helped shape and move the MEC's assumptions about who the poor were and, consequently, informed how it might more effectively engage the poor evangelistically.

By 1903, in offering a general survey of the work of the society, North concluded his comments by heralding the success of the Bowery "Rescue Mission." He called it "worthy of the spirit of John Wesley, and of the pioneers in our own land."[43] By invoking Wesley and the early American Methodists, North also hinted that here was work that carried forward the same noble values that buttressed the civilization previous generations of Methodist heroes helped create in the United States. In doing this, he

40. *Report of the New York City Church Extension and Missionary Society of the Methodist Episcopal Church for the Year Ending March 31, 1894*, 22.

41. Broder, *Tramps, Unfit Mothers, and Neglected Children*, 15–18; and Sandage, *Born Losers*, 17.

42. *Report of the New York City Church Extension and Missionary Society of the Methodist Episcopal Church for the Year Ending March 31, 1894*, 23.

43. *Year Book for the Year Ending April 30th, 1903*, 38.

made a claim that allows us to classify the society's work as pure American evangelism.

City Evangelism and the Rich

Original caption: Our church at Hamden Plains, Connecticut (new residential section of New Haven), was alert to the problems of rapid suburban growth, and, with Centenary help, put up this adequate plant

Even as the New York society came to recognize the critical work of evangelizing the poor, it also made an intentional effort to focus on the rich. The fact was that both the poor and the rich operated out of value structures beneath the ideal of Christian American civilization. It was the white *middle-class* native born Americans who held the ideal values and patterns of life. If some of the poor failed because they demonstrated by their poverty that they refused to work hard in order to succeed in the economic climate fostered by middle-class values, the rich failed by ignoring the plight of the needy or, worse yet, exacerbating it for their own financial gain. So it was that Banks in his address to the New York society was able to state, "These 'devil's poor' are just as good as 'the devil's rich,' and we must get it into our hearts that there are none of them, rich or poor, who rightfully belong to Satan, but God wants them saved."[44]

44. *Report of the New York City Church Extension and Missionary Society of the Methodist Episcopal Church for the Year Ending March 31, 1894*, 22.

R. L. Dashiell directed the New York society to the problem of the apathetic wealthy in 1874 when he condemned one popular, yet appalling view of the church held by Methodists of that era: "[T]he church is a beautiful and comfortable Christian home, for good, well-to-do people, through which they may pass by easy stages to eternal rest. There are multitudes of people—aye, in the Methodist Episcopal Church—who have no higher notion of the Christian life than personal comfort and happiness. These all fall infinitely below the Gospel ideal, ignoring the fact which lies at the foundation of the church, the specific purpose of its institution—to seek and save the lost."[45]

The most common way that the New York society, as well as the Chicago society, sought to redeem wealthy individuals from their compassionless existence was through appealing for funds. In every annual report, in addition to the presentation of the financial statistics of the society, there were appeals for more money. Often these appeals came in the form of specific funds created by the societies, such as the contingency fund the Chicago society created to help Methodist societies in Cook County who suddenly found themselves in financial difficulty or the fund for paying down the society's indebtedness established by the New York society. To give to these funds, or to the societies generally, was redemptive for the wealthy because the societies held that this giving was on a par with the actual mission work the societies undertook. This meant that the wealthy were beginning to demonstrate the generous nature of the middle-class in seeking to share the salvation that came from teaching others to live according to WMCNB values and patterns of life. North helped make this point in 1906 when, during his eulogy for the missionaries in the city, he included the donors to city missions as the equals of the missionaries: "No braver sons and daughters of the church ever bore her banners than they who have gone forward on this crusade, no friends of Christ, more living or more pure, ever told by word and life that story for which a weary world is ever waiting. God bless them both—the men who plan and give, the men who plead and serve."[46]

The Chicago society came later to the recognition of the need to care for the poor and the rich, since its primary focus was on the construction of new buildings and the refinancing of existing buildings. However, when it arrived at this conclusion, it engaged in it full bore. In 1916 the society

45. *Report of the New York City Church Extension and Missionary Society of the Methodist Episcopal Church for the Year Ending March, 1874, 10.*

46. *Year Book for the Year Ending April 30th, 1906, 50.*

brought Rev. Dan G. Batey, a MEC minister who once "had sunk as low as the worst," but was brought to conversion and restoration to civilization through a city mission to the poor, as the coordinator to launch rescue mission work in Cook County. While this work specifically sought to reach the poor, the society also saw it as a means of forging connections between the poor and rich in order to civilize both. As the article in the society's annual publication explained it: "Methodists must have one hand on the best families and most cultured youths of the land, holding them steady in the slippery paths of prosperity, while her other hand must be reached down to rescue from the dens of iniquity and the haunts of sin; she must also minister to all that lie within the embrace of these two hands stretched to the extremes of society."[47]

Within this embrace, Methodism drew the (presumably white, native) poor back to the civilization, which was theirs by birthright: "But it must be remembered that in this rescue mission work we find many of those who have fallen are from the higher walks of life, and have gone through college and university, and who, in their early days, were connected with good families, members of young people's societies, and of the Christian Church. In an evil hour they fell and we find them to-day wrecks of humanity on the backwash of city life. But for such as these Jesus died . . . Jesus Christ can magnify his grace most wondrously in saving from the midst of vilest conditions."[48] It seems that to be saved by Christ from these vile conditions involved more than repentance and forgiveness, but a re-entry into the more prosperous ways of Christian American civilization as the saved one re-imbibed and re-embodied the values of that civilization.

The rescue mission touched the rich by heightening their sensitivity to the plight of the poor and the heroic endeavors of the rescue mission workers. This heightened sensitivity was meant to result in an increased generosity on the part of the rich toward this effort, as the society itself acknowledged:

> We ask the Methodists of this city, as they meet in their comfortable churches and tarry before the Lord, to kindly remember our mission work in their prayers and let us have a place in their sympathy. And in the late hours of night when retiring to rest do not forget that at these very times the rescue mission workers of the Chicago Home Missionary Society are out in search of some mother's daughter or some wandering boy. Pray for this work.

47. *City Foursquare*, 9.
48. Ibid.

> Send in your special contributions for it. There can only be ad-
> equate support as we get special help, for the ordinary income of
> the society is not as yet equal to this undertaking.[49]

In addition to offering the wealthy a way of giving their prayers and money to the rescue missions, the Chicago society also hit upon a means of connecting the wealthy to the poor by establishing the Methodist Mutual Aid Union. Through the Union the wealthy could donate second-hand items that were damaged beyond use so that the poor could repair the items and sell them. The Chicago society acknowledged that several local churches in Chicago engaged in this sort of ministry for years prior to the society's organization of the union. However, the development of the union clearly brought the importance of ministering to the poor to a new level of consciousness for the Chicago society. This is evident in the society's desire for the union: "Through this [the union] we hope to respond more adequately to the needs of the poor in the densely crowded sections of the city."[50]

In many ways, this development of the union is highly symbolic of the close connection WMCNB Americans saw among employment, industrial goods and participation in Christian American civilization. If the ability to amass and use industrial goods properly belonged to those whose values and lifestyles reflected the best of Christian American civilization, it was also necessary that these people substantiate their participation in that civilization by sharing, rather than hoarding, those goods with people who sought entry (or re-entry) into that civilization. However, as appropriate to the failed ability the poor had demonstrated to take advantage of the benefits the civilization offered them by the fact they had become poor, the wealthy would only allow the poor access to broken industrial goods. If the poor could prove themselves by engaging in honest labor through which they took those broken goods and made them functional again, then the poor showed themselves worthy of participating in Christian American civilization. Redemption was thus available to the poor through how they handled industrial goods and to the rich through donating the industrial goods that provided the opportunity for the poor to claim their identity as hard-working Christian Americans again. In effect, both were given an opportunity to act as middle-class Americans. The Annual Report of the Chicago society superintendent explained as much:

49. Ibid.

50. Ibid., 6.

We hope to take girls who have never had any chance in life and boys who have been handicapped by an unfavorable environment, and others of maturer years and teach them hat trimming, garment making, shoe repairing, furniture fixing and start them on other lines of activity by which they may come to self-respecting independent manhood and womanhood and have a means of earning their own living. We believe that if our wealthy laymen could once get a vision of the social and economic redemption possible to thousands of people through this department they would be willing to give it generous supports, as laymen in other cities have done.[51]

This kind of innovative work of the city societies directly influenced the work of the denomination as a whole. In 1920 the General Conference formed Goodwill Industries with the explicit instructions that "the Bureau [of Goodwill Industries] shall support and indorse only those local industries which are organized and conducted according to its established rules and regulations, and these local industries shall be administered as far as practicable in cooperation with local City Societies."[52]

City Evangelism and Children

In this week-day religious education class,
Gary, Indiana, thirty-eight nationalities are represented

51. Ibid., 23.

52. Mills, *Journal of the Twenty-Eighth Delegated General Conference of the Methodist Episcopal Church Held in Des Moines, Iowa, 1920*, 607.

Original caption: Today's investment for tomorrow among the Portuguese.
A student from Boston University teaches this Sunday-school class

The final group that the Methodist urban societies targeted in their evangelistic efforts was children, especially the children of immigrants. Dashiell in his 1874 address to the New York society explained why this group was so important. According to him,

> to save these masses we must reach and win childhood. It is a great thing to plant the cross by the rapids, when old men are rushing down the darkening tide—but you will save time and labor to plant that cross at the head of the stream, where the fountain spring is starting its gentle current. No system of truth will reach and shape the civilization of a people which does not plant itself deep in the heart and mind of childhood. There is not much to attract you in that little tattered fragment of our humanity, who, with tangled hair and dirty brow, confronts you with its sad presence in the streets; but the possibilities and probabilities of that life—what he may be, and ought to be, and will be, if you and I do our duty.[53]

53. *Report of the New York City Church Extension and Missionary Society of the Methodist Episcopal Church for the Year Ending March, 1874*, 11.

A Japanese Boy with His American Toys, Seattle, Wash.

In making this claim, especially through the reference to what the child of the streets would become apart from the aid of Methodists to convert him to a civilized life, Dashiell and many other Methodists sounded much like other Protestant urban reformers of their day. The general belief was that children who were left to the streets would grow to become criminals, if boys, and prostitutes, if girls.[54] As a result, children, particularly the children of the poor and immigrants (two groups that often overlapped substantially), needed to have significant social controls established around them so that they could be indoctrinated with WMCNB

54. Broder, *Tramps, Unfit Mothers, and Neglected Children*, 37–45.

values and patterns of life. These children would then grow up to become productive members of the Christian American civilization, casting off the values of their parents. Labor historian Roy Rosenzweig (1983) listed the values that Protestant reformers hoped poor and immigrant children would develop simply through having access to structured playgrounds: "Loyalty, courtesy, justice, helpfulness, friendship, courage, sympathy, morality, cleanliness, citizenship, seriousness, patience, honesty, mutual understanding, and higher ideals were among the virtues promised."[55]

The New York society addressed the need to reach children by promoting Sunday schools and other forms of children's groups. The deaconesses, who established a home in New York City in 1889, especially supported the Sunday schools. As the deaconesses visited the people in the city, often moving from house-to-house or apartment-to-apartment to inquire about the spiritual and physical health of the occupants, they always encouraged the parents they encountered to send their children to Sunday school. By 1891, the deaconesses reported the parents of approximately seven hundred children had promised to send their children to Sunday school.

More than these Sunday schools, however, the New York society was proud of the Kindergartens connected to MEC congregations in New York City. In 1902 North boasted of five Kindergartens, three of them in what he termed "mission churches," which were large congregations that offered a variety of ministries to the people in the surrounding neighborhood, such as medical care, various classes in domestic and industrial training, and direct aid to the poor. The two other Kindergartens were located in the Italian missions that the Methodists maintained in the city. These were, according to North, the only two Kindergartens for Italians in New York. North explained: "Each morning at our two chapels . . . sixty to seventy-five of these odd little strangers are learning love, life, and religion, by the precept, example and companionship of the cultured women who, with cheerful self-sacrifice, give themselves to this ministry to neglected childhood."[56] While North did not specifically mention American civilization in this comment, the subject ("love, life, and religion") the children learned are consistent with what WMCNB Americans would want their children to learn and embody. Moreover, that it was Italian, hence Catholic, children that the Methodists lavished such effort on is telling.

55. Rosenzweig, *Eight Hours for What We Will*, 147.

56. *Year Book for the Year Ending March 31st, 1902 Containing the Thirty-Sixth Annual Report of the New York City Church Extension and Missionary Society of the Methodist Episcopal Church*, 15.

Fun in playroom of Chinese kindergarten,
Church of All Nations, New York City

The Chicago society was not as involved with Kindergartens, but was a strong proponent of the congregations it supported developing Sunday schools and various forms of children's clubs, including the Boy Scouts for boys and the Junior League for girls. In doing this, the society stated that its primary reason for promoting such children's activities was grounded in its desire to Americanize the various immigrants making Chicago their home, priding itself on the fact that the children of immigrants often desired to participate in its congregations' children's activities because these foreign children wanted to become Americanized. The society reported: "Many of the children of all nationalities that come among us prefer to become Americanized as early as possible. All are required to attend our English public schools, and many attend our English-speaking Sunday-schools, and unite with our English-speaking churches, and adopt our American customs. Many thousands of these are among our most useful members in all our Protestant churches."[57]

57. *Annual Report of the Chicago Home Missionary and Church Extension Society for 1889, 6.*

Story hour in the kindergarten—
Halsted Street Church, Chicago

It seems that the Chicago society was not overly idealistic in this assessment, as other Methodist agencies likewise attested to the movement of younger generations of immigrants toward Americanization. This was most noticeable in how these younger people left the ethnic mission congregations of their parents, where their native tongues were spoken, and moved into English-speaking MEC congregations. One example of this is in a 1908 report to the General Conference from the Epworth League, a Methodist organization tasked with forming young people to be loyal Methodists. This report attested to how effectively the Methodists Americanized the German population by setting up German-speaking congregations and then providing the means for the children in those congregations to enter English-speaking congregations.

> In the United States, with her hundreds of thousands of Germans, in country and city life, we still have a great mission. As loyal American citizens, we can accomplish this mission only by proclaiming the cross of Jesus Christ to our fellow-countrymen in the mother tongue of their fatherland. Hundreds of our people, especially of the younger generation, quietly enter the American Mother Church and become a salt and light there. English pastors east and west have told me repeatedly that some of their most conscientious church members, the most

heroic givers, and the best personal workers in their congregations came from our ranks, and were converted at our German
altars.[58]

Likewise, in an article in *Methodism and the Republic*, a Swedish
Methodist pastor agreed that it was the desire of most Swedish Methodists
to have not only their children, but all their generations, become thoroughly Americanized:

> I mention the fact that we are in America, and thank God that
> we are here, most of us, by choice and not by accident. Here all is
> American; that is, American in thinking, in practice, in language
> (English). The tendencies of all our environments, commercial,
> social and political, are to Americanize us. Our children attend
> the English-speaking public schools and colleges, and we speak
> English largely in our families. Our neighbors are Americans.
> In our travels the English is used, so that the tendencies are al-
> together in this direction, and what is more, we would not have
> it otherwise if we could; for our intention is not to establish a
> Sweden in America, but to become thorough Americans, and,
> if possible, the best type of Americans. The only difference,
> my English-speaking brother, between your Americanism and
> mine, is this: you came over the day before yesterday in the
> person of your ancestors, and I came yesterday in my own dis-
> tinguished person. But we are both Americans—Americans to
> the core.[59]

In sum, Methodist evangelization of the city took manifold forms
under the auspices of various agencies and individuals, including deaconesses, missionaries, pastors, and wealthy patrons. This manifold group of
evangelists and their variety of ways to carry out their purpose was called
forth by the diversity of urban dwellers and the unique conditions that
formed the lives of those people. However, even with all of these variables
in place, the Methodists unswervingly remained committed to bringing
the various constituencies they sought to evangelize in line with WMCNB
values and patterns of life.

Even though many Methodists who engaged in urban ministry became more open to challenging cultural assumptions about such groups
as immigrants and the poor, they did not go so far as to challenge the
culture itself. They still assumed that the United States set the benchmark

58. Hingeley, ed., *Journal of the Twenty-Fifth General Conference*, 1396.
59. Nelson, "Future of Swedish Methodism," 291–92.

for Christian civilization and that they had to spread this civilization for people to share in the fullness of God's salvation through a better quality of life in this world.

Protecting the Civilization from the City

Even as the Methodists sought to make inroads into the city, hoping to save urban dwellers by making them participants in Christian American civilization, they also came to conclude that the cities represented a significant threat to that very civilization. Beyond the continuing Methodist concern that the immigrants might become political liabilities to the Republic if they were not Americanized quickly enough, the city harbored the possibility of engaging in any number of immoral activities, such as alcohol consumption and Sabbath-desecration, that could quickly pollute even the most virtuous WMCNB American. Even more dangerous, the city had the capacity to spread beyond its borders, exerting its deleterious influence on people who might never even set foot in a city. As a result, Methodists began to consider how they might erect a barrier between the city and WMCNB Americans in order to protect the civilization from the immoral values emanating from the city.

City vs. Country

Many Methodists came to discuss the potential of the city to bring down Christian American civilization by contrasting the wicked city to the righteous country. Methodists, most of whom could claim the rural regions of the United States as their birthplaces in either the north or south, had an ideal image of the country. It was in the country the Methodists came into their own as tamers of the American frontier. It was also in the country that the yeoman Methodist worked hard and handed down his values to his family, ensuring prosperity for his children and for his nation. As a result, Methodists reasoned that if the cities had the capacity to upset this rural bastion of WMCNB values, it had the capacity to upend the entire civilization. The bishops wrote in 1908: "The problems of the cities are inextricably interwoven with those of the country. In concentrating opportunity it concentrates temptation. Faith seems to be born most easily under the whole dome of the stars and in the naked spaces. The city holds men to earth. There they can have little open vision of the awakening and creative forces. Much of the best life of the cities is that which reaches them from the country. The two greatest problems before us are the re-demption of the cities from vice and the salvation of the small country places from Paganism."[60]

A key reason for this leaching of what Sydney Ahlstrom (2004) termed "urban values"[61] into the civilization protected by the country was the growing propensity for the populations in each area to encounter the other. Ironically, it was the very technology that the Methodists heralded as part of Christian American civilization's capacity to evangelize the world that facilitated these encounters. Pointing to the growing ease of travel between the city and the country thanks to the mechanization of transportation, the bishops stated in 1912, "The trolley and automobile have so connected the city and the country that the formerly urban problems of desecrating the Sabbath and recreation have spilled over into the country because the country folks can easily access the city and urban dwellers can easily reach the country."[62] This problem of integrating the urban and rural populations only grew in the coming years, as shown by the fact the bishops reiterated in their concern about the same issue in their addresses of 1916 and 1920.

On the local level, the city societies were well aware of the impact urban sprawl was having on the surrounding countryside. This is especially true of the Chicago society, which oversaw all the home missionary work in Cook County, some of which remained rural through the early twentieth century. As early as 1885, the society's corresponding secretary described the moral state of the various neighborhoods of Chicago thusly, "you would be surprised at the growing tendency to utter neglect of all religious work, or religious experiences, and how soon moral people, and some professed Christians, forget God and His Sabbaths, and fall into the habits of the irreligious and ungodly around them."[63] Two years later, after devoting nearly two pages to describing the growing number of cable cars and steam engines making their way into the city from the suburbs of Cook County, the corresponding secretary declared that the worst traits of the city of Chicago could easily infest the surrounding areas if no evangelism occurred to stymie this process.

60. Hingeley, ed., *Journal of the Twenty-Fifth General Conference*, 143.

61. Ahlstrom, *Religious History of the American People*, 915.

62. Hingeley, ed., *Journal of the Twenty-Sixth Delegated General Conference of the Methodist Episcopal Church Held in Minneapolis, MN, 1912*, 204.

63. *Articles of Incorporation of the Chicago Home Missionary and Church Extension Society, with Reports for 1885 and 1886*, 3.

> It is easy to see how the two or three millions of people that
> will soon crowd this country, can by a few moments extra time
> and a few cents extra money, reach beautiful and commodious
> homes, and raise their families amidst the flowers and trees of
> their own planting, and enjoy the purity and freshness of the
> country air, and the refined society of Christian homes . . . But
> to prevent these communities from growing up into irreligion
> and forgetfulness of God, now is our time to sow the good seed
> of the Kingdom, that shall bear fruit of a hundred fold in the
> near future.[64]

The bishops and the corresponding secretary of the Chicago society
were in good company in voicing their concerns. In 1908, Theodore Roosevelt convened a Commission on Rural Life to explore how to improve the
quality of life among farmers in the United States. In his letter authorizing
the commission, Roosevelt wrote, "There is but one person whose welfare
is as vital to the welfare of the whole country as is that of the wage worker
who does manual labor; and that is the tiller of the soil, the farmer. If
there is one lesson taught by history, it is that the permanent greatness of
any States must ultimately depend more upon the character of its country
population than upon anything else. No growth of cities, no growth of
wealth, can make up for a loss in either the number or the character of the
farming population."[65]

For Roosevelt, as for the Methodist bishops, a primary way of protecting against the destruction of the character of the country population,
and thus of Christian American civilization, was through making the city
a less alluring destination for those in the country. According to Roosevelt, "There is too much belief among all our people that the prizes of life
lie away from the farm. I am therefore anxious to bring before the people
of the United States the question of securing better business and better living on the farm, whether by co-operation between the famers for buying,
selling, and borrowing, by promoting social advantages and opportunities
in the country, or by any other legitimate means that will help to make
country life more gainful, more attractive, and fuller of opportunities,
pleasures, and rewards for the men, women, and children of the farms."[66]
The bishops made the same plea in their address of 1920, calling on the

---

64. *Annual Report of the Chicago Home Missionary and Church Extension Society for 1887*, 18.

65. "Roosevelt Plans Better Farm Life," 4.

66. Ibid.

denomination to evangelize the country by "bring[ing] interest, art, music, social life to persons who otherwise will not have it."[67]

By the time the bishops penned these words, the MEC already had an official mechanism in place to act on it. The General Conference of 1912 created the Department on Rural Churches as one of the five major departments of the Board of Home Missions and Church Extension. The General Conference tasked the department to "seek in every possible manner to furnish inspiration and information, methods and plans, to aid the district superintendents and country pastors of Methodism... Further, that the theological seminaries, Church periodicals, and the Methodist Federation for Social Service, be called upon to aid in restoring the standing and efficiency of the rural church as the center of the social, intellectual, and spiritual life of every community."[68]

The wording of this mandate is instructive. The MEC did not simply desire to restore the country, but to restore the rural churches as the backbone of a restored country. This clearly points to how worried the MEC leaders were about losing their WMCNB base in the country. It also suggests that these leaders recognized that if they lost their base in the rural areas, they had nowhere left to go because of their relative weakness in the cities. As they saw it, the people might not only leave the country in favor of the city, they would likely leave the MEC altogether in making that transition. To avoid this scenario the MEC needed to keep the country dwellers in the country and connected to their local churches. This avoided a hemorrhage of rural population to the city where they might be lost permanently to Methodism and civilization, and established a potent, church-organized defense against urban values making their way into the country.

One of the ironies in this is that the bishops and others were struggling to make the rural way of life more interesting and engaging for the population while at the same time holding up the existing patterns of life in the country as ideal. The MEC leadership seemed to miss the point that the patterns of life that helped sustain the Christian American civilization were changing, and hanging on to the older rural culture would ultimately be a losing battle. More than this, as they would ultimately realize, Christian American civilization was ephemeral since it was couched in very specific historic-cultural context. It would take until the 1920s for this to become apparent, however.

67. Mills, *Journal of the Twenty-Eighth Delegated General Conference*, 191.
68. Hingeley, ed., *Journal of the Twenty-Sixth Delegated General Conference*, 691.

So it was that the MEC rediscovered the country as a mission field because of their fear of the city. Prior to the growth of the cities, the denomination largely took the country for granted. While it worked hard to construct church buildings and form societies in it, it never thought to nuance its understanding of what specific needs or concerns might face those in the country. It always assumed that the country would be filled with those who were easily integrated into Christian American civilization because they accepted the values associated with that civilization as a matter of course. Only when the city and its influences demonstrated that the country was not a staid and unmoving entity did the Methodists begin to consider the importance of re-energizing and refocusing their work in the country.

Immorality in the City

This renewed emphasis on the country did not undermine the work of the MEC to address the issues of immorality in the cities themselves. The city societies were well aware of the immorality in their respective cities and strove to combat it. As the corresponding secretary of the Chicago society stated in his 1891 report, graphically drawing in three of the four groups that the society specifically sought to evangelize (i.e., the immigrant, the poor, and children): "No one who has the spirit of Him who was continually found going about doing good, or who has an anxious thought about rescuing the perishing, or caring for the dying, can look without pain upon these concentrated foreignized centers of iniquity in which the furnace fires of hell are already kindled and daily and hourly becoming hotter and hotter. These seething caldrons of vice, these open gateways to death, must have material with which to ply their infernal traffic, and this material is usually the fair youth of the land."[69]

The following year, the secretary made certain to include the rich in his list of groups impacted by immorality, stating, "we go to the refined and rich, living in homes of elegance and luxury, yet destitute of the refining, mellowing and uplifting influences of the grace of Christ."[70] While this description of immorality might sound far milder that what he would later term in the same report, "the great unwashed in the rum-ridden and licen-

69. *Annual Report of the Chicago Home Missionary and Church Extension Society for 1891*, 8.

70. *Annual Report of the Chicago Home Missionary and Church Extension Society for 1892*, 7.

tiously cursed portion of our great city," the fact is that both descriptions are of people who fall below the moral values of a Christian American civilization: the latter because of their engagement in immoral activities, the former because of their lack of Christian commitment to uplift the needy. The rich and the poor alike stood in need of WMCNB values and patterns of life to connect them to Christian American civilization.

The New York society was of a like mind, with its corresponding secretary stating: "The agencies of evil are multiplied with a still more rapid increase than those of good. With such a steady increase of worldliness, Sabbath breaking, inebriety, and sin, a corresponding increase in just the work being done by this Society is imperatively demanded to counteract it . . . the armies of sin are boldly marching on, while the tide of depravity is constantly rising, threatening to invade our homes, and by its pernicious undercurrent bear away our sons and daughters."[71]

Following this harrowing description, the secretary then placed the work of the society to meet this swell of immorality firmly on the ground of pure American evangelism as he described the cultural values, led by the encouragement of private property and domestic peace, that the society promoted. In doing this, he reminded his audience that they were not only called to this work by Christ, but by virtue of their citizenship: "Citizens of New York, there is not a property holder within its bounds, there is not a resident that walks its streets, but what is benefited by the noble, conservative work done by this Society . . . to rescue the perishing, to raise the fallen, and to carry peace and happiness into thousands of homes in this city, now blighted by sin."[72]

The primary mechanism the city societies used to deal with immorality was to work through the local congregations and missions. The societies believed strongly that the existence of a local congregation, particularly when housed in a suitable church building, was a potent force for overcoming immorality. More than that, the corresponding secretary for the Chicago society in 1886 argued that the presence of such congregations was a necessary condition for overcoming immorality. Pointing to the efforts of the best-known and most far-reaching evangelists and evangelical Christian organizations that were dedicated to overcoming immorality in the city, he claimed that they would have had no sustainable, positive impact apart from the local congregation aiding them:

71. *Report of the New York City Church Extension and Missionary Society of the Methodist Episcopal Church for the Year Ending December 31st, 1884*, 34–35.

72. Ibid., 35.

> What could [Dwight L.] Moody or [Sam] Jones, or any of the
> evangelists of the present day accomplish if the different Chris-
> tian Churches should stand aloof from them? It is because
> there are strong churches already established in our cities, and
> because they unite their strength to aid these evangelists, that
> they are able to succeed in bringing so many souls to Christ. It
> is because the strong churches of our country throw their influ-
> ence in favor of the Young Men's Christian Association that they
> are a success in our midst. This fact is recognized by the best
> workers in that body of enterprising Christian men.[73]

It was out of these local congregations and missions that Methodist
pastors, deaconesses, and laypeople could labor against the immoralities
of their day by building sustainable relationships with individuals and with
entire urban neighborhoods. Out of the credibility that these relationships
offered, these dedicated Methodist workers could then turn people away
from immorality. The New York society recorded, for example, the importance of pastors from these congregations holding temperance meetings,
encouraging individuals to sign pledges of abstinence from alcohol, and
providing entertainment through reading rooms in their local church
buildings that would draw young men away from the "grog-shops."[74] In
its report for 1874 the New York society included several anecdotes of
individuals who had their personal morality transformed through the
work connected to local congregations. In each case, the transformation
took place either through the efforts of a missionary sent out from a local congregation or by the penitent individual coming to "the altar" in a
church building. In both cases, an established congregation was necessary
as a base of operations for these ministrations to occur.[75]

The WHMS was also active in its effort to combat immorality in the
cities, focusing on immoral activities perpetrated upon women and girls.
The members of the WHMS were particularly concerned with "white
slavery," the term they deployed to describe prostitution. From 1911 to
1913, Mrs. George O. Robinson, the president of the WHMS, led the organization in developing an intentional response to this immoral practice.

73. *Articles of Incorporation of the Chicago Home Missionary and Church Extension Society*, 15.

74. *Report of the New York City Church Extension and Missionary Society of the
Methodist Episcopal Church for the Year Ending December 31st, 1884*, 34–35.

75. *Report of the New York City Church Extension and Missionary Society of the
Methodist Episcopal Church for the Year Ending March, 1874*, 36–40.

This culminated in the formation of the Bureau of Social Hygiene, which oversaw the work of local WHMS auxiliaries seeking to end prostitution.

As the term "white slavery" indicated, the WHMS believed that the women engaged in prostitution were largely innocents forced into their degraded profession by the basest desires of men. Citing the example of a girl who was a dedicated member of a Methodist youth society who disappeared when traveling near her home in Boston, the President of the WHMS luridly explained, "Greed and lust—the worst passions of men— are fighting for this terrible vice. It is not alone the weak and desolate, the evil-disposed that are affected; no rank in life is without danger to its daughters." In the same report, she pointed to the cities of the United States as the primary location for this practice, calling out Philadelphia and New York as particularly worthy of shame. Most appalling to the president was that "eighty-three per cent" of all prostitutes discovered in the United States by reformers were "American-born."[76] Clearly this was a problem that stood in direct conflict with the ideal vision Methodists held of the United States as a Christian American civilization.

The WHMS deployed both a rescue operation and a systemic response to the practice of white slavery. The rescue operation entailed dispatching teams of Methodist women to the railroad stations and ports where young women, especially immigrants, often could be found traveling alone. The WHMS operatives watched for single girls or women and, when they spotted such a traveler, hurried over to her to ascertain if she had a secure family with which to stay. If she did not, the operatives directed her to a WHMS-sponsored house where she would be safe and could make connections with honest employers before moving into her own place. Additionally, when no operatives were available, the WHMS partnered with such organizations as the Young Women's Christian Association to post flyers around railroad stations and ports to warn unsuspecting women of particularly dangerous men, businesses, and parts of town. Notably, the WHMS was so thoroughly against the sex trade that in spite of the terminology they used ("white slavery") they did not only focus on white immigrants, but on any single females they found at the stations and ports. They were especially active in the ports of the western cities where they searched for Chinese and Japanese girls who often came to the States because they were duped by brothel owners about the possibility of having good work when they arrived.

76. Women's Home Missionary Society, *Thirty-Second Annual Report*, 110–11.

The success the WHMS enjoyed in this work became apparent from the reaction it received as a result of it. The pushback came from the very men that the women of the WHMS so vilified. In one instance, deaconesses who went to a train station in San Francisco had a group of men who "threatened them with violence, using coarse, obscene language because some girls just arriving from the inland towns were warned not to go to certain streets and were directed to respectable boarding houses."[77] As disconcerting as this encounter no doubt was, it proved the efficacy of the rescue work the WHMS did on behalf of women who might be trapped in the sex trade. It also showed the vicious nature of uncivilized men compared to the civilized deaconesses sent out by the WHMS.

On a systemic level, WHMS President Robinson offered an economic solution: The way to defend the American home, and especially Victorian womanhood, was through providing a living wage for both men and women. Honest workingmen needed this wage in order to sustain a household in which they could adequately care for the needs of their daughters and wives, thus protecting them from unscrupulous men who might prey on the household's need for extra income. Women needed this wage so that, if forced to provide for themselves, they could do so through honest work. Quoting an article in the *New York Christian Advocate*, Robinson reported, "It can not be debated at all that the under-pay of men and women alike creates a system under which all girls who are poor, ignorant, exhausted, and disheartened are finding it as hard as possible to be chaste, and as easy as possible to be unchaste."[78] So it was that the United States, to be a Christian American civilization, needed not only morally upstanding people living within its borders, but a way of equitably distributing wealth to those people so that they might remain honest.

There is little wonder that the WHMS found white slavery repulsive. White slavery was the epitome of all that stood against Christian American civilization. Like Mormonism, it degraded the Victorian role of true womanhood and the Victorian family.[79] Like African slavery in the South, it degraded human equality and the American ideal of liberty. And, like both Mormonism and African slavery, it rejected the authority

77. Women's Home Missionary Society, *Thirtieth Annual Report*, 96.

78. Women's Home Missionary Society, *Thirty-Second Annual Report*, 111.

79. In the episcopal address of 1912 the bishops explicitly connected white slavery to the polygamy of Mormonism. Hingeley, ed., *Journal of the Twenty-Sixth Delegated General Conference of the Methodist Episcopal Church Held in Minneapolis, MN, 1912*, 219-220.

of the Republican government.[80] In all, then, it demanded an evangelistic response that sought to overthrow it with the powerful WMCNB values of Christian American civilization. This is precisely what the WHMS provided.

THE EXPANSION OF CITY EVANGELISM

These local efforts to stamp out immorality in the city helped instigate and refine many of the national crusades for moral purity that the MEC engaged in during this era, including inveighing against the evils of alcohol, divorce, amusements, and the strife between capital and labor. For example, it is during this time that the General Conferences heavily debated the content of the so-called "amusements paragraph" in the *Book of Discipline*. It was also during this time that the denomination led the national charge in favor of temperance by sending some of its most talented men and women, not least who of was Frances Willard, to serve in the Women's Christian Temperance Union or the Anti-Saloon League. Each of these issues and organizations had a life of its own beyond the city, though the cities often served as the launching points from which Methodists supported their favored causes. More than that, they also caused the MEC to begin rethinking its traditional views of evangelism on a much broader scale.

Progressivism and Post-Millennialism

A significant reason for this expansion of city evangelism was the influence of progressivism in the United States. As the late nineteenth century gave way to the early twentieth century, the MEC found itself in agreement with the work of the progressives who believed "if the nation was to be reformed, it would be first by seizing the social possibilities of the cities."[81] This progressive idea centered largely on the reform of political and economic systems, seeking to move from the systems in municipalities to ever-larger systems. Robert Wiebe (1967) described in detail how the progressives engaged in a systematic growth from work in municipal governments, to work in state governments, to work on the national

---

80. The Congress had passed a law entitled "The White Slave Traffic Act" in June 1910 prohibiting the importation of women across international or state lines for the purpose of prostitution.

81. Rodgers, *Atlantic Crossings*, 112.

level, especially during the presidency of Theodore Roosevelt.[82] According to Wiebe, on the municipal level the progressives pressed for an end to inefficient government, for the establishment of basic services, especially in the realm of public health, for general social well-being, and for the scientific expertise of middle-class professionals in maintaining consistent economic and political policies. This sort of activity was perfectly in accord with pure American evangelism, based as it was on WMCNB values and patterns of life.

Not surprisingly, the MEC responded with gusto to the progressive agenda, believing that the fate of the nation hung on the reformation of the city. The Chicago society noted in its report, "The conquest of Chicago means the salvation of the state, and the state will never be free as long as our city is fettered by sin."[83] Appealing to eschatological imagery, Frank Mason North exclaimed the point more grandly when first taking office as the Corresponding Secretary for the New York society: "The kingdom of Christ must be established in the great social, commercial, industrial, and intellectual centers and dominate their life, or be relegated to the rank of a fourth rate power among the forces which control human destiny. This is true of all the cities, and both Church and world have at last recognized the battle ground upon which the contest must be fought out. It is true of New York in particular. Convert the whole country and leave this city unsaved, and soon the land would be lost again."[84]

Strongly influenced by postmillennial theology in thinking about the salvation of the cities, some Methodists went so far as to suggest that the only means of God bringing the Kingdom of God on earth was for God to save the cities. This led one partisan of city evangelization to declare at the New York society "As we love our country and divine Master, it is our paramount duty to Christianize New York. I firmly believe God means to save this world, and I do not believe that he, even with almighty power, can do it without saving this city."[85]

MEC leaders also agreed with the problem of corruption in municipal governments. No one less than the bishops made this agreement explicit when they stated in their address of 1900, "colossal evils . . . menace our civilization . . . the corruption and venality charged upon much of our

82. Wiebe, *Search for Order, 1877–1920*, 164–195.

83. *Annual Report of the Chicago Home Missionary and Church Extension Society 1907–1908*, 15.

84. *Report of the New York City Church Extension and Missionary Society of the Methodist Episcopal Church for the Year Ending March 31, 1892*, 20.

85. Ibid., 17.

political life, the political ownership of cities and States by one man or a few men whose will is law."[86]

In earlier years, the Methodists would have sought to address this corruption by personally evangelizing the corrupt politicians themselves. The New York society heard this very point from C. H. Parkhurst, the keynote speaker at the society's annual meeting in 1890. He explained, "The trouble in New York is not wickedness—it is wicked men, concrete and individual, each for himself. There is nothing that will change the character of New York unless there is something that will change the character of the men that make up New York . . . Now, the sovereign antidote to individual iniquity is . . . the Gospel of Jesus Christ preached individualizingly, as one man with a heart full of glad power and confidence in his Saviour goes to one man who has no such power and comfort and confidence, and tells him the story of his own Friend and Redeemer."[87]

However, by the turn of the twentieth century, the Methodists found this answer less and less satisfying, in part because they saw the percentage of city residents who claimed to be Methodist shrinking and the problems in the city rise. As a result, they were ready to search for a new way of doing evangelism in the cities and, by extension, in the nation. North presciently caught this readiness to change on the part of the denomination in the introduction to his 1901 address to the New York society:

> Thus, for nearly half a century, has the genius of Methodism been seeking out the best methods for embodying its faith and purpose in the evangelization of this metropolis. Fruitful, indeed, have been the years not only in the actual products of ministry, which may be seen on every side, but in the preparation for that fuller and richer service to which the new century invites us . . . Foundations should be laid, upon which generations to come shall find it profitable to build. A newness of life—out of which should come courage, self-denial, faith, victory—is penetrating the purpose of the church.[88]

In this call for something new, North was not suggesting there was a need for a new set of beliefs and values to undergird the ministry of the MEC. He was only stating that the MEC needed to be innovative in how it

86. Monroe, *Journal of the General Conference of the Methodist Episcopal Church Held in Chicago, Illinois, 1900*, 76.

87. *Report of the New York City Church Extension and Missionary Society of the Methodist Episcopal Church for the Year Ending March 31, 1889*, 27.

88. *Thirty-fifth Annual Report of the New York City Extension and Missionary Society of the Methodist Episcopal Church*, 15, 19.

presented its existing beliefs to be more relevant and effective in the new urban reality it faced. In making this point, he tacitly reminded his listeners of the success of WMCNB American values that were "penetrating the purpose of the church" in the past and, presumably, would continue to in the future.

Temperance Booth where People Could Sign Pledges to Abstain from Alcohol

Social Witness and an Evolving Understanding of Evangelism

The new way of doing ministry that North advocated involved the MEC expanding its view of what evangelism entailed. Given the clearly broken systems that ensnared the people of the city, the MEC began to recognize that evangelism required the conversion of social, political, and economic systems along with the conversion of individuals in order to bring about a Christian American civilization. In addition to the decreasing number of urban Methodists, it is likely the interaction of the MEC home missionaries with those in the urban settings helped convince the church of the need to address social systems. The problems faced by individuals were not always due to the individuals' personal faults, but were sometimes forced on individuals by unjust systems. The direct contact with the immigrants, for example, taught the city societies to nuance their understanding of immigration to the point of even arguing in favor of open immigration because of the benefits many immigrants brought to the United States. Likewise, direct contact with the poor began to erode traditional Victorian categorizations of whom among the poor deserved aid and who did not.

This new view of evangelism called for the denomination to undertake two new forms of activities: humanitarian aid and social witness. Humanitarian aid went beyond the individual help that many home missionaries were already providing to people within their care. It involved creating new structures that would augment the political, economic, and social systems so that those systems might be more humane. It included the establishment of Methodist hospitals in all the major cities in the United States. These hospitals were required to provide the best treatment possible free of charge to all who needed it, and were often staffed by deaconesses who trained as nurses. Homes for the aged and orphanages were also part of this work.

In 1892, the bishops bestowed their approbation on these works of humanitarian aid in their episcopal address. They went so far as to suggest that these new institutions were indicative of God's millennial activity in the United States.

> It is a matter of special thanksgiving that the Church is more and more taking on the sense of the importance of the humanitarian work which was so conspicuously taught by our Lord, and which from the first has distinguished his spirit. Hospitals for the sick and unfortunate, orphanages for the parentless and

> neglected children, and industrial and Churchly agencies for
> the care of the poor, are becoming more numerous and efficient
> in our great cities. These naturally are a later growth of our
> Church-life, but it may be hoped will become a rapid and vigor-
> ous development as our people increase in wealth . . . [They] are
> the harbingers of a time not far distant when ample provisions
> will be made for all the unfortunate who need and deserve such
> ministries.[89]

So it was that Methodist evangelism in the cities through the establishment of MEC humanitarian institutions pointed to the coming of Christ's
Kingdom on earth.

Humanitarian work was not enough on its own, however. While it
might create new structures that cared for the needy, it did not challenge
the existing systems that were unjust to the needy. This latter work required social witness. The denomination's chief means of addressing this
was to create the Methodist Social Federation. This new denominational
agency made its initial mark on the American landscape when it helped
draft and pass the Methodist Social Creed in 1908. The creed advocated
for the laboring class, demanding better working conditions and pay, as
well as the abolition of child labor.

In 1912, the Federation followed up with a pointed report to General
Conference. This report signaled a significant shift in how the MEC understood and practiced evangelism. Presented in a question-and-answer
format, the report re-envisioned the mission of the denomination and its
agencies to focus on converting systems more than on converting people.

The first question was, "What principles and measures of social reform are so evidently righteous and Christian as to demand the specific
approval and support of the church?"[90] The Federation's answer to this
was to proclaim several systemic issues that needed to correction. These
included the over-work of laborers through the establishment of an eight-
hour day and at least one day a week for rest, the complete cessation
of child labor in the factories, and the removal of "the social causes of
destitution."

The second question in the report spoke to how the MEC must
modify its existing structure to provide the necessary support for advancing these solutions to social ills: "How can the agencies of the Methodist

---

89. "Address of the Bishops of the Methodist Episcopal Church and the Reports
of Missionary Bishops Thoburn and Taylor, to the General Conference of 1892, at
Omaha, Neb," 11–12.

90. Hingeley, ed., *Journal of the Twenty-Sixth Delegated General Conference*, 1324.

Episcopal Church be wisely used or altered with a view to promoting the principles and measures thus approved?"[91] In answering this question, the Federation called on the denomination to keep pace with "the best practices of modern business," especially in its role as landlord and employer through its various agencies. It charged pastors to "acquaint themselves with every social group" in order to preach the denomination's moral standards more effectively to every group. It suggested that local congregations divide themselves by age and gender to learn about the plight of those less fortunate than themselves in their own demographic. Children in Sunday school, for example, would learn about child labor, while the Ladies' Society would learn about the difficulties facing girls and women. Both local congregations and annual conferences should have social service committees that would keep abreast of pertinent legal and economic issues that the church should address and rally to support appropriately. These committees would also help forge connections with like-minded organizations, whether from other denominations or that were only civic, to help coordinate these political efforts. Finally, the denomination as a whole should develop a curriculum for its seminaries, colleges, youth members, and children to teach about social problems and to organize the students at all levels to participate in rectifying these problems.

Here was clear recognition of the systemic problems of the age in which the MEC was set as well as an undeniable call for the church to expand its understanding of evangelism to include social witness. However, even in this dramatic change, the Methodists did not depart from engaging in pure American evangelism. The Federation made this clear in the concluding sentence of its report: "These, our findings, we present in the belief that, in the social crisis now confronting Christianity, the urgent need and duty of the church is to develop an evangelism which shall recognize the possibility and the imperative necessity of accomplishing the regeneration of communities as well as persons, whose goal shall be the perfection both of society and of the individual."[92]

The goal remained a perfected society and a perfected person. While less jingoistic in its call for civilization, the clear motivation of uplifting society through evangelism so that it operated by the values seen as normative by WMCNB Methodists, demonstrated that even the most socially conscious Methodists of the early twentieth century were operating in a way that can be described as pure American evangelism.

91. Ibid., 1327.
92. Ibid., 1331–1332.

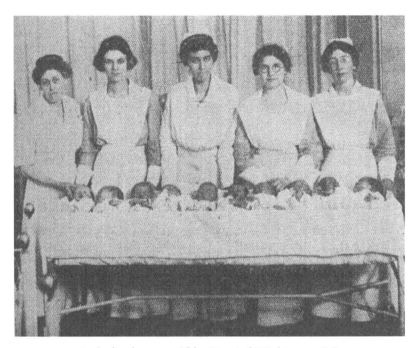

In the bawl-room—Sibley Hospital, Washington, DC

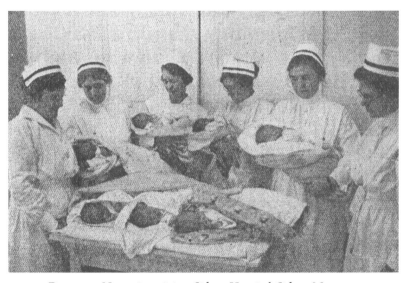

Deaconess Nurses in training, Sidney Hospital, Sidney Montana

Original caption: The orphanage is more than an orphanage:
it is a home

Original caption: A happy old age guaranteed
by the Old People's Home

THE CITIES AS CATALYST FOR
DENOMINATIONAL REFLECTION

The city proved to be the most complex of all home mission fronts for the Methodist Episcopal Church. As the bishops explained in their address to General Conference in 1920: "Nowhere else is Christian work more difficult, more fruitful or more important."[93] Full of promise and potential because of the ways its economic and political power demonstrated the might of Christian American civilization to the world; it nonetheless fostered a culture in which its own residents were denied access to that civilization. Worse yet, it exported the very immoral activities that Methodists most sought to combat to the rest of the country. This combination demanded that the Methodists employ a combination of evangelistic practices: those that sought to transform the peoples in the cities and that sought to protect Christian American civilization, especially in rural areas, from urban values. Both these sets of activities are part of pure American evangelism. The former, as in all other home mission fronts, sought to inculcate people excluded from Christian American civilization with WMCNB values and patterns of life. The latter sought to sustain Christian American civilization in a pristine form so that its values could continue to shine for the nation.

Even in the midst of this proliferation of evangelistic activities, the cities forced the Methodists to come to grips with yet another realization: the newly developed focus on evangelizing whole groups of people was not enough to bring about Christian American civilization. The Methodists needed to consider the systems in which those peoples operated, since the systems often demanded that those people live according to values that were well beneath those of Christian American civilization. As a result, the Methodists augmented their practice of evangelism by working with progressives to purify the social, economic and political systems so that, through them, the glory of the civilization the MEC championed would shine not only to all Americans, but to the world.

This willingness on the part of Methodists to modify their understanding and practice of evangelism, often because they came into direct contact with those who were most repressed by the various systems at work in the city, suggests that the Methodists were more malleable and robust in their evangelism than historians have described. Often, historians have

93. Mills, *Journal of the Twenty-Eighth Delegated General Conference of the Methodist Episcopal Church Held in Des Moines, Iowa, 1920*, 191.

suggested that Methodist evangelism after the Civil War suffered from the Methodists increasing in respectability, that this improvement in social location caused them to reject the poor and outcast in favor of simply attempting to shore up what they already had. In fact, the Methodists of this era were deeply concerned with the poor and the outcast, and they intentionally sought to work out ways to evangelize the poor effectively.

While the Methodist Episcopal Church proved less capable of reaching the working class in the years after the Civil War than in the years before it, it is a mistake to argue that this stemmed from a lack of reflection on their social location or a lack of compassion for those in need. The cities demanded both this kind of reflection and this kind of compassion, and the MEC sought to respond as best it could for the evangelization and civilization of as many urban dwellers as possible and for the transformation of the cities themselves.

In many ways, the growing excitement the Methodists expressed as they engaged in urban evangelism laid the groundwork for a final home mission that would carry with it massive eschatological expectations. This was the MEC evangelistic involvement in the First World War. It was through the war the Methodists believed Christian American civilization would expand throughout the world by the force of American military arms.

6

The First World War and the Centenary Campaign

WITH EACH OF THE regions the Methodist Episcopal Church engaged in home missions in it seems that the prize for success increased. To bring Christian American civilization to the South was to reclaim the full Republic. To convert, or reclaim, the inhabitants of the West was to establish a continent-spanning Christian American civilization that could stand against rival civilizations. To purify the people and structures of the cities was to bring the Kingdom of God in the United States. These heightening expectations found their summit in the early twentieth century, as the United States entered the First World War. The global scale of the war led Methodists to hope for the Kingdom of God to come throughout the earth as a result of it, and prompted the MEC to engage in massive evangelistic activities alongside of the nation's war effort. As global as these expectations were, the MEC actions surrounding the war are still best understood as part of my concept of pure American evangelism because they never strayed from holding that WMCNB values and patterns of life were normative models in which the world needed to be formed.

The reason the First World War had such an impact on the MEC's understanding and practice of evangelism is because of how immediately and viscerally it connected the Methodists to their vision of Christian American civilization. While the MEC initially rejected the idea of the United States entering armed conflict, advocating the more civilized process of mediation among nations to work out international problems, they quickly rallied to the cause when Woodrow Wilson exhorted the nation to war. Sharing the optimism of the progressives, who hoped the war would sweep the world clean in order to establish an international utopia based on progressive American social policies, the Methodists looked to how the war might be the very engine God would use to destroy the feudal Catholic civilizations of Europe, allowing Christian American civilization to be established across the globe.

The MEC supported this millennial vision of the war with all its evangelistic might. Through its home missions it prepared American soldiers to be effective ambassadors of Christian American civilization overseas. Through its foreign missions, it believed the generous and peace-loving nature of Americans in the form of humanitarian aid would demonstrate the superior values of WMCNB Americans to the rest of the world. As grand as these hopes were, they were ultimately dashed when the actual terms of the armistice that concluded the First World War failed to abide by WMCNB values. This, coupled with a host of other failures to see Christian American civilization take hold in Europe in the wake of war led to a deep disillusionment on the part of many Americans, including the Methodists, and sucked the energy out of the MEC's evangelistic dreams.

A direct byproduct of the initial excitement among Methodists early in the war was the Centenary, the name Methodists gave to the campaign held from 1918 to 1919 to celebrate the one-hundredth anniversary of the MEC founding its missionary society in 1819. Conceived of on a grand scale, with promotion from every Methodist agency, and culminating in an exhibition the size of a world's fair, the goal of the campaign was to capitalize on the enthusiasm Methodists displayed during the war by raising tens of millions of dollars in order to advance MEC missions domestically and overseas. Although the Centenary initially seemed to be successful, it ultimately fell far short of the goals denominational leaders set for it. The impact of this was to engender vast disappointment among denominational leaders, who decided by the early 1920s to focus on conserving what resources and excitement they did generate through the campaign while curtailing any further attempts at helping peoples participate in Christian American civilization. As a result, the practice and understanding of evangelism I describe as pure American evangelism was officially at an end.

The First World War

The Holiness of Arbitration

During the last decade of the nineteenth century and the first decade of the twentieth century, WMCNB American values led many Methodists to decry participation in armed conflict.[1] The bishops enunciated this position as early as 1896, declaring

> [W]e believe that the whole diplomatic and moral power of our government should be put forth to bring these gigantic wrongs to a sudden end. For the settlement of disputes between . . . different nations of the earth, we believe that the spirit of our Saviour set forth by our Church demands that the great principle of arbitration shall be tried to its utmost, and that the great majority of disputes can be happily settled in that way.[2]

Not surprisingly, the bishops held up the United States as the exemplar of a civilized nation that eschewed war. They stated later in the same address, "The United States has already set an example to the world by decorously submitting to arbitration nearly fifty occasions of differences with other nations."[3]

The bishops reiterated this stance in 1908, giving their approval both to Teddy Roosevelt for arbitrating an end to the Russo-Japanese War and to the construction of the Hague tribunal building in the Netherlands based on a grant from Andrew Carnegie. In view of both of these activities, the bishops were optimistic that Christian American civilization was spreading its values to such an extent that war might be eradicated. They opined, "it is yet evident by the creation of the Hague Tribunal and by the revision of the laws of war, that the consciences of the nations are more sensitive as to the wickedness of war than at any other time; that strong efforts are being made to diminish its evils, both on sea and on land, and that the spread of democratic ideas is such that very soon rulers will not

---

1. While I will not deal with it here, the Spanish-American War proved a notable exception to this. However, the reason Methodists made this exception is in concert with pure American evangelism. The idea of liberating people under the thumb of Roman Catholic Spain would strike Methodists as a highly appropriate use of American military power.

2. "General Conference of the Methodist Episcopal Church: The Episcopal Address, 1896," 24.

3. Ibid.

be able to go to war without the consent of those whose bodies must pay the cost in labor, wounds, and death."[4]

At the same General Conference the Methodist Federation for Social Service sought to apply the bishops' approbation of international arbitration when it called on the Methodist Episcopal Church to be involved in an active campaign "for international peace. To secure such international agreements as shall lessen the probability of war."[5]

It is clear from these passages that through the first decade of the twentieth century the Methodist Episcopal Church believed standing against war and for international arbitration was a social witness that would best present the values associated with Christian American civilization. Since the Methodists connected their view of holiness to this civilization, their support of international arbitration was a means of carrying out the charge to spread scriptural holiness over not only their own continent, but the entire globe. This logic, however, could swing both ways. Peaceful arbitration was a means to the end of bringing about Christian American civilization across the Earth. If a different, more effective means could be found to accomplish this end, it was incumbent on the MEC to adopt this new means even if the new means was incompatible with the current means.

Making the Case for War

As news of the horrors visited upon soldiers and civilians alike made its way to the United States after fighting broke out in Europe in 1914, Methodists began the process of providing nuances to their absolute stance against war, and specifically against the United States being involved in a war. While the various spokesmen of the denomination abhorred the mass loss of life and rampant destruction war caused, they also began to consider the possibilities available to the United States, and specifically to Methodism, made available through the immediate war in Europe. The MEC had not anticipated that the current war, destructive as it was, also created opportunities for Americans to present a social witness that would be visible and meaningful for a far larger mass of the global population than would ever be possible in peacetime. Since, for Methodists, being American and being Methodist were the hallmarks of civilization, this realization left the door open to consider how the current war might be

4. Hingeley, *Journal of the Twenty-Fifth General Conference*, 134–35.

5. Ibid., 1326.

a divine gift allowing Americans, especially Methodist Americans, the capacity to accomplish their mission of civilizing the world more forcefully and quickly than through long years of being a moral exemplar to the other nations. Put in millennial terminology, the Methodists had to leave room for the possibility that God allowed the First World War as the mechanism by which to establish God's Kingdom on earth using the United States as the template for how the world would be ordered in this Kingdom.

The General Conference of 1916, the only General Conference held during the actual fighting of the First World War, is where the leaders of the Methodist Episcopal Church developed and expressed their growing openness to the idea of the war as a useful instrument in carrying out the Methodist's mandate to draw all people into a Christian American civilization. The most explicit treatment of the war on this score was in the episcopal address, which offered a five-part analysis of the war.

First, consistent with the social witness they enunciated two decades before, the bishops condemned the war and its attendant atrocities. The bishops wrapped this condemnation in language related to civilization, specifically decrying how the war disrupted the work of Methodist conferences and missions in Europe. They explained that the war was the height of "lawless" (i.e., uncivilized) behavior and therefore endangered the worldwide Methodist communion, which the bishops tacitly understood as the height of civilization: "The strife and upheaval of nations has distracted the minds of all men everywhere. Never have so many millions of people been 'scattered and peeled' by the shameless perfidies and terrifying cruelties of an utterly lawless war. Thousands of the members of our own communion are impoverished and bereaved by the losses of relatives and friends."[6]

Second, however, the bishops found reason for encouragement in the midst of this horrific situation. The primary reason for this was the compassionate response welling up out of the United States to the benefit of those blighted by the war.

> There is a rising up of the better nature of both men and nations which pours forth sympathy with the helpless and bereaved; seeks the unoffending but comfortless hearts which are hidden away under the heavy clouds of sorrow with which the brutal passions of inhuman men have invested them. No greater evidence of this sympathy could have been expressed than was

---

6. Locke, *Journal of the Twenty-Seventh Delegated General Conference*, 156.

manifested in the unparalleled giving of multi-millions of dollars, which the American people have contributed so generously to the relief impartially of the sufferers in all the warring nations and which was so extensively supplemented by the personal service of American physicians and nurses in hospitals and on battlefields.[7]

Third, the bishops tied the generosity of Americans during the war directly to a millennial hope that the American people, who were synonymous with the Christian Church, could construct the Kingdom of God on earth out of the broken European civilizations. They stated confidently, "There never was a war in which the Son of Man was defeated. Out of the ruins of our vaunted civilization shall rise the surer foundation of His eternal Kingdom. He shall not fail nor be discouraged till He hath set judgment in the earth and the isles shall wait for His law . . . And He hath committed unto us the word of reconciliation—'We are the ancients of the earth and in the morning of the times!' It is the opportunity of the Christian Church, and of the American people."[8]

Fourth, after connecting the American nation with the Christian Church explicitly, the bishops suggested that the church still had a responsibility separate from the state. The church needed to be the conscience of the state, guaranteeing that the state would not descend into the kind of destructive, uncivilized ways of living that allowed for war in the first place. They argued, "Certain it is the Christian Church only can furnish tranquility to the State. When human nature is paralyzed and outraged in its highest faculties and instincts, only the Church is possessed of the privilege to deliver it from the dark thralldom of passion and overpowering bondage of sin."[9] Presumably, the bishops meant to suggest that the church must become this conscience for the states in Europe, not for the United States, since they already effectively had asserted that United States possessed this conscience built into its national character.

Finally, the bishops singled out the MEC as uniquely suited to take on this role of civilizing the world because of its polity. Specifically, the bishops believed that because the MEC had general superintendents (i.e., bishops) that came from the United States, but traveled around the world to visit the Methodist conferences and missions that existed in several different nations, the Methodists were better able than any other denomination

7. Ibid.
8. Ibid., 157.
9. Ibid.

to understand and sympathize with the situations faced by the people in any given nation while still providing clear Christian American leadership to those people. This suggests that their protestation of neutrality in the current war only extended to the MEC's official position, but did not signal their lack of interest in shaping the outcome of it.

> The connectional spirit, the interests held in common, and the itinerant General Superintendency of the Methodist Episcopal Church afford us greater privilege than is given to any other communion for making common cause with all the sufferers, knitting our hearts in closer bonds and tenderly relieving the distress with brotherly and substantial aid. Neutral as the Church has been and should be, we should have much influence in making peace between dissevered Methodists and possibly between the hostile states. Special care should be given to the reports from all our distressed communions in Europe. Very much then depends upon the delicacy and wisdom of our action in this General Conference. But whatever may be done, our people at home and abroad should feel that the Methodist Episcopal Church, in all lands and under all flags, stands for world righteousness and world peace, the ultimate disarmament of all nations, the social redemption of all peoples as a practical application of the teachings of Jesus Christ, the Redeemer of mankind.[10]

This address set the tone for all other comments about the war made during this General Conference, allowing for Methodists simultaneously to declare their disgust for war while allowing them to describe their peculiar hope for this particular war as a springboard for the advance of Christ's Kingdom. The Board of Foreign Missions issued a statement that described some of the terrible consequences of the war and then explained how these consequences created an environment the Methodists could capitalize on to win over the hearts and minds of the Europeans:

> Accumulated misery and wretchedness have spread over wider areas, hunger and disease—ever following in the wake of war— are reaping their sad harvests of death among the aged and the feeble, bereaved women, and helpless, homeless children. Countless homes have been destroyed, tens of thousands of children orphaned, official members of our churches and heads of families have been incapacitated by wounds . . . Churches have lost their pastors . . . If a recurrence of the cataclysmic

10. Ibid., 157–58.

conflict which is now shaking the foundations of human society on every continent is to be rendered impossible, the work of foreign missions should be enlarged and strengthened in every land. Though our churches have been dismembered and our ministries and laymen called to the battle front, our opportunities for Christlike ministries even now are literally unbounded. Help now will do more to win the hearts of the people than ten thousand kindly acts when the war is over.[11]

So, while the foreign missions board deplored war and its associated ills, it also saw a redemptive purpose in the current war that the Methodists could bend to their own purposes.

A separate report on World Conditions, commissioned specifically for this General Conference, expanded the argument of the Board of Foreign Missions by claiming that the war called not only the Methodist Episcopal Church, but the United States as a nation, to fulfill their common mission to the world. In stating this, the authors of this report assumed that the national identity of the United States was perfectly aligned with the work of God on earth, even citing American military involvement in Mexico as an example of this. They also assumed that the United States was governed primarily by Christians whose only goal was to bring about the Kingdom of God on earth.

An American people, having the mind of Christ and conforming to His will in all its dealings with Mexican disturbers, in all relations to South American countries and in all its diplomatic negotiations with governments beyond the oceans, will be seeking as the end of its endeavor, not so much a mightier United States, as a better world. An impoverished and bleeding world presents to the one powerful nation remaining which knows Jesus Christ, abides in peace and abounds in the resources of both matter and mind, a divine opportunity. If America should now seek to save her life by withholding her services she would lose her life, and deserve to lose it. The supreme concern of Christian citizens in this fateful hour should be to know the duty and mission of their own nation, and by all the powers of consecrated citizenship to help their nation in the performance of its task . . . it should promote just and enduring peace in the spirit of Jesus Christ according to his teachings . . . throughout the earth.[12]

11. Ibid., 1193.
12. Ibid., 719.

It was precisely because of the Christian leadership guiding the United States that the report argued the American people should seek to lead the world into this new epoch of peace and justice. Moreover, the responsibility of this leadership demanded that the American people avoid foreclosing any activities that might aid in bringing the nations of the world to a more civilized existence. As the report stated, "without committing ourselves to definite policies or assuming to prescribe methods of procedure, we express our conviction that the time is ripe for the United States of America to take the lead in the establishment of a league or federation of nations which shall be so constituted, sustained, empowered, and operated as to protect weak people from outrage and oppression, and restrain strong peoples from breaking the peace of the world."[13]

Presumably, this even allowed for armed conflict if necessary to curtail the oppressive (i.e., uncivilized) powers from seeking to stymie the Christian American civilization that otherwise would spread throughout the globe. That this Christian American civilization was the same as the Kingdom of God was clear in the report's conclusion: "It is certain that in this frenzy of the peoples there is working the statesmanship of God. By this chastisement of the nations for the crimes of history, by the fine fervor of unselfish devotion which comes when life is stripped of its illusions and men come face to face with spiritual reality, and by the destruction of many an old abuse in the fierce fires of political revolution, God is doubtless fertilizing the fields of human society for fairer growths of Christian civilization."[14]

So it was that in 1916 the Methodist Episcopal Church began a perceptible shift in its stance toward war. While continuing to condemn the terrible human cost of war, denominational leaders made allowances for how both the United States and the MEC might capitalize on the current war in Europe. They even hinted at being willing to accept the United States becoming a belligerent so long as it did so to facilitate the coming of the Kingdom.

What is striking about this shift is that it continued to resound with the logic of pure American evangelism. The chief end of pure American evangelism was to help peoples share in the quality of life that Christian American civilization made possible by teaching them to follow the WMCNB values and patterns of life that undergirded this civilization. During the last decade of the nineteenth century and the first decade of

13. Ibid.
14. Ibid., 720.

the twentieth century, championing international arbitration was seen as the best way to teach these values on an international stage because arbitration demonstrated the American capacity to check savage passions in favor of valuing peace. The hope was that others would see the moral greatness of what the United States was doing and would follow suit. However, as the MEC's leaders worked through their reasoning about war, they came to recognize that any mechanism that disseminated WMCNB American values and brought people to participate in Christian American civilization was a legitimate means to that end. As a result, the MEC could deploy the same reasoning they used to advocate for arbitration to support a war in which the United States acted to bring all peoples and nations to share in the benefits of Christian American civilization.

The First World War presented the Methodists with such a war. It promised to demolish the remnants of Europe's feudal Catholic civilizations while simultaneously creating the conditions for the United States to plant Christian American civilization among the European peoples. So it was that the MEC could use its practice of pure American evangelism as a framework for understanding how the First World War could be redemptive for the world.

The Methodists were in the company of many other WMCNB Americans, especially those who were progressives, in finding a redemptive and civilizing rationale for the First World War. Daniel T. Rodgers (1998) detailed the ways that the progressives reacted to the war, observing that while "most American progressives experienced the war's onset with acute bewilderment and dismay," they quickly saw great opportunities for massive reorganizations of society during wartime that peacetime would not allow.[15] Domestically, many progressives entered the federal government through the Wilson Administration intent on bringing a progressive agenda to bear on major social, political and economic problems. They soon found that the war offered unique opportunities for both refining and advancing their plans. Utilizing lessons they learned from how both Britain and Germany ordered their societies during the early years of the war, and, later, tapping the sweeping wartime powers the federal government put in place to maintain civil and economic tranquility in the United States, they implemented new regulations on such massive and contentious domestic issues as labor and housing.[16]

15. Rodgers, *Atlantic Crossings*, 273.
16. Ibid., 285–86.

Beyond this domestic agenda, the progressives also set their sights on the possibility of extending a beneficent American presence across the world. This purpose found its ultimate expression on 2 April 1917 when Woodrow Wilson, the chief progressive, addressed Congress to ask for a declaration of war against Germany. In his address, Wilson first made clear that the government of Germany was not simply at war against other European powers, but against civilization itself. Specifically referring to the German announcement that it would use its submarines against any vessel seeking entrance into a European port controlled by Allied powers, Wilson declared the German government was acting in contradiction to "humane practices of civilized nations." Broadening this, he stated, "The present German submarine warfare against commerce is a warfare against mankind."[17]

Such a global attack on civilization demanded an equally global righteousness to countermand it. This is precisely what Wilson argued the United States could offer by becoming a belligerent in the war:

> Our object now, as then, is to vindicate the principles of peace and justice in the life of the world as against selfish and autocratic power and to set up among the really free and self-governed peoples of the world such a concert of purpose and of action as will henceforth ensure the observance of those principles . . . The world must be made safe for democracy. Its peace must be planted upon the tested foundations of political liberty. We have no selfish ends to serve. We desire no conquest, no dominion. We seek no indemnities for ourselves, no material compensation for the sacrifices we shall freely make. We are but one of the champions of the rights of mankind. We shall be satisfied when those rights have been made as secure as the faith and the freedom of nations can make them.[18]

For Wilson, as for the progressives who rallied to his call, the entrance of the United States into the First World War was to serve the greater good. And, while Wilson rejected the idea that the United States stood to claim any spoils from the war, he also made clear that the great American hope was that the world would be remade in American civilization's image following the war.

---

17. Wilson, "Making the World Safe for Democracy: Woodrow Wilson Asks for War," § 6.

18. Ibid. § 17.

Based on this reasoning, the Methodists could stand together with the progressives in the vanguard of those who supported their nation going to war. Indeed, the entrance of the United States into the war was the final, appropriate action to guarantee the spread of Christian American civilization in the world following the destruction of the old order in Europe. This was the conclusion drawn by several MEC periodicals of the day. The editors of the *New York Christian Advocate* declared on 5 April 1917, "Whatever have been the opinions of Americans in the thirty-two months since the war burst upon the world . . . the course of events has brought with it a revolutionary change of mind—there can now be but one purpose, the prosecution of this righteous undertaking."[19] The following week, the editors harkened back to the MEC's support of the Union during the Civil War, suggesting that while war itself is an ugly and unchristian thing, this specific war presented an opportunity for Methodists to once again prove their deep support of God and country through their generous giving of money, prayers and personal service. They explained, "We believe that the righteousness of the cause will warrant any sacrifice, and that though some stages of the way be marked by blood and tears, at the end of it lies a larger prospect of freedom and peace than any which the world has ever known."[20]

The *Northwestern Christian Advocate*'s editors also admitted to a change of heart in reference to the United States entering the war, "We confess to a personal revision of thought and outlook upon the momentous events transpiring all about . . . We see it now as we did not, indeed, could not, some months ago. Time served to accumulate evidence against Germany until it became overwhelming and we entered irrevocably. We are at war." They followed this confession with a statement on the promise the war held, "Personally, we believe the present world conflict is pregnant with the vastest possibilities that have been presented to humanity since the advent of Christ . . . We are praying God . . . that his Kingdom may come and his will be done on earth in larger accord with heavenly standards."[21]

The editors of the *Western Christian Advocate* likewise stood in line to support the war. Addressing a large German immigrant population in their readership, they turned to the favorite home missions' issue of the Americanization of immigrants. Using sharp language, they suggested that

19. "America Enters the War Against War," 324.
20. "Christian's Duty," 354–55.
21. "New World Opening," *Northwestern Christian Advocate*, 364.

the war presented an opportunity for immigrants to claim their American identity and reject their previous national allegiances. To do anything less would be perilously close to treasonous. They wrote:

> Now that war has been declared let us commend ourselves to steadfast honor. Bitterness should be banished, hatred shunned, treachery discredited, and a stern resolution to stand by the flag registered. A patriotic citizen always follows his country's flag in his devotion. Wherever it goes, whether in war or peace, whether against my convictions or judgment, it is still my country's flag. I must support it, lest I come to stand in heart among those called traitors. There is but one country now to all men who have taken out papers of American citizenship. Let no man in heart allegiance do anything that will in the future shame his face when he looks upon "Old Glory." Now is the time to break all old-world ties and cut the die forever for America, the land of youth and freedom.[22]

Methodist Evangelism During the First World War

Once the Methodists made the decision to support the United States entering armed conflict, they were ready to bring their full evangelistic effort to bear in order to convey Christian American civilization to both the nation's fighting men and to the world. The *Western Christian Advocate*'s editorial decision to emphasize a home mission theme in its article proved prescient, since the MEC turned to the Board of Home Missions and Church Extension (BHM&CE) and the Women's Home Missionary Society (WHMS) to prosecute its evangelistic work meant to convey Christian American civilization throughout the world.

Following Congress' declaration of war, the BHM&CE moved to form a National War Council of the Methodist Episcopal Church, which it tellingly situated under the board's Department of Evangelism. The war council set about raising one million dollars with the goal of using these funds to evangelize citizens directly impacted by the war effort. This evangelism occurred in four ways: (1) By sending clergy to visit citizens who became soldiers in military camps stateside, (2) By providing wholesome activities for soldiers in the camps so that they would not be tempted to drink alcohol or seek the services of prostitutes, (3) By advocating for

---

22. "Current Comments," *Western Christian Advocate*, 338.

better work conditions and housing for civilians in the United States engaged in war industry work, and (4) By sending chaplains to the front.[23]

The WHMS followed suit, joining with its sister organization, the Women's Foreign Missionary Society, to develop the Woman's War Council of the Methodist Episcopal Church. It likewise had four duties: (1) To generate publicity in churches and through church papers in favor of the war effort, (2) To foster local woman's war councils in congregations that would discuss the humanitarian needs created by the war and solicit donations to meet those needs, (3) To provide hospitality for women and children coming to visit soldiers stationed in domestic camps, and (4) To provide afghans, pillows and care packages (containing such items as jams, jellies, and cookies) for soldiers in hospitals or for soldiers and/or soldiers' families who were church visitors on Sunday mornings.[24]

The MEC's evangelistic strategy is not hard to unravel here. Believing that American soldiers would serve as missionaries of Christian American civilization overseas, the Methodists sought to make American soldiers become paragons of the values that undergirded that civilization. The work of the Department of Evangelism's War Council guaranteed the soldiers received traditional calls to Christian faith through the presence of the chaplains and pastors, as well as inculcation in the WMCNB values that the Methodists held as critical to Christian American civilization. They backed up this exhortation by their work in and around the camps aimed at protecting soldiers from the evils of various immoral amusements, especially alcohol and prostitution. Finally, the Woman's War Council facilitated the means for men to remain in contact with their wives and children. This was not only an act of hospitality; it also reminded the soldiers of their commitments to their families, thus helping them continue to value domesticity even in the midst of an all-male military setting.

Pure American evangelism, especially as it developed in the cities, is also visible in how the Methodists sought to maintain a social witness among Americans more broadly during the war. The Department of Evangelism's War Council maintained this witness by their work to support civilian laborers at home. The Woman's War Council did this through its humanitarian work. By raising the awareness of the common Methodist through both church publications and local committees as to the devastation wrought by war, and by offering concrete donations for the alleviation

---

23. Sweet, *Methodism in American History*, 376.

24. The work of the Woman's War Council is described in detail in Mills, *Journal of the Twenty-Eighth Delegated General Conference*, 1124.

of the humanitarian need caused by the war, the women were in line with the work that the deaconesses did in the cities. They demonstrated the palpable concern and generous nature of Methodists, setting a moral example for other Americans.

In addition to the work of these specifically Methodist organizations, the MEC also supported the war effort through several ecumenical and non-sectarian agencies. This included participating in the Federal Council of Churches' creation of the General Wartime Commission, which helped supply chaplains, wholesome reading material (especially Bibles and morally-uplifting tracts), and appropriate camp activities for soldiers. The denomination also provided the chairman to the United Fund Drive in the person of John R. Mott. The drive successfully raised $200 million from Jewish, Catholic and Protestant sources to support religious work in the war effort.[25] This cooperative work might be seen as out-of-step with the MEC viewing the war effort as a means of spreading the values prized by specifically American Methodists, except that the Methodists led this effort. Rather than dilute their mission, the Methodists were leading what they perceived to be less-civilized groups within the nation (*viz.*, the Jews and Roman Catholics) to be more fully engaged with Christian American civilization even as they aided the nation in its holy work of spreading Christian American civilization across the seas.

As it had during the Civil War, the MEC once again assumed that the federal government embodied the best ideals of Christian American civilization. This meant that the denomination not only wanted to direct its evangelistic work toward undergirding the government's wartime activities as much as possible, but that it wanted to support the federal government in every way. As with the Civil War, the Methodists offered this support through their money, their lives, and their publications: by selling Liberty Loans in their congregations, encouraging their young men to become recruits for the army, and disseminating pro-war-effort propaganda.[26]

It is likely that the MEC easily fell in with the federal government because the government's training of the soldiers paralleled the MEC's own

---

25. While this joint work with Catholics might initially seem opposed to pure American evangelism, I would argue that the Methodists saw the Catholic cooperation in this effort as a salutary movement of the Catholics toward Christian American civilization and away from the papacy. As such, the Methodists could be proud of their leadership over this fund both because of its support of the war effort and because of how it was converting Catholics to see the better civilization.

26. Ahlstrom, *Religious History of the American People*, 889–92.

activities. Like the MEC, the progressives in the American military "imbued their troops with a clear idea of what distinguished the U.S. Army from all others by cataloging the superior qualities of the American soldier for their wartime recruits."[27] This indoctrination was seen as critical because the American soldier, more than any other group of individuals, would have "many chances to promote American methods of fighting and the American way of life" in Europe.[28] As a result, it was necessary to equip the soldiers to be good conveyors of American civilization.

Along these same lines, the progressives felt it was critical that the nation shield its soldiers from engaging in immoral activities lest "army life . . . rob men of this generation of their moral imperative by exposing them to the contaminating influence often associated with army life."[29] To this end, Wilson created the Commission on Training Camp Activities (CTCA), which he tasked with rigorously enforced the laws "which forbade the sale of liquor to men in uniform and enabled the president to outlaw prostitution in broad zones around each camp." Along with this work, the CTCA launched a massive program to combat illicit sex by soldiers. This program included sexual education classes as well as athletic programs, especially boxing, intended to re-direct the soldiers' pent-up sexual energy.[30]

The desire to draw people into the quality of life provided by Christian American civilization is visible in the MEC's primary evangelistic work, its cooperative work with other groups, and its general support of the government's war effort. The consistent goal was to create a situation in which soldiers could experience the full benefits of Christian American civilization in how their lives on camp were regulated. Blessed by this experience, these soldiers would then be ardent missionaries of the values undergirding this civilization when they arrived in Europe.

The CDA and CCWD

The great hopes the MEC hung on the First World War were most fully expressed in the dual publication by the Methodist Book Concern of the books *Christian Democracy for America* (CDA) and *The Christian Crusade for World Democracy* (CCWD) in 1918. These books were "designed for

27. Keene, *Doughboys, the Great War, and the Remaking of America*, 105.

28. Ibid.

29. Ibid., 24.

30. Ibid., 25, 40–41.

use in Mission Study classes, in Epworth Leagues, young people's societies, church groups, and Sunday schools, as well as for general reading."[31] While each book had discreet authors, the Board of Home Missions and Church Extension and the Board of Foreign Missions had significant influence over the content in them.

Above all, these books were proponents of linking the church and the United States as jointly forging a Christian American civilization at home and abroad. As the authors explained in the introduction of *CDA*, calling upon the very institutions that the Methodists most supported in their efforts to evangelize and civilize the various groups in the United States, "The public school, the home and the church have worked as one in promulgating the principles which now are the rock-bed foundation of our national ideals."[32] These principles, which were synonymous with WMCNB values, in turn became the seedbed for American-style democracy. Indeed, democracy was impossible apart from these principles because these alone were grounded in the will of God and, as the authors of the *CCWD* asserted, "this order of life can never be realized till it rests on the foundation of the world's first and greatest democrat—Jesus Christ."[33]

While all Protestant denominations had some hand in this formation of a Christian American civilization, the authors averred that the MEC had more claim than any other. The authors of *CDA* pointed to the frontier experience of the Methodists as providing the most formative definition of national values and inserted a lengthy quote from Theodore Roosevelt in support of this. According to Roosevelt,

> The Methodist Church plays a great part in many lands; and yet I think I can say that in none other has it played so great and peculiar a part as here in the United States. Its history is indissolubly interwoven with the history of our country . . . Its essential democracy, its fiery and restless energy of spirit, and the wide play that it gave to individual initiative all tended to make it peculiarly congenial to a hardy and virile folk, democratic to the core, prizing individual independence above all earthly possessions, and engaged in the rough and stern work of

31. This quote is found in the Foreword of both volumes. Forsyth and Keeler, *Christian Democracy for America*, 11; and Taylor and Luccock, *Christian Crusade for World Democracy*, 7.

32. Forsyth and Keeler, *Christian Democracy for America*, 17.

33. Taylor and Luccock, *Christian Crusade for World Democracy*, 26.

conquering a continent . . . The whole country is under a debt of gratitude to the Methodist.[34]

Both sets of authors argued that by the beginning of the twentieth century this Methodist-forged nation needed to take leadership in spreading its Christian American civilization to the rest of the world in the form democracy. As the authors of *CDA* explained, "America has become spokesman for world democracy . . . From, the national capital of the United States of America has gone forth the challenge which is to change the status of human relationships the world over . . . The minds of men are aflame with the fires of a new day. And America . . . is leading the way to a practical application of all that the term 'democracy' means."[35]

Based on this charge to the nation, the authors of *CDA* spent the balance of their book describing specific home missions and explaining, somewhat awkwardly at times, how the MEC could bring the vision of democracy to the various groups living within the United States. Likewise, the authors of the *CCWD* considered how the MEC might participate in the national mission to inculcate WMCNB values in the peoples of the world to foster the growth of democracy in all nations.

The war served as the catalyst that allowed the authors of *CDA* and the *CCWD* to promote the advance of democracy. As the authors of *CDA* described it, the war raised existential questions of the most basic sort that prepared people in the United States and around the world to hear the message of the gospel in conjunction with the call to Christian American civilization.

> War has clouded the sky and added to the inability of our own and every land to hear the voice of God in the affairs of men. Questionings which had lain dormant are now active in the thinking of countless hundreds of thousands. Does God still exist? Has Christianity utterly failed? Does God hear the prayers of opposing armies when they plead for his assistances? Is he mindful of the men slain on the field of battle? Is he concerned over the homes made lonely by the taking away of their men? Will the church ever be able to answer the new demands made upon it? . . . No superficial answer will satisfy. It must be an answer that will vitalize faith and stimulate to service. Every phase of human living is involved. Every human relationship is affected . . . The Church of Jesus Christ must reconsecrate itself to the needs of to-day. As in times past it must be the steadying

34. Forsyth and Keeler, *Christian Democracy for America*, 19–20.
35. Ibid., 15.

force of the nation. Its message must be proclaimed in every place where men and women are to be found . . . Out of the horrors and devastation of war a new day must dawn. The character of that day depends upon those who claim Jesus Christ as their Saviour and Lord.[36]

As before, the authors of *CDA* followed this broader point by gesturing toward the MEC as uniquely suited to this task:

This is no new challenge to the Methodist Episcopal Church . . . the church which for several generations has adapted itself to the changing needs of the times will respond now with full-hearted loyalty. It is awake to the needs of our national life. It recognizes the Kingdom's necessities. It has called its ministry and membership to service which is adapted to the conditions and needs. It is pointing them to the way they may best help in a task the doing of which will bless not only our own land, but also every land where our boasted democracy gains foothold.[37]

The authors of the *CCWD* were in full agreement with this assessment, writing, "In a day of democratic striving the world over, a church born of democratic ideals, a force for social progress in its very birth hour, and during all its history a church of the common people, cannot escape the responsibility of world-service for democracy . . . Methodism must answer the call for service and leadership in that struggle for which her birthright and experience have so splendidly fitted her."[38]

Even more pointedly, the authors of the *CCWD* explained the undertaking Christians and Americans alike were called to:

The task of the hour is one task. In it the two great passions of the human heart join and fuse—patriotism and religion. *On the patriotic side* it is to rid the world of the menace of the rampant despotism of Germany and her allies; to free democracy from the material obstacle of aggressive autocracy. *On the religious side* it may best be stated by the reversal of President Wilson's words, *to make democracy safe for the world*; to set at work those forces of education, moral control and religion among the backward peoples of the world without which democracy is a "destruction walking at noonday."[39]

---

36. Ibid., 191–92.

37. Ibid., 192–93.

38. Taylor and Luccock, *Christian Crusade for World Democracy*, 178-179.

39. Ibid., 22.

Here is the case for pure American evangelism in its starkest terms: the Christian American serving both God and nation by supporting the patriotic workings of the nation's government and by uplifting the peoples of the world to share the values and forms of Christian American civilization. In this light, supporting the nation in war was not only appropriate, it was a moral obligation, for "the nation has embarked on a great, unselfish, spiritual crusade to clear the pathway for God and it follows its sons across the sea with prayer."[40]

It was with such enthusiasm that the Methodist Episcopal Church first resisted and then embraced the entrance of the United States into the First World War. It was out of this enthusiasm that the denomination also launched the most ambitious plan in its history to fund a massive expansion of home and world missions during the war.

40. Ibid., 23.

The Centenary

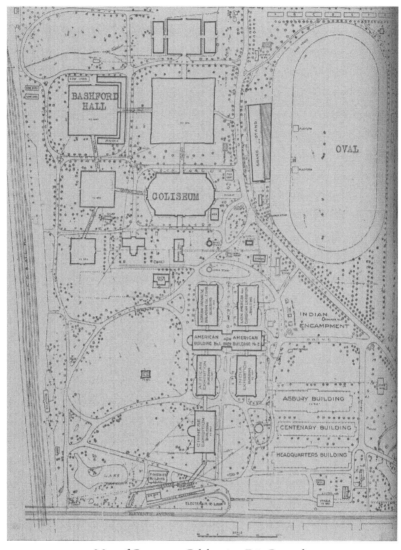

Map of Centenary Celebration Fair Grounds

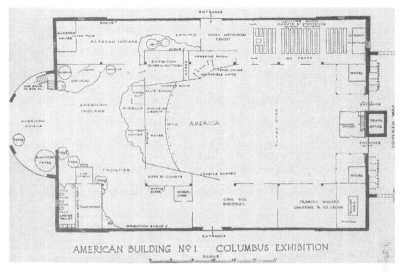

Diagram of the First Building Showcasing
Home Missions at the Centenary Celebration

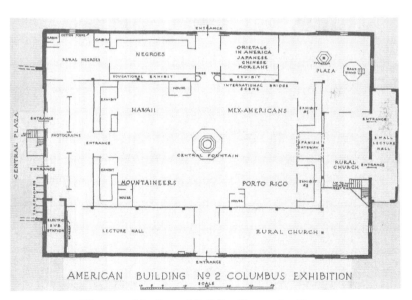

Diagram of the Second Building Showcasing Home
Missions at the Centenary Celebration

The Administrative Office of the Centenary Celebration
with the Cross and U.S. Flag Intermixed

The Centenary Cadets, an Armed Police Force Employed
by the MEC to Guard the Celebration

The Wayfarer

Envisioning the Centenary

The groundwork for celebrating the Centenary was laid during the General Conference of 1916, the same General Conference that saw the Methodists moving toward supporting war as an acceptable means to extend the influence of Christian American civilization. That the bishops used similar logic in supporting both the potential for armed conflict and the Centenary is clear from the episcopal address, which introduced the idea of celebrating the Centenary by stating, "The cross of Christ makes deep appeals to humanity. As the Church prays belated races and nationalities shall catch new visions, kings and princes shall dream new dreams, nations shall behold with joy a new heaven and a new earth."[41] In addition to this call for prayer, the bishops suggested that the denomination pledge itself to raise $10 million in funds for home and foreign missions.

Virtually every denominational agency greeted the possibility of the Centenary with enthusiasm, offering additions and amendments throughout the conference session to what the Centenary would include. The Committee on Foreign Missions, for example, called on the Board of Foreign Missions and the Women's Foreign Missionary Society to anticipate the Centenary monies by doubling the amount of their expenditures in the coming year as well as by identifying additional special projects they would like to fund. It also recommended that MEC capital projects should be planned around the world and that an endowment fund should be established to cover administrative costs associated with overseeing this massive new inflow of money.[42]

In the end, the program ballooned to something far larger than the bishops initially envisioned. The final form of the Centenary, as put forth by a committee of one hundred in their report to the General Conference, entailed ten objectives. According to their report, these were:

1. That the Methodist Episcopal Church now take its full share in the evangelization of the world, according to facts of need as definitely ascertained and presented.

2. That eight million dollars ($8,000,000) a year for five years be secured to cover askings of foreign fields, to establish permanent funds to meet overhead expenses, retiring allowances for missionaries and relief for their widows and orphans. That this amount ($40,000,000) be put with the amounts needed for home missions.

---

41. Locke, *Journal of the Twenty-Seventh Delegated General Conference*, 200.
42. Ibid., 630.

3. That the Centenary Commission conduct a joint campaign (1918–1919) under the auspices of the Boards of Foreign and Home Missions.

4. That a powerful church-wide educational campaign be prosecuted, by means of press, picture, and pulpit.

5. That a vital missionary organization be carried from Area, Conference and District, down to the last church.

6. That every local church be made dominantly evangelistic at home and missionary in its outreach.

7. That the teaching of stewardship of life, character, and possessions (the tithe) be taught as fundamental to Christianity.

8. That the prayer life of the church be zealously cultivated.

9. That a denomination-wide celebration be held on the State Fair Grounds at Columbus, Ohio in June, 1919, as the culmination of the Centenary, to be followed by echo meetings in every section.

10. When approved by the Board of Bishops and the Boards of Foreign and Home Missions, the authorities of the Methodist Episcopal Church, South, be asked to co-operate.[43]

What becomes clear from this report is that the General Conference came to see the Centenary not simply as a way to raise money, but as a way to condition the membership of the MEC to become tireless, dedicated, generous givers to the cause of missions.

The authors of *CCWD* were among the cheerleaders for the Centenary, arguing that it was the means by which the MEC would complete its moral crusade to establish the values necessary for democracy throughout the world. They explained that through the Centenary the MEC "girded itself to face adequately its share of the world task . . . [by estimating] what it needs for a five-year term to attempt in a fair measure the Christianization of the one hundred and fifty millions in the non-Christian world for which it is solely responsible."[44] The authors then staked out the ground of pure American evangelism in no uncertain terms when they put forward a remarkable juxtaposition of images, arguing that war was an apt metaphor for explaining how God called the church to share the love of Christ at this particular moment in history:

---

43. Sweet, *Methodism in American History*, 381–82.
44. Taylor and Luccock, *Christian Crusade for World Democracy*, 30.

> For this hour, the Centenary World Program of Methodism
> is the organized strategy of the love of Christ. It must stir the
> Church as the voice of God . . . The hour has struck when the
> Christian Church must get on with the business of establishing
> the kingdom of God by an aggressive warfare in deadly earnest
> if she is to hold the allegiance of men. In her total task she has
> what the world so direly needs, "The moral equivalent of war";
> and only as she utilizes all her resources for that one tremendous
> objective can she lead a world which has become accustomed to
> a war footing. There is no other idea large enough to serve "as a
> moral equivalent to war" than the adventure of applying Chris-
> tianity to a desperately needy world. All the "war virtues," far-
> sighted planning, quick initiative, unselfish courage, disciplined
> leadership, obedience, *esprit de corps* and effective cooperation,
> may find permanent and satisfying place in the crusade of the
> kingdom of God. The task to which the church calls men must
> be large enough to make room for these virtues, else it will not
> appear worth while . . . Merely dabbling with its task will rally no
> army to the standard of the church. The church must be saved by
> her faith, a militant and aggressive faith in the world-kingdom
> of God, to which she dedicates her all.[45]

Lest the readers forget that the Christian Church was joined with the
nation in this "moral equivalent to war," the authors reminded them a few
pages later, "Surely, it is God's time to place before the newly discovered
and released capacities in the manhood and womanhood of America for
sacrifice, leadership, and devotion, the Christian crusade for the world's
true freedom."[46] The Centenary was the chief source of funds and manpower for that crusade.

With such sentiments, the Centenary struck a chord throughout
Methodism. William Warren Sweet recorded that numerous pastors enthusiastically took up the summons to promote the Centenary in their
local congregations and to take subscriptions for it. To aid in this, the denomination put out vast quantities of printed material, much of it using
the best advertising techniques of the day, to encourage both members
and friends of the MEC to pledge their funds, time and prayers to the
support of this endeavor. The denominational leaders were gratified to see
an overwhelmingly positive response to this effort, and so continued to
increase the dollar amount they hoped to raise for Methodist evangelistic

45. Ibid., 180–81.
46. Ibid., 185.

missions at home and abroad, with the final goal settling at an astonishing $100 million dollars.[47]

The Methodists were not alone in their excitement and grand ambitions during the First World War. Ahlstrom noted that following the war a great many of the evangelical denominations sought to continue with their record-setting wartime fundraising and voluntarism through campaigns meant to mobilize their respective congregations to keep the momentum going.[48] Handy, in an article (1960) surveying the histories that explained the lead up to the ultimate "religious depression" that would strike American Protestantism during the 1920s, explained, "During and just after the first World War there was an intensification of this synthesis through an emphasis on 'Christian Americanization,' by which was meant growth toward national democratic and spiritual ideals, of which the churches were the best custodians."[49] While this was the case, the Methodist Centenary was set apart by its sheer size, particularly in reference to the culminating celebration in Columbus.

The Centenary Celebration

Alonzo E. Wilson, who chronicled the actual events of the Columbus celebration in a 393-page scrapbook for the Methodist Episcopal Church Division of Special Days and Events, provided an excellent insight into how wide-ranging the celebration was.[50] Comparing it to the size of the world's fairs and expositions of his day, Wilson described the Centenary as an event that required the construction of seven large buildings to house missionary exhibitions for each of the following regions: (1) Africa, (2) China, (3) India, (4) Japan, (5) Latin America and Europe, (6) and (7) the United States (which was in a double-building). These buildings housed a total of twenty-seven auditoriums, each of which hosted anywhere from 200 to 700 meetings over the three weeks of the event, totaling approximately 2,900 meetings in sum. Beyond this, the buildings offered several exotic peeks into the regions the buildings represented, including elephant rides outside the India building, tours of life-sized African huts in the Af-

47. Norwood, *Story of American Methodism*, 376–77. Sweet, *Methodism in American History*, 382–83.

48. Ahlstrom, *Religious History of the American People*, 892, 898.

49. Handy, "American Religious Depression, 1925–1935," 7.

50. All statistics and citations in the following description of the Centenary celebration are from A. Wilson, *Methodist Centenary Celebration*.

rica building, and milk-bars and soda fountains in place of saloons in a mock-up city-street-of-the-future in the American building.

In addition to these exhibition buildings, there were eleven other auditoriums housed in ten other venues, including a moving picture hall, a bandstand, three large tents, two additional halls, the Grand Stand and the Coliseum. The Grand Stand was the largest of all the venues, attracting 1,050,000 attendees during the three weeks and hosting several major productions, including a Wild West show, various pageants, and many of the keynote speakers (such as Secretary of the Navy Josephus Daniels and popular orator William Jennings Bryan). The most technologically advanced display was a 135-foot tall outdoor movie screen, which required a special "lantern" for displaying slides at the size of 115 foot square. In all, the celebration used 611,452 square feet for its events.

The most representative of the exhibits was a three-act pageant entitled "The Wayfarer: A Pageant of the Kingdom" that enlisted over 2,000 people as part of the cast and chorus and was put on several times in the Coliseum. In the first act, the Wayfarer views the devastation on the earth brought by the First World War and shares his pessimism at the state of the world. A woman named "Understanding" comes to Wayfarer and reveals to him the analogy between the world's current situation and that of the exiled Jews in Babylon. She explains to him how the exile offered the Jews the opportunity to receive more readily the promise of the coming Messiah. Likewise, she claims that the current war is preparing the world for the coming of the Kingdom of Christ. In the next act, Wayfarer watches the life of Jesus Christ and is particularly fixated on how Jesus faced a seemingly hopeless situation in his crucifixion and yet overcame it in his resurrection. From these lessons, Wayfarer realizes "that the most discouraging situation is but the prelude to a glorious triumph." The final act depicts Wayfarer as "committed . . . to the program of world conquest." During the act, Wayfarer watches a series of nine scenes, each of which demonstrate the increasing influence of Jesus Christ over the population of the world until, in the finale, all 2,000 cast members in various ethnic garbs representing the whole of humanity come forward to pay tribute to Christ.

If "The Wayfarer" best enacted the millennial hopes of pure American evangelism, the Centenary as a whole was a testament to the strident optimism Methodists had that such hopes were soon to be realized. Alonzo E. Wilson succinctly captured this in his brief summarization of the mission he believed the Centenary celebration set before all Christian Americans:

"This is a dawn of a new day. The American people are interested in the problems of life, of living conditions, of humanity throughout the world . . . the exalting of the fatherhood of God and the brotherhood of man is to-day's program for the church, the theater, the fair and exposition; and the uplifting of those millions now in ignorance and poverty to education, right living, and Christianity is our triumph for to-morrow."[51]

The Centenary was thus a means of bolstering what Methodists believed Americans both were and could be. It was a monument to Christian American civilization and a launching point for the final, victorious thrust of Methodist evangelism which would spread that civilization and its values not only across the United States, but into the entire world. To this extent, it is difficult to imagine an event more perfectly aligned with the concept of pure American evangelism.

The Aftermath

Organizing to Conserve Success

The MEC embarked on both the First World War and the Centenary with towering expectations for what they would accomplish. In both cases, they were bitterly disappointed. This disappointment dawned on the MEC gradually, but as it did, it became corrosive, dissolving away the connection between the church and the culture that had undergirded pure American evangelism for the preceding half-century. What made the disappointment especially poignant was that the initial results of both the First World War and the Centenary seemed so positive.

With the signing of the Versailles Peace Treaty and the completion of the Centenary, the Methodists had reason to believe they were entering the 1920s on a high note. No single day was more indicative of this than 28 June 1919, the date the Treaty of Versailles was signed and one of the days during the Centenary celebration in Ohio. As reported by the *New York Christian Advocate*: "When word was received that the peace treaty had been signed a spontaneous celebration was started, trumpeters rode through the grounds shouting glad tidings and calling the people to assemble at the band stand, near the Coliseum. There a band struck up patriotic airs, bells rang and the siren sounded."[52]

---

51. A. Wilson, *Methodist Centenary Celebration*, 5.
52. "Church Brings the Ends of the World Together at Columbus," 851.

Those who made their way to the band stand heard the peace treaty interpreted in terms of the advance of Christian American civilization:

> Bishop Stuntz opened the peace celebration by leading the crowd in singing "Faith of Our Fathers, Living Still." He then said, "Brothers and sisters, the war is over—right! Let us bow our heads in silent prayer." After prayer he continued: "It is a triumph for the Church of Jesus Christ our Lord. I believe in peace, but not peace at any price. The Lord never promised peace except to those who behaved themselves." Continuing, he stated that his hand and the hand of every Christian in the United States on that day signed the peace treaty, President Wilson acting as our representative.[53]

Everything about the way Bishop Stuntz conducted this impromptu gathering has the markings of pure American evangelism. He lumped the mission of the church and the mission of the nation together when he proclaimed that the victory of the Allied forces was a victory for Jesus Christ and the Church. The hymn he chose bolstered that point, suggesting that the victorious peace won by the Allied forces allowed for the continuation of the Christian heritage the Methodists so treasured. Following this, he gave the United States and the values of WMCNB Americans pride-of-place by singling out of Wilson as the chief signer of the treaty and imposing the clearly Arminian notion that the nations needed to remain responsible in order to retain the God-given blessing of peace. All together, then, Stuntz signaled that the Christian Church could celebrate this victory because the United States, which he understood as a Christian nation, had led the Allied forces to victory and was also the chief architect of the peace that would result from it. He believed that the same motivations for MEC evangelism were the motivations that had orchestrated the peace agreement ending the First World War.

A few weeks following this event, the Methodists would find another reason to celebrate. The Centenary seemed to have been successful even beyond the ever-increasing goal they had set for it. At the conclusion of the exhibition in Columbus, no less than $115,003,375 was subscribed to the various causes connected to it, and by April 1920 $15,279,480 of those subscriptions had been paid. This allowed the denomination to cover the costs incurred to underwrite all aspects of the Centenary celebration ($4,656,949) and still have over $10 million left for evangelistic efforts.[54]

---

53. Ibid., 851.

54. Mills, *Journal of the Twenty-Eighth Delegated General Conference*, 699, 701.

In addition to this, over one million people attended the event, including such notables as all the bishops from both the MEC and the MECS, former president William Henry Taft, William Jennings Bryan, the governors of several states, thousands of preachers, and hundreds of thousands of lay members of the MEC.

So great was the success of the Centenary that, even before the Columbus event concluded, the denomination sought ways to encourage the continuation of the work of the Centenary Campaign. For this purpose, on 24 and 25 June 1919, the Joint Centenary Committee, a committee consisting of members of both the Board of Foreign Missions and the Board of Home Missions and Church Extension, met with a large number of bishops and district superintendents from around the country. At this meeting, they adopted a "conservation program" that entailed 1) emphasis on financial stewardship among Methodists, 2) encouragement for young people to enter Christian service, 3) further study of how to accomplish the goals of all home missions, and 4) a challenge to evangelize one million souls by 1 May 1920 through a denomination-wide revival. The last of these points brought the most excitement from the attendees at this meeting, being adopted "by a rising unanimous vote." When the vote was registered, no one less than seventy-year-old Brother Van, in attendance as a representative from the North Montana Conference, rose to lead the assembly in the hymn "Palms of Victory."[55]

At this high-water mark of pure American evangelism, when it seemed entirely possible that the MEC would succeed incorporating all peoples into Christian American civilization, it is odd that the Joint Centenary Committee chose to call its plan a "conservation program." Even more out of step with the enthusiasm of the time is that there are several activities interspersed within the plan aimed at the MEC simply trying to hold onto its existing resources. While this sort of planning is hardly indicative of a major shift in thinking—it is only natural that the Methodists would want to create programs to help them sustain the success of the Centenary and to manage the resources it raised—it did suggest the MEC had reached a critical point in its history. It had become successful enough in learning how to mobilize its membership and gather funds that it needed to put nearly as much energy into administering the generosity of its membership as it did into the evangelistic work the gifts of the membership were meant to support. As such, conservation of resources

---

55. "After the Centenary, What?," 849–50.

became as important to the denomination as being able to engage in its evangelistic work.

Less than a year after the Joint Centenary Committee met, the General Conference of 1920 had as its main point of business organizing the denomination to carry out this "conservation program." As usual, the bishops led the way, declaring in their episcopal address the importance of "extending, perpetuating, and conserving the outstanding features of stewardship, intercession and world vision brought to the church in the Centenary movement." Expanding on this, they explained:

> To have done a commanding thing once is magnificent, but to make the Centenary principles temporary would be a disaster. A church with the world always before its eyes and on its heart; a church permanently committed to stewardship of possessions and of life; a church ever practicing intercession as the Master ever lives to intercede; a church all at it, always at it and completely at it ought to be the outcome, the large result of the Centenary. To lapse back into our old, small ways and small days would be tragic. This Conference must see to it that the spirit and features which have so greatly profited the church are made permanent.[56]

The bishops, as the Joint Centenary Committee before them, split their focus on conserving the resources the denomination realized from the Centenary while also deploying those resources for evangelistic work. To make certain their listeners did not lose sight of the latter, the bishops specifically called out evangelism as being of primary consideration later in their address:

> In particular should the spirit of evangelism now being stressed with such emphasis and being blessed with such results become the crowning feature of its life. We do not plead for an evangelistic ministry alone, nor for occasional evangelism and special evangelists but for an evangelistic church, always and in all its activities seeking to fulfill Christ's redemptive purpose in the world. The effort to bring people to Christ is at the heart of our task. Thus must go on with increasing fervor and power through the years. The shout over the redeemed must never be allowed to die in our camp.[57]

---

56. Mills, *Journal of the Twenty-Eighth Delegated General Conference*, 192.
57. Ibid., 192.

The Board of Foreign Missions and the Board of Home Mission and Church Extension stood in full agreement with the bishops as to the need for continuing the work of the Centenary. Like the bishops, they also split their emphasis between advancing and conserving, describing how the Centenary funds allowed the boards to carry out their respective pre-existing programs. While these programs were vast and stood to increase their capacity to evangelize and civilize the peoples where they were situated, it is nonetheless notable that these boards did not put forward any new work beyond what was already in place. The Centenary essentially let the board fulfill their existing ideas rather than allowing them to dream beyond them.

The Board of Foreign Missions declared, "The Methodist Missionary Century began with a great faith in which a few devoted, far-seeing spirits shared; it ended with a great achievement to which the intercession, in consecration of life, of time, of money, in individual and group service . . . contributed." It then laid out three ways in which the Centenary had been especially useful in foreign missions: (1) It provided a cash buffer that allowed the Board to continue funding missionaries and missions at the same level in spite of a significant weakness in the dollar and a rise in inflation in other countries following the First World War. On this score alone, the board stated that the Centenary was a "most brilliant success." (2) It provided the board sufficient funds to complete "unfinished business," especially erecting mission buildings on vacant properties the MEC had purchased in the past and supplying missionaries to work in them. (3) It allowed the board to commission several comprehensive studies meant to make the board more effective in its evangelistic efforts in various countries. As the Board wrote, "We have had surveys, we are now getting blue prints."[58]

The board's excitement at these results was palpable. It suggested that these successes of the Centenary not only provided a foundation for the next five years of Methodist missions, "but, far beyond this, [would be] the new constructive program which will give among the peoples of the world a place of action for the Gospel of our Lord for a thousand years."[59] This sort of grand claim demonstrates that the board still operated out of pure American evangelism, seeking to bring the soteriological benefits of Christian American civilization to all under its auspices. By the same token, it must be observed that all three of the results it identified from the

---

58. Ibid., 1048–50.
59. Ibid., 1050.

Centenary were nothing more than improving upon existing Methodist missions. The board simply hoped to conserve and upgrade what was already within its realm rather than advancing beyond these.

The Board of Home Missions and Church Extension filled the last four pages of its report with activities that it claimed the Centenary made possible. Again, however, these activities were not new advances as much as they were continuations of efforts in existing home fields, and these activities continued to emphasize extending Christian American civilization through well-established practices of pure American evangelism. Fully a third of the money went to the construction of new buildings, demonstrating the continuing commitment by Methodists to engage in civilizing the frontiers of the nation (whether in the West or in the cities) through church extension. In addition, the Board described work among African Americans, Mexicans in the Southwest, Native Americans, and foreign-speaking populations in the cities, explaining its on-going efforts to teach these groups the values essential to Christian American civilization. On this score, the board singled out its work among immigrants as particularly worthy:

> The program for Americanization work is most interesting. The amount appropriated for this work for 1920 is $2,532,002. Of this amount $1,773,398 is for church buildings and community houses, and $758,604 for the support of workers, including pastors. Support is provided in whole or in part for 102 English-speaking pastors doing work among foreign-speaking peoples, 283 language-pastors, 142 women-workers, 56 directors of religious education, 39 deaconesses, and 46 special workers. And the whole range of help includes work with Armenians, Chinese, Finns, Germans, Greeks, Jews, Italians, Japanese, Latin-Americans, Norwegian-Danish peoples, Portuguese, Poles, Czechs, Russians, Slavs, Slovacks, Swedes, Syrians, and polyglot communities. Some 349 projects are in growing polyglot communities, 218 in the cities and 131 in rural industrial sections. It is noteworthy that provision is made for several workers among the Jews. Special attention is being give to community houses among all these people, with a program that ministers to every need not provided for in the crowded sections where they live.[60]

Backing up this rhetoric with dollars, the board budgeted slightly more than one-half of the Board's total budget in 1919 for what it categorized as Americanization ministries in 1920. At the same time, the

60. Ibid., 1113–14.

fact that the board simply sought to increase its existing budget line items rather than re-working its budget shows a desire to continue its work relatively unchanged. This work clearly continued in the vein of pure American evangelism precisely because the board sought to conserve its current modes of operation rather than to explore new forms of evangelistic ministry.

Adding to these reports, the General Conference delegates voted in concert with the bishops' suggestion to do something that would make the features of the Centenary permanent. In the spirit of the bishops' dual-focus between pressing ahead in evangelism while conserving the vast resources the Centenary made available for that evangelism, they did this by forming the oxymoronically named Committee on Conservation and Advance. They tasked this committee with distributing the money raised by the Centenary to appropriate causes within the denomination. So it was that, at the end of the General Conference of 1920, the MEC was flush with success and enthusiasm, but was also straddling two realities. While it was ready to make the final push so that all peoples in the United States, and even around the world, would participate in Christian American civilization, it also was carefully avoiding new ways of engaging in evangelism. It wanted to sustain its existing mission and the generosity of its membership to that mission rather than looking to new vistas with its significant new resources.

Conservation Overtakes Missions

The conservatism of the General Conference in seeking to build the capacity of the MEC's existing mission is certainly understandable. The MEC had been at this work for decades and now seemed to have cultivated the support base necessary to bring it to a successful completion. However, the General Conference may have had more reason than good planning practices for seeking to shore up the Centenary-inspired support for the MEC's missionary work. The bishops hinted at this in the conclusion of their address in 1920:

> The fever of the disturbed world is in the veins of the church and it is not well to have it so. Somebody must be able to calm the tossing waves of human life. A perturbed, fretted church cannot do it. We cannot accomplish a spiritual triumph if we are ourselves paralyzed with fear, or overwhelmed by dread of catastrophe. The church must possess the strength of the eternal God in

the peace that passes understanding . . . The world breaks at the point of its character. Our ministry is to the world's character. Our supreme need today is a Christlike character of our own. We must 'keep the soul of the world alive.[61]

Here the bishops accurately diagnosed the position of the Methodist Episcopal Church—ready to meet the world at its deepest need, but also dependent on people who themselves were impacted by the values and trends of the world. So it was that substantial conservation efforts were necessary lest the capacity to move ahead in evangelistic mission crumble. And, as it turned out, they were precariously close to crumbling.

As the first few years of the 1920s concluded, the initial splendid indications the Centenary gave to the MEC quickly evaporated. By 1 April 1923 only $55,878,201 of the subscriptions pledged during the Centenary campaign had come in as actual donations. Recognizing that the donations were not arriving quickly enough to match either the total amount subscribed or even the amount ultimately set as the goal for the campaign, the Committee on Conservation and Advance ran another media blitz of the MEC membership, hoping to spur their generosity. This included publishing the capacious *The World Service of the Methodist Episcopal Church*, which surveyed each mission field where the MEC was active, both domestically and overseas. Using the language of evangelism that had been commonplace for Methodists since the Civil War, it besought its readers to bring civilization to every people living in the United States and throughout the world. It also included specific amounts each home mission field or foreign mission field needed in order to accomplish its work. It added to these dollar amounts the warning that, if the promised Centenary donations either were delayed or did not come at all, it would leave a great many people languishing in uncivilized situations.

While such efforts did help increase the total amount donated to Centenary missions, when the MEC finally closed the books on the Centenary only seventy percent of the total subscribed materialized as actual donations.[62] More than just prove to be a disappointment, this withholding of funds by one-time enthusiastic givers began a negative domino effect within the church. The conservation mechanisms created by General Conference began to take precedence in the denomination as the leadership sought to retain what funds the denomination did have. This led to a double reduction in expenditures on mission: the first because the

61. Ibid., 195–96.

62. Norwood, *Story of American Methodism*, 377.

expected money from the Centenary had not materialized, the second because the MEC further tightened the budgets of its mission agencies in order to preserve denominational capital. As a result, the Methodist presence in mission contracted domestically and abroad. Most symbolic of this contraction was that the denomination soon brought missions under the broader category of "benevolences." This not only distanced the MEC from its historic identification with evangelism, it also signaled to the members of the MEC that missions were a secondary concern, subsumed to broader do-goodism.[63]

The fever in the Methodists' veins not only caused them to underfund denominationally organized missions, it led to a downturn in the quality and follow-through of local evangelism. When the Joint Centenary Committee voted to launch the ambitious program of drawing one million new souls to the MEC during the year following the Centenary celebration, Methodists diligently set out recruiting people to their local congregations. This local evangelistic effort seemed to bear exceptional fruit as, by the end of the allotted time, Methodists boasted over 1.8 million new people attending their services or Sunday schools. However, as with the amount of money subscribed to the Centenary campaign, this number was not what it seemed. Beneath it were two sizable and systematic problems.

First, the Department of Evangelism proved to be wholly impotent in this evangelistic effort. In spite of its mandate, the department reported to the General Conference of 1920 that "the war has made impossible evangelistic continuity in the local church" because of the highly mobile nature of the American population caused by troop deployments. As a result, rather than encouraging local congregations to engage in evangelism, the department promoted the war effort. The department reported, "Special military days and weeks were urged in the local churches and public meetings were held which combined both patriotism and evangelism."[64] While this focus was in keeping with the effort to extend Christian American civilization, and did provide a Christian witness to the American people during the war years, it was also ephemeral. Following the war, these efforts provided no platform for advancing evangelism among people at home or abroad. Moreover, the department's war focus made it out-of-step with whatever evangelistic work was being accomplished by local congregations. Worse than that, the lack of innovative thinking about how to address the tran-

---

63. Stevens, *Compendious History of American Methodism*, 384–86.

64. Mills, *Journal of the Twenty-Eighth Delegated General Conference*, 1110.

sient American population created by the war meant that the department had no means of equipping congregations to engage in evangelism once the war was over. This meant that congregations would be unprepared to engage in effective evangelism.

This lack of effective training in evangelism explains the second problem, which became apparent in reference to the 1.8 million new people that had come into the church after the Centenary: Methodist evangelism was no longer effective at generating denominational loyalty among its converts. The majority of converts, both adults and children, came to local congregations through Sunday schools. While this point of entry was not problematic (the Sunday school had long served as an important and effective entryway for new people to come into to the MEC), the lack of training most individual Methodists had in evangelism often meant that the Sunday schools were not well equipped to handle these new converts or move them into the broader life of the congregation. This became clear in a study by the Board of Sunday Schools analyzing the trends related to the post-Centenary evangelism program.

The board maintained that of the 1.8 million converts only 551,000 had become members of the MEC. The rest, the board stated baldly, were allowed to "drift away from the church." Based on this sobering analysis, the board went on to argue:

> Our work is not done when the converts are counted; they must be cared for, taught, and trained for Christian living. Methodism has been successful in winning converts, but not successful in holding them . . . If the present evangelistic campaign shall merely result in a great ingathering of numbers who will not be taught or trained by the church, who will find no opportunity for Christian expression or definite forms of Christian service, the campaign will fail and it were better it had never been projected. It is not enough that we win a million souls to Christ, they must be permanently built into the life of Christ and the church.[65]

The board did end its report on a positive note, suggesting that Christian education through the Sunday schools could provide the necessary means of holding the converts within the Methodist fold. However, even with this hope, the emphasis in the report clearly shifted away from reaching people outside of the church so that they could participate in Christian American civilization to conserving the people who already

65. Ibid., 1261–62.

were interested in the MEC. This move ran directly counter to the idea of pure American evangelism, which consistently pressed for an advance of Christian American civilization and the values attached to it to new populations.

By the mid-1920s, as the denominational leaders of the MEC looked back at how the Methodists withdrew their support for missions, they came to view the Centenary as a failure. Even the Centenary's biggest boosters acknowledged its shortcomings. Halford Luccock, who was half the authorial team of *WWCD*, co-authored *The Story of Methodism* (1926) in which he struggled to figure out what had gone wrong with the program he once lauded as "the moral equivalent to war." In this new book, he first cast about looking for positive results of the Centenary. Among these, he opined that it brought American Methodists to recognize the global scale of their denomination, it raised Methodists' awareness of how many people around the world had not yet heard the gospel, it set a high standard for giving to the church, it excited young people about the possibility of serving in missions, and it provided for the erection of numerous church buildings and for the launching of some new church programs around the world. After relating these positives, however, he resigned himself to the fact that the Centenary simply did not live up to his expectations:

> That the Centenary was not all permanent advance will be admitted. There was, it is probable, too much use of the war psychology . . . Much that had been projected, and even pledged, under the enthusiastic spell of the days just after the armistice, was found impossible of fulfillment in the cold gray light of the postwar depression. Moreover, the Centenary did, by certain of its promotional methods, tend to make shoddy thinkers believe that the task of building the kingdom of God is simply a task of perfecting a high-pressure organization of churches and ministers for the raising of certain definitely ascertainable sums of money. In these, and perhaps some other ways, an atmosphere of false excitement and achievement was created, which could not be kept up. Gradually this promotional fever evaporated. With its passing there were left certain problems of adjustment which have perplexed many leaders, and many whom the church had commissioned for work in various difficult fields. The solution of these problems is a matter of time and hard thinking. When the readjustments are completed, the permanent benefit which has grown out of the Centenary will be clear.[66]

66. Luccock and Hutchinson, *Story of Methodism*, 487.

The "problems of adjustment," as Luccock called them, were essentially problems of conservation. The denomination needed to roll back the extensive evangelistic undertakings that it had envisioned through the Centenary when the Methodist membership did not remain committed to that vision. This, then, was the historical legacy of the Centenary: it displaced uplifting people to participate in the quality of life made possible through Christian American civilization with conserving denominational assets—whether in the form of dollars or people. To what extent this displacement could be called a "permanent benefit" is open to debate.

> **NO RETREAT !**
>
> The Board of Home Missions and Church Extension steadfastly refuses to beat a retreat and as steadfastly refuses to listen to timid and visionless counsel. It is profoundly convinced that Christ is calling the church to join him in a conquering crusade that shall end only when the social organism has been thoroughly Christianized. The board believes that the great body of Methodists join in this conviction.

Follow up Centenary Fundraising Notice
to Encourage People to Pay Their Pledges

A Shift in the Understanding of Evangelism

Following the Centenary fiasco, the MEC was not simply scaling back its missionary work, it was revising its understanding of evangelism. It is the combination of these changes that ended pure American evangelism.

In the above passage, Luccock provided two good insights as to why the Methodists were beginning to reevaluate their understanding of evangelism. One was that the "war psychology" in the United States quickly faded following the war; bringing the enthusiasm Methodists felt both for American participation in the First World War and for the Centenary to an end. In its place, Luccock stated, there was a "postwar depression." The second was that the Centenary was more form than substance. It was too much a slick advertising campaign that crassly exploited millennial hopes in order to raise funds, and not enough actual engagement in mission to bring about the new civilization the people desired. This effectively played on the emotions for a short time but ultimately proved false, as became evident in the years following the Centenary.

The disappointment of the MEC membership fits with the mood of WMCNB Americans more broadly as they were entering the 1920s.

During the late nineteenth century and early twentieth century, this group was idealistic and enthusiastic, launching the progressive movement as a means to perfect the United States on municipal, state, and federal levels. At the outset of the First World War, this group embraced Wilson's rhetoric of making the world safe for democracy and rallied to the cause. However, after the war, public opinion in the United States, with this group in the lead, turned against that crusading mentality. The American people as a whole wearied of wartime sacrifices and became jaded toward what they perceived as broken wartime promises.

Historians offer several explanations for the growing distaste Americans felt toward the mantle of being an activist world leader. A common theme through all of these explanations is the failure of the First World War to live up to the promise Wilson and the progressives connected to it. This failure took several forms. First, the Treaty of Versailles proved to be far short of Wilson's "peace without victory" ideal, as the Allied powers in Europe demanded exorbitant reparations on the part of Germany and carved up the lesser powers of Europe by dismantling and creating various countries. As this became known to Americans, many of them questioned to what extent their involvement in the war had made the "world safe for democracy" and to what extent it simply propped up old world European powers. As Senator Homer T. Bone expostulated, "the Great War . . . was utter social insanity, and was a crazy war, and we had no business in it at all."[67]

Not only did the war fail to spread enlightened American civilization across the world, progressives were bitterly disillusioned when the United States refused to participate in the League of Nations. The League was to be the progressives' crowning achievement, wreathing the globe with the efficiency and morality of American civilization. However, by the time the Senate voted on the Treaty of Versailles, the influence of a relatively small group of individuals, whom Wiebe termed the "profit-oriented," had begun to eclipse an enfeebled President Wilson and fragmented Democratic Party. This group, which loathed losing the natural economic advantages the United States held over Europe after the war by joining an organization that would work for world equality, successfully lobbied to have the treaty defeated.[68]

---

67. Doenecke and Wilz, *From Isolation to War, 1931–1941*, 6–7, and Wiebe, *Search for Order*, 277.

68. Doenecke and Wilz, *From Isolation to War, 1931–1941*, 7, and Wiebe, *Search for Order*, 281.

This ignoble end to the League of Nations lent itself to the theory that Wilson and the Congress may have been at the mercy of the major financial magnates in deciding to go to war, which, had it been true, would have eviscerated the progressive support for the war. While no proof surfaced to support this claim, a popular notion of war-profiteering by those firms that lent enormous sums of money to the Allies led some Americans to believe that the United States entered the war to protect the investment of these firms when it appeared that the Central Powers might be victorious.[69]

Adding insult to injury, the progressives also watched as their work during the war on domestic labor issues dissipated in the wake of the Bolshevik Revolution. While labor initially hoped to make permanent the stronger position it received during the war, and engaged in several strikes during 1919 as a means to this end, the fear of Bolshevism crippled this endeavor. Desiring to avoid any appearance of radicalism, such powerful unions as the American Federation of Labor and the United Mine Workers quickly voted out the leaders in their ranks that might be seen as socialist. Consequently, progressives had no partner within the unions to work for labor reform and faced an American population that was highly skeptical of anything smacking of European statism or Russian Communism.[70]

Finally, a great many Americans became frustrated with the federal government's treatment of the veterans who served in the war. Not only did it take much longer than anticipated for the soldiers deployed overseas to return home after the armistice, the depression following the war left many of these soldiers without work. Additionally, the veterans fell significantly behind the civilian population in wealth. While the war had brought a boom to American manufacturing and had allowed for a significant increase in civilian wages, those in the military earned a much lower wage. One result of this was to make veterans and their families much less capable of weathering the Great Depression when it arrived. This led to the rancor over the possibility of bonus pay for the veterans that would culminate in the Bonus March of 1932.[71]

For all these reasons, the American people, and specifically the progressives who hoped to chart a new vision of global cooperation and peace through American participation in the First World War, entered the 1920s with a growing sense of disappointment. Their greatest efforts had not only failed to bear the fruit they hoped for, they backfired as both Europe

69. Doenecke and Wilz, *From Isolation to War, 1931–1941*, 8–9.

70. Rodgers, *Atlantic Crossings*, 301–16.

71. Keene, *Doughboys, the Great War, and the Remaking of America*, 170–78.

and the United States seemingly turned away from the last few steps to achieving a civilized world. Thus staggered, the progressives retreated and supported the new calls for American isolation in the 1920s.

Members of the MEC, many of whom were progressives, had even greater reason for despair. For them, the realization that the federal government, including President Wilson, could lose its Christian character was a tremendous shock. For years, the MEC had appealed to the government as the great protector of Christian American civilization. Now, the church found that the government was riddled with corruption to the point of sabotaging the possibility of expanding the blessings of the United States to the rest of the world. This was a betrayal of the highest order.

With the failure of their mission to help the peoples of the world live into the salvation Christian American civilization could bring at the very moment success seemed so certain, the MEC was left without a clear mission. All they could do was abandon the pure American evangelism they had undertaken so fervently as a failure. The various plans for conservation that the Methodists laid even before they were ready to give up on advancing Christian American civilization proved an ideal mechanism for this retrenchment.

Exceptions that Prove the Rule

There are two important exceptions to the Methodist Episcopal Church's move away from pure American evangelism toward conserving existing resources. The first is the Woman's Home Missionary Society. The second is the Board of Temperance, Prohibition and Public Morals.

While the denominational agencies quickly shifted their attention toward retaining what resources they already had, the WHMS continued on its mission of evangelizing and civilizing the home mission fields unabated well into the 1920s. There are two reasons for this. The first was the relative independence the WHMS enjoyed from the denomination. Ironically, the denomination's unwillingness to include the WHMS as a full denominational agency, thus forcing it to raise its own funds and volunteers independently from denominational largesse, buffered the agency from the denomination's straits following the Centenary. This left the WHMS free to focus on its own concerns. The extent of this freedom is especially clear in the minutes of the WHMS annual meeting of 1920. Held just a year after the Centenary celebration concluded, it would be reasonable to expect a report on the WHMS's participation in the grand event. However, there is not a single reference to the Centenary. Instead, the women were celebrating the fortieth anniversary of their own society. While the rest of the denomination was trying to work out the mixed results of the Centenary in 1920, the members of the WHMS occupied themselves with their agency's own milestone.

The second reason was that the women of the WHMS were celebrating the ratification of the Nineteenth Amendment to the United States Constitution granting women full suffrage rights in state and federal elections (ratified August 1920). With this new potential to engage the political structures, the women of the WHMS had more reason than ever to advance their vision of what a Christian American civilization should be. As the corresponding secretary wrote in her report given at the WHMS annual meeting in 1920, "Let us therefore accept the privilege and responsibility, and perform the duties of citizenship in this great republic. Let no one of our women say, 'let the men look after politics,' but let Christian women everywhere say, "As a God-fearing citizen I accept this sacred right in the interest of my nation, my State, my community, my home, my children, and myself.""[72]

The Board of Temperance, Prohibition and Public Morals likewise had reason to celebrate. The states ratified the Eighteenth Amendment, which outlawed trade in spirituous liquor in the United States, in January 1920. Buoyed by this legislative success, the board pressed for more sweeping reforms in the United States, laying out a nine-point plan to reach all of these goals. This plan included continued political agitation for the strictest enforcement of the Eighteenth Amendment, a call for the end to beer consumption in the United States, the prohibition of German immigration to the United States until Germany paid all war reparations, the demand for English to be the only language used in American newspapers, a total abstinence pledge-signing campaign among all Americans, a ban on tobacco cigarettes, an insistence on reinstating the Bible as a required text in public schools, a return to Sabbath observance, and support for anti-gambling, anti-prostitution, and anti-prizefighting efforts. Several of these items clearly have pure American evangelism motivating them. Indeed, in introducing this plan, the board made clear that establishing a Christian American civilization was its primary aim. Contrasting the United States to Germany, it wrote: "We ought to see that Uncle Sam puts his feet on every one of these steps by which Germany went to ruin, and

72. Women's Home Missionary Society, *Women's Home Missionary Society of the Methodist Episcopal Church Thirty-Ninth Annual Report*, 67–68.

walks in the opposite direction—upstairs! If we do not wish to go the way Germany went, we must urge that American civilization pause, get her direction, and build on the foundations that Germany rejected. This will be program enough for the reformers of the United States for the next decade or two."[73]

Drawing directly from the rhetoric President Wilson deployed, which depicted Germany as a nation that had heard the Protestant faith, but had turned away from its civilizing power, the board urged Americans to learn from this cautionary tale and choose the better way. As representatives of those who were doubly-victorious, both as Americans in the war and as prohibitionists in the legal battle over alcohol, the board was confident to prescribe how the United States ought to move forward to live up to its nature as a Christian American civilization.

The WHMS and the Board of Temperance, Prohibition, and Public Morals bucked the denominational trend toward conservation of resources as well as the shift away from pure American evangelism, instead trumpeting a loud advance of Christian American civilization as they headed into the 1920s. However, these agencies were not representative of the MEC as a whole by this point in time. This was true for two reasons. First, both agencies catered to specific constituencies who could celebrate unique political victories for their respective causes and who, based on this, were optimistic about Christian American civilization taking hold in the future. The denomination as a whole, however, in watching both the dollars and converts it thought were secure begin to disappear, was in a much less aggressive state of mind.

Second, both of these organizations had their origins in the late nineteenth century when the MEC was brimming with zeal to advance Christian American civilization. More than that, Methodists established both of them specifically to safeguard aspects of Christian American civilization—Victorian domesticity in the case of the WHMS and personal morality in the case of the board. As such, it was part of the very character and mission of these organizations to continue with this agenda. It would have been odd indeed if these particular agencies had failed to continue using the rhetoric of civilization and uplift.

Ultimately, however, the anachronistic nature of these agencies would catch up to them. This occurred as the denomination decided to phase out both agencies, absorbing them into larger denominational agencies geared more toward denominational conservation of resources. In the

---

73. Mills, *Journal of the Twenty-Eighth Delegated General Conference*, 1333–34.

merger of the MEC, MECS, and Methodist Protestant Church to form the Methodist Church in 1939 the WHMS merged with the WFMS as well as its counterpart agencies in the other denominations, thus losing its distinctive emphasis on carrying WMCNB values and patterns of life into the home mission field. By 1964, the denomination further curtailed women's missions when it delegated much of the mission work previously under the women's jurisdiction to a new denominational mission agency. The Board of Temperance, Prohibition, and Public Morals likewise ceased to exist, handing its trust to the General Board of Church and Society of the newly created United Methodist Church (formed in 1968 from the merger of the Methodist Church and the Evangelical United Brethren Church).

By the late twentieth century, then, the Methodist Episcopal Church and its successors had divested themselves of all remnants of the crusading desire to advance Christian American civilization by instilling WMCNB values and patterns of life through its home missions. While it still held out hopes for influencing the nation politically on certain moral and ethical issues, and it continued to engage in ministries to African Americans, Native Americans, Mexicans, and various immigrant groups, the desire to advance a specific understanding of Christian American civilization was no longer part of that activity. Instead, the chief hope of the activity was to hold onto the inroads that previous generations had already made in order to retain denominational strength.

The final chapter of MEC evangelism during this era, then, is one of massive investment followed by massive loss. The Methodists, following their soteriology to connect their evangelistic efforts to the civilizing purposes of the United States, mortgaged their entire denominational energy and resources to back what seemed like a sure means of bringing God's Kingdom to earth: the First World War. In doing this, they demonstrated that the logic of what I have called pure American evangelism was at the center of their thinking. They demonstrated pure American evangelism again by their move to close down their home mission work so quickly on the heels of the failure of Christian American civilization to take hold following the war. Without the eschatological hope of the United States to drive their mission, specifically as manifested in the inability of the MEC to trust the federal government as a pure upholder of Christian American civilization, all they could do was hope to conserve what the denomination had been able to gain during the great Centenary campaign.

Conclusion

HISTORIANS OFTEN PRESENT THE story of the Methodist Episcopal Church throughout the nineteenth century and into the early part of the twentieth century in terms of success and failure. Following this line of interpretation, the church succeeded socio-economically and failed in its mission with perhaps a few heroic examples of progressive individuals and agencies seeking to stem the church's embourgeoisement. This interpretation is insufficient, however, in that it assumes a natural antipathy between a higher social location and missional commitment. The story of the MEC during this period is the story of a highly adaptive people seeking to use their evangelistic activities to promote what they believed were the greatest gifts of God for humanity. For them, these gifts consisted of salvation in the world to come as well as participation in Christian American civilization in the present world. As the delegates to General Conference heard in the Report on the Pastoral Address in 1872: "Suffer us to remind you, dear brethren, that the increase of our sphere of labor and opportunity imposes upon us increased responsibilities. From the Atlantic to the Pacific, and from Alaska to Texas, an open door is set before us, as a denomination, to proclaim and present, free, and full salvation all over our land and to lay strong foundations for Christian civilization."[1] In short, the MEC home missionary work during this era is best described as pure American evangelism.

This idea of pure American evangelism points to intriguing new ways of charting the historiography of not only American Methodism, but the history of mission. Much of the history available today still follows the model H. Richard Niebuhr envisioned in his landmark *Christ and Culture*. Describing five typologies of how Christians relate to culture, Niebuhr suggested that either cultural values or the gospel must take precedence over the other. While historians can rightly identify situations in which

---

1. Harris and Woodruff, *Journal of the General Conference of the Methodist Episcopal Church, Held in Brooklyn, N.Y., 1872*, 444.

the church and the larger culture have clearly influenced the other, the negotiation of the church with the culture is much more nuanced than each side simply seeking to overcome the other. This realization pushes historians past the either/or narration of history, so reminiscent of the croakers' assertions that either the MEC could maintain spiritual vitality or it could acquiesce to social prestige, to consider how the church is a participant in culture even as it seeks to transform that culture. Pure American evangelism is one such story of how a specific denomination claimed this role of being a product of American culture, an interpreter of that culture to others, and an evangelist calling people to share in what they believed was God's salvific work through that culture.[2]

In making the case for pure American evangelism, it is important to remember that I am not suggesting the MEC abandoned its biblical message of calling people to Jesus. Using its unique soteriology it created an American gospel by wedding the biblical assurance of eternal life to the quality of life enjoyed by most WMCNB Americans. As Methodists invited people to share in the eternal benefits of repentance and forgiveness through Jesus Christ, they also sought to train people to participate in the blessings of a Christian American civilization. These blessings were technological, economic and political, allowing for a higher quality of life than elsewhere in the world.

Equally potent with the desire to bless people by bringing them into Christian American civilization was the fear that groups who held to values or patterns of life different than WMCNB Americans might have the power to overthrow the blessed life Christian American civilization offered. This spurred the MEC to engage in home missions with all the peoples that they most feared could topple the civilization: white southerners, African Americans freed from slavery, white settlers in the West, Native Americans, Mexicans and other Spanish-speaking peoples, immigrants, the poor, the rich, and other city dwellers.

THEMES DRAWN FROM PURE AMERICAN EVANGELISM

In describing pure American evangelism, it is easy to write off the Methodists of the late nineteenth century and early twentieth century as simply jingoistic and racist imperialists. To be sure, these terms describe much

---

2. Andrae Crouch's work on culture-making, while in the realm of sociology instead of history, likewise speaks to the need to reconsider the relationship of the church and culture. Crouch, *Culture Making*.

of what the Methodists did during this period. At the same time, it is clear that pure American evangelism cannot be circumscribed by such words. The MEC's evangelism was concerned with the well-being of the evangelized, and this allowed the MEC to avoid being nothing more than unthinking proponents of the economic, political and moral norms of the United States. Even as pure American evangelism prompted MEC home missionaries to share WMCNB values and patterns of life as salvific, it also allowed the MEC to be sensitive, critical, intentional, and open.

First, pure American evangelism sensitized the MEC to the needs of those they evangelized by building relationships between the home missionaries and the evangelized. This resulted in the church seeing the world at least partially from the perspectives of those they evangelized and modifying their ministries to fit better with the needs of the people. This was true of Thomas Harwood taking the time to learn Spanish and live with the Mexicans, Brother Van and Tom Iliff wearing western attire and changing their names to fit in with the western settlers, the deaconesses who nursed the sick and visited house-to-house, and the city society that hired a former street person to serve as the director of one of its rescue missions.

Second, pure American evangelism granted Methodists the ability to be critical of the "America" that they both presented and represented. While the Methodists were unanimous in their belief that the United States was blessed by God, having the soul of the Protestant church within it and the power of human achievement in its technology, political structure and economic might, this did not mean the Methodists were unaware of or unconcerned with the flaws in the nation. They saw these flaws clearly in the lack of education offered to African Americans, in the broken treaties with the Native Americans, in the nativism that viewed all immigrants as dangerous, and in the various systems that trapped the city laborers and their families. They then spoke out against these flaws and called on the United States to live up to the ideal nation they believed it should be.

Third, pure American evangelism was intentional. As much as the Methodists reflected their place and time in history in terms of the values they sought to impress on others, the practice of evangelism itself required an intentional effort. The high level of commitment that the denomination demanded of its home missionaries proves this. Whether it was the preachers who itinerated around vast, undeveloped land in the West with little remuneration, the women who served as WHMS missionaries or deaconesses who battled with the sex traffickers, or the enormous work the General Conferences undertook to create the FAS, CES, and other de-nominational agencies, the church intentionally pledged its time, money, personnel, and effort to its evangelistic mission. The Centenary stands as the highlight of this intentional commitment to mission.

Finally, pure American evangelism was a powerful force to open the MEC beyond its cultural, racial, and sexual biases. In some ways, this is counterintuitive, since the goal of pure American evangelism was to cre-ate a homogenous civilization based on common WMCNB values and patterns of life. Yet, the work engendered by pure American evangelism allowed the denomination to explore new ways of being. That the FAS could argue successfully to have an African American take leadership in the agency as a director even when the denomination as a whole was seg-regated points to this. The work of the Methodist Federation for Social Service in creating the Social Creed so the church could stand with the needs of the laboring class in spite of the middle class's fear of immigrant anarchists overthrowing Christian American civilization is another exam-ple. In both cases, the church used pure American evangelism as a means to explore alternative ways of being institutionally and socially even while holding to a specific WMCNB perspective.

This openness is especially visible in how the MEC allowed for the contributions of women. The MEC provided them a national platform for their activity even as it refused to ordain women, claimed women's primary sphere was domestic, and denied direct funding to the Methodist women's societies. In fact, pure American evangelism proved to be a per-fect motivating force to spur late-Victorian Methodist women to action. Believing in the God-given glory of the nation they inhabited, that the home was the heart of the nation, and that the woman was the heart of the home, they embraced the evangelizing and civilizing home missions of the denomination with vigor. They gave generously of their money (the WHMS had a total appropriations budget of over $1.4 million in 1920) and their service. This service took on manifold forms, including becom-ing deaconesses or missionaries in some parts of the nation that were least hospitable to women, and staying keenly involved with current political and economic events, such as lobbying for constitutional amendments against polygamy and alcohol.

The zeal, remarkable organizational abilities and deeply generous spirit of the Methodist women made them indispensable to pure Ameri-can evangelism. Apart from the women's activities, it is unlikely that pure American evangelism would have been as far-reaching or as long-lived as it was.

In recognizing the sensitivity, capacity to criticize, intentionality, and openness that pure American evangelism engendered in the MEC, we come to a startling conclusion. Pure American evangelism, with all of the cultural and racial superiority it carried with it, helped lay the groundwork for the more progressive form of American Methodism that The United Methodist Church has come to express. While UMC members today would find much to disagree with in the content of pure American evangelism, they would also find much in the practice of ministry to affirm. The current United Methodist emphasis on caring for the needy, speaking against unjust social, political, and economic structures, and making room for participation from unexpected quarters of the church are all traits that the UMC can trace back to its MEC predecessors who were so keen to spread the American gospel. The practitioners of pure American evangelism might be pleased to know that, while their message may have faltered, their ethic of engagement with culture continues.

Bibliography

"After the Centenary, What?" *The Christian Advocate* (July 3, 1919) 849–50.

Ahlstrom, Sydney E. *A Religious History of the American People*. 2nd ed. New Haven: Yale University Press, 2004.

"America Enters the War Against War." *The Christian Advocate* (April 5, 1917) 324.

Annual Reports of the Chicago Home Missionary and Church Extension Society for 1887–1913. Chicago: multiple publishers, 1889–1913.

Articles of Incorporation of the Chicago Home Missionary and Church Extension Society, with Reports for 1885 and 1886. Chicago: Dunn, 1887.

Asbury, Francis. *The Journal and Letters of Francis Asbury*. Edited by Elmer T. Clark, J. Manning Potts, and Jacob S. Payton. 3 vols. Nashville: Abingdon, 1958.

Bailyn, Bernard. *The Ideological Origins of the American Revolution*. Enlarged ed. Cambridge, MA: Belknap, 1992.

Bangs, Nathan. *The Life of the Rev. Freeborn Garrettson: Compiled from His Printed and Manuscript Journals, and Other Authentic Documents*. 4th ed. New York: Lane & Tippett, 1845.

Barclay, Wade Crawford. *History of Methodist Missions: Part One: Early American Methodism, 1769–1844*. Vol. 1, *Missionary Motivation and Expansion*. New York: Board of Missions and Church Extension of The Methodist Church, 1949.

———. *History of Methodist Missions: Part Two: The Methodist Episcopal Church, 1845–1939*. Vol. 3 *Widening Horizons, 1845–95*. New York: Board of Missions and Church Extension of The Methodist Church, 1957.

Bederman, Gail. *Manliness & Civilization: A Cultural History of Gender and Race in the United States, 1880–1917*. Chicago: University of Chicago Press, 1995.

Benjamin, Walter W., and Leland Scott. "The Methodist Episcopal Church in the Postwar Era." In *The History of American Methodism*, 2:315–90. Nashville: Abingdon, 1964.

Blight, David W. *Race and Reunion: The Civil War in American Memory*. Cambridge, MA: Belknap, 2001.

Bosch, David J. *Transforming Mission*. Maryknoll, NY: Orbis, 1991.

Boswell, Charles M. "Methodism and the Cities." In *Methodism and the Republic*, 309–22. Philadelphia: Board of Home Missions and Church Extension of the Methodist Episcopal Church, 1908.

Broder, Sherri. *Tramps, Unfit Mothers, and Neglected Children: Negotiating the Family in Nineteenth-Century Philadelphia*. Philadelphia: University of Pennsylvania Press, 2002.

Brummitt, Stella W. *Brother Van*. Cincinnati: Methodist Book Concern, 1919.

Bryan, William Jennings. *Speeches of William Jennings Bryan*. Vol. 2. New York: Funk & Wagnalls, 1909.

Bucke, Emory Stevens, editor. *The History of American Methodism.* 3 vols. Nashville: Abingdon, 1964.

Buckley, James M. *A History of Methodism in the United States.* 2 vols. New York: Harper, 1898.

Campbell, Ted A. *The Gospel in Christian Traditions.* New York: Oxford University Press, 2008.

———. *Wesleyan Beliefs: Formal and Popular Expressions of the Core Beliefs of Wesleyan Communities.* Nashville: Kingswood, 2010.

Cartwright, Peter. *Autobiography of Peter Cartwright.* Nashville: Abingdon, 1984.

Carwardine, Richard J. "Methodists, Politics, and the Coming of the American Civil War." In *Methodism and the Shaping of American Culture,* edited by Nathan O. Hatch and John H. Wigger, 309–42. Nashville: Kingswood, 2001.

Chandler, Alfred D. *The Visible Hand: The Managerial Revolution in American Business.* Cambridge: Belknap, 1977.

"The Christian's Duty." *The Christian Advocate* (April 12, 1917) 354–55.

"The Church Brings the Ends of the World Together at Columbus." *The Christian Advocate* (July 3, 1919) 851.

"Church Extension." *Western Christian Advocate* (January 8, 1868) 10.

The City Foursquare. Chicago: Chicago Home Missionary and Church Extension Society, January 1916.

Clapp, Rodney. *A Peculiar People: The Church as Culture in a Post-Christian Society.* Downers Grove, IL: InterVarsity, 1996.

Coke, Thomas, and Francis Asbury. *The Doctrines and Discipline of the Methodist Episcopal Church, in America, with Explanatory Notes, by Thomas Coke and Francis Asbury.* Philadelphia: Tuckniss, 1798.

———. *A form of discipline, for the ministers, preachers, and members of the Methodist Episcopal Church in America: Considered and approved at a conference held at Baltimore, in the state of Maryland, on Monday the 27th of December, 1784: in which the Reverend Thomas Coke, L.L.D. and the Reverend Francis Asbury, presided. Arranged under proper heads, and methodized in a more acceptable and easy manner.* New York: Printed by W. Ross, in Broad-Street, 1787.

Cole, Charles C., Jr. *The Social Ideas of Northern Evangelists, 1826–1860.* New York: Columbia University Press, 1954.

Crouch, Andrae. *Culture Making: Recovering Our Creative Calling.* Downers Grove, IL: InterVarsity, 2008.

"Current Comments." *Western Christian Advocate* (April 11, 1917) 338.

Davis, Morris L. *The Methodist Unification: Christianity and the Politics of Race in the Jim Crow Era.* New York: New York University Press, 2008.

Deverell, William F. "Church and State Issues in the Period of the Civil War." In *Church and State in America: A Bibliographical Guide the Civil War to the Present,* edited by John. F. Wilson, 1–32. New York: Greenwood, 1987.

Doenecke, Justus, and John E. Wilz. *From Isolation to War, 1931–1941.* 3rd ed. American History Series. Wheeling, IL: Davidson, 2003.

Dorsey, Bruce. *Reforming Men and Women: Gender in the Antebellum City.* Ithaca, NY: Cornell University Press, 2006.

Edwards, B. B. "The Conversion of Immigrants." *Western Christian Advocate* (November 11, 1842) 20.

Farrish, Hunter Dickinson. *The Circuit Rider Dismounts: A Social History of Southern Methodism, 1865–1900*. Richmond, VA: The Dietz, 1938.

Ferguson, Charles W. *Methodists and the Making of America: Organizing to Beat the Devil*. Bicentennial ed. Austin, TX: Eakin, 1983.

Fisher, H. D. "Methodism in Utah." *Western Christian Advocate* (June 2, 1880) 172.

Foley, Neil. *The White Scourge: Mexicans, Blacks, and Poor Whites in Texas Cotton Culture*. Berkeley: University of California Press, 1997.

Foner, Eric. *A Short History of Reconstruction, 1863–1877*. New York: Harper & Row, 1990.

Forbes, Robert. "Methodism and the Republic." In *Methodism and the Republic*, 9–24. Philadelphia: Board of Home Missions and Church Extension of the Methodist Episcopal Church, 1908.

Forsyth, David D., and Ralph Welles Keeler. *Christian Democracy for America*. New York: Methodist Book Concern, 1918.

"The Fraternal Address." *Western Christian Advocate* (May 24, 1882) 161.

Freedmen's Aid Society. *First–Fourteenth Annual Reports of the Freedmen's Aid Society of the Methodist Episcopal Church*. Cincinnati: Western Methodist Book Concern, 1869–1882.

"General Conference of the Methodist Episcopal Church: The Episcopal Address, 1896." New York: Eaton & Mains, 1896.

Goen, C. C. *Broken Churches, Broken Nation: Denominational Schisms and the Coming of the Civil War*. Macon, GA: Mercer University Press, 1985.

Guernsey, Alice M. *Lands of Sunshine*. New York: Woman's Home Missionary Society, 1916.

Hagood, L. M. *The Colored Man in the Methodist Episcopal Church*. New York: Hunt & Eaton, 1890.

Handy, Robert T. "The American Religious Depression, 1925–1935." *Church History* 29, no. 1 (1960) 3–16.

———. *A Christian America: Protestant Hopes and Historical Realities*. New York: Oxford University Press, 1984.

Harris, William L., editor. *Journal of the General Conference of the Methodist Episcopal Church, Held in Philadelphia, PA, 1864*. New York: Carlton & Porter, 1864.

———. *Journal of the General Conference of the Methodist Episcopal Church, Held in Chicago, Ill., 1868*. New York: Carlton & Lanahan, 1868.

Harris, William L. and G. W. Woodruff, editors. *Journal of the General Conference of the Methodist Episcopal Church, Held in Brooklyn, N.Y., 1872*. New York: Nelson & Phillips, 1872.

Harwood, Thomas. *History of New Mexico Spanish and English Missions of the Methodist Episcopal Church from 1850 to 1910*. 2 vols. Albuquerque: El Abogado, 1908.

Hatch, Nathan O. *The Democratization of American Christianity*. New Haven: Yale University Press, 1989.

Hempton, David. *Methodism: Empire of the Spirit*. New Haven: Yale University Press, 2005.

Hildebrand, Reginald. F. *The Times Were Strange and Stirring: Methodist Preachers and the Crisis of Emancipation*. Durham, NC: Duke University Press, 1995.

Hingeley, Joseph B., editor. *Journal of the Twenty-Fourth General Conference of the Methodist Episcopal Church, Held in Los Angeles, California, 1904*. New York: Eaton & Mains, 1904.

———. *Journal of the Twenty-Fifth General Conference of the Methodist Episcopal Church, Held in Baltimore, MD, 1908*. New York: Eaton & Mains, 1908.

———. *Journal of the Twenty-Sixth Delegated General Conference of the Methodist Episcopal Church Held in Minneapolis, MN, 1912*. New York: The Methodist Book Concern, 1912.

Jacobson, Matthew Frye. *Barbarian Virtues: The United States Encounters Foreign Peoples at Home and Abroad, 1876–1917*. New York: Hill & Wang, 2000.

Jones, Scott J. *The Evangelistic Love of God and Neighbor: A Theology of Witness and Discipleship*. Nashville: Abingdon, 2003.

Journal of the General Conference of the Methodist Episcopal Church Held in the City of New-York, 1844. In *Journals of the General Conference of the Methodist Episcopal Church*, 2:1–240. 1840, 1844. New York: Carlton & Phillips, 1855.

Kallenberg, Brad J. *Live to Tell: Evangelism for a Postmodern Age*. Grand Rapids: Brazos, 2002.

Kasson, John F. *Civilizing the Machine: Technology and Republican Values in America, 1776–1900*. New York: Hill & Wang, 1976.

Keene, Jennifer D. *Doughboys, the Great War, and the Remaking of America*. Baltimore: Johns Hopkins University Press, 2001.

Kirby, James E., Russell E. Richey, and Kenneth E. Rowe. *The Methodists*. Westport, CT: Greenwood, 1996.

Kynett, Alpha G. "Our Church Extension Work." In *Methodism and the Republic*, 114–28. Philadelphia: Board of Home Missions and Church Extension of the Methodist Episcopal Church, 1908.

Kynett, Alpha G., editor. *The Methodist Forward Movement in the United States*. Annual of the Board of Home Missions and Church Extension of the Methodist Episcopal Church, 1907–1908. Philadelphia: Board of Home Missions and Church Extension of the Methodist Episcopal Church, 1908.

Literary Notices. *The Ladies' Repository* 26 (September 1866) 573.

Leonard, Bill J. "Evangelism and Contemporary American Life." In *The Study of Evangelism: Exploring a Missional Practice of the Church*, edited by Paul W. Chilcote and Laceye C. Warner, 101–16. Grand Rapids: Eerdmans, 2008.

Lincoln, Abraham. *The Writings of Abraham Lincoln*. Edited by Arthur Brooks Lapsley et al. New York: Lamb, 1906.

Litwack, Leon F. *Been in the Storm So Long: The Aftermath of Slavery*. New York: Vintage, 1979.

Locke, Edwin, editor. *Journal of the Twenty-Seventh Delegated General Conference of the Methodist Episcopal Church Held in Saratoga Springs, NY, 1916*. New York: Methodist Book Concern, 1916.

Loud, Grover C. *Evangelized America*. New York: Dial, 1928.

Luccock, Halford E., and Webb Garrison. *Endless Line of Splendor*. Nashville: United Methodist Communications, 1992.

Luccock, Halford E., and Paul Hutchinson. *The Story of Methodism*. New York: Methodist Book Concern, 1926.

Luchetti, Cathy. *Under God's Spell: Frontier Evangelists, 1772–1915*. New York: Harcourt Brace Jovanovich, 1989.

Marsden, George M. *Fundamentalism and American Culture*. New ed. New York: Oxford University Press, 2006.

————. *The Outrageous Ideal of Christian Scholarship*. New York: Oxford University Press, 1997.

Marty, Martin E. *Righteous Empire: The Protestant Experience in America*. New York: Dial, 1970.

May, James W. "The War Years." In *The History of American Methodism*, 2:206–56. Nashville: Abingdon, 1964.

McLoughlin, William G. *Revivals, Awakenings, and Reform*. Chicago History of American Religion. Chicago: University of Chicago Press, 1978.

Mills, Edmund M., editor. *Journal of the Twenty-Eighth Delegated General Conference of the Methodist Episcopal Church Held in Des Moines, Iowa, 1920*. New York: Methodist Book Concern, 1920.

Monroe, David S., editor. *Journal of the General Conference of the Methodist Episcopal Church, Held in Philadelphia, PA, 1884*. New York: Phillips & Hunt, 1884.

————. *Journal of the General Conference of the Methodist Episcopal Church, Held in New York, 1888*. New York: Phillips & Hunt, 1888.

————. *Journal of the General Conference of the Methodist Episcopal Church, Held in Chicago, Illinois, 1900*. New York: Eaton & Mains, 1900.

Moore, H. H. *The Republic to Methodism, Debtor*. New York: Hunt & Eaton, 1891.

Moorehead, James H. *World without End: Mainstream American Protestant Visions of the Last Things, 1880–1925*. Bloomington: Indiana University Press, 1999.

Nash, Gary B. *The Unknown American Revolution: The Unruly Birth of Democracy and the Struggle to Create America*. New York: Penguin, 2006.

Neely, Thomas B. *American Methodism: Its Divisions and Unification*. New York: Revell, 1915.

Nelson, C. G. "The Future of Swedish Methodism." In *Methodism and the Republic*, 284–98. Philadelphia: Board of Home Missions and Church Extension of the Methodist Episcopal Church, 1908.

"A New World Opening." *Northwestern Christian Advocate* (April 11, 1917) 364.

Niebuhr, H. Richard. *The Kingdom of God in America*. Chicago: Willett, Clark, 1937.

Norwood, Frederick A. *The Story of American Methodism*. Nashville: Abingdon, 1974.

Nye, David E. *Electrifying America: Social Meanings of a New Technology, 1880–1940*. Cambridge: MIT Press, 1990.

Packard, William. *Evangelism in America: From Tents to TV*. New York: Paragon House, 1988.

"Plan for Consolidating Church Benevolences; Report of the Commission Appointed at the Latest M.E. General Conference—Three Great Societies." *The New York Times* (April 27, 1903) 6.

Platt, Ward. *Methodism and the Republic: A View of the Home Field, Present Conditions, Needs and Possibilities*. Philadelphia: Board of Home Missions and Church Extension of the Methodist Episcopal Church, 1908.

Rader, Daniel L. "The Pacific Northwest." In *Methodism and the Republic*, 63–78. Philadelphia: The Board of Home Missions and Church Extension of the Methodist Episcopal Church, 1908.

Reports of the New York City Church Extension and Missionary Society of the Methodist Episcopal Church for the Years Ending March, 1887—March 1901. New York: multiple publishers, 1874–1901.

Richey, Russell E. *The Methodist Conference in America: A History*. Nashville: Kingswood, 1996.

Riggin, F. A. "Piegan Indian Mission: An Example of What Is Being Done." In *Methodism and the Republic*, 299–308. Philadelphia: Board of Home Missions and Church Extension of the Methodist Episcopal Church, 1908.

Rodgers, Daniel T. *Atlantic Crossings: Social Politics in a Progressive Age*. Cambridge: Belknap Press of Harvard University Press, 1998.

Roosevelt, Theodore. "True Americanism." Theodore Roosevelt Collection. MS Am 1785.4 (48). Houghton Library, Harvard University, n.d. Online: http://www.theodorerooseveltcenter.org/Research/Digital-Library/Record. aspx?libID=0280950.

Rosenzweig, Roy. *Eight Hours for What We Will: Workers & Leisure in an Industrial City, 1870–1920*. New York: Cambridge University Press, 1983.

Salter, Darius. *American Evangelism: Its Theology and Practice*. Grand Rapids: Baker, 1996.

Sandage, Scott A. *Born Losers: A History of Failure in the America*. Cambridge: Harvard University Press, 2005.

Schmidt, Leigh Eric. *Holy Fairs: Scotland and the Making of American Revivalism*. 2nd ed. Grand Rapids: Eerdmans, 2001.

Scott, Leland. "The Message of Early American Methodism." In *The History of American Methodism*, 1:291–359. Nashville: Abingdon, 1964.

Sellers, Charles. *The Market Revolution*. New York: Oxford University Press, 1991.

Simpson, Matthew. *A Hundred Years of Methodism*. New York: Nelson & Phillips, 1876.

Sklansky, Jeffrey. *The Soul's Economy: Market Society and Selfhood in American Thought, 1820–1920*. Chapel Hill: University of North Carolina Press, 2002.

Smith, Alson Jesse. *Brother Van: A Biography of the Rev. William Wesley Van Orsdel*. Nashville: Abingdon, 1948.

Smith, Timothy L. *Revivalism and Social Reform: American Protestantism on the Eve of the Civil War*. Baltimore: Johns Hopkins University Press, 1980.

Stanley, Brian. "Defining the Boundaries of Christendom: The Two Worlds of the World Missionary Conference, 1910." *IBMR* 30, no. 4 (2006) 171–76.

Stevens, Abel. *Compendious History of American Methodism*. New York: Eaton & Mains, 1868.

Stowell, Daniel W. *Rebuilding Zion: The Religious Reconstruction of the South, 1863–1877*. New York: Oxford University Press, 1998.

Sullivan, Winnifred F. "Religion and Law in the United States: 1870 to the Present." In *Church and State in America: A Bibliographical Guide the Civil War to the Present*, edited by John F. Wilson, 339–72. New York: Greenwood, 1987.

Sweet, William Warren. *Methodism in American History*. New York: Methodist Book Concern, 1933.

Talbot, H. J. "The Methodist Episcopal Church in Utah." In *Methodism and the Republic*, 79–97. Philadelphia: Board of Home Missions and Church Extension of the Methodist Episcopal Church, 1908.

Taylor, Alan. *American Colonies: The Settling of North America*. Penguin History of the United States. New York: Penguin, 2002.

Taylor, S. Earl, and Halford E. Luccock. *The Christian Crusade for World Democracy*. New York: Methodist Book Concern, 1918.

Teasdale, Mark R. "Peter Cartwright and the Emerging National Identity in Antebellum America." *Methodist History* 46, no. 2 (2008) 101–13.

"Theory and Practice." *Central Christian Advocate* (March 2, 1887) 2.

Thirkield, Wilbur P. "The Mountain Whites of the South." In *The Methodist Forward Movement in the United States: Annual of the Board of Home Missions and Church Extension of the Methodist Episcopal Church*, edited by Alpha G.Kynett, 1907–1908. Philadelphia: Board of Home Missions and Church Extension of the Methodist Episcopal Church, 1908.

Tigert, John J. *A Constitutional History of American Episcopal Methodism.* 4th ed. Nashville: Publishing House of the Methodist Episcopal Church, South, 1911.

Tomkinson, Laura E. *Twenty Years' History of the Women's Home Missionary Society of the Methodist Episcopal Church 1880-1900.* Cincinnati: Woman's Home Missionary Society of the Methodist Episcopal Church, 1903.

Turner, Frederick Jackson. *History, Frontier and Section: Three Essays by Frederick Jackson Turner.* Albuquerque: University of New Mexico Press, 1993.

The United Methodist Church. "The General Rules of the Methodist Church." Online: http://archives.umc.org/interior.asp?mid=1648.

United Methodist General Commission on Archives and History. "United Methodist Membership Compared to United States Census Population." Online: http://www.gcah.org/site/?c=ghKJI0PHI0E&b=3828783.

Van Marter, Martha. "The Woman's Home Missionary Society." In *Methodism and the Republic*, 323–46. Philadelphia: Board of Home Missions and Church Extension of the Methodist Episcopal Church, 1908.

Wade, R. J. editor. *The World Service of the Methodist Episcopal Church.* Chicago: Methodist Book Concern, 1924.

Warner, Laceye C. *Saving Women: Retrieving Evangelistic Theology and Practice.* Waco, TX: Baylor University Press, 2007.

Watters, William. *A Short Account of the Christian Experience and Ministereal Labours of William Watters.* Alexandria, VA: Snowden, 1806.

Wesley, John. *The Methodist Societies, The Minutes of Conference.* Edited by Henry D. Rack. Vol. 10 of *The Bicentennial Edition of the Works of John Wesley.* Nashville: Abingdon, 1993.

Wiebe, Robert H. *The Search for Order, 1877-1920.* New York: Hill & Wang, 1967.

Wigger, John H. *Taking Heaven by Storm: Methodism and the Rise of Popular Christianity in America.* Urbana: University of Illinois Press, 1998.

Willentz, Sean. *The Rise of American Democracy: Jefferson to Lincoln.* New York: Norton, 2005.

Wilson, Alonzo E. *Methodist Centenary Celebration: State Fair Grounds, Columbus, Ohio, June 20–July 13, 1919: Official Reports and Records.* Unpublished report located in the Vault at the United Library at Garrett-Evangelical Theological Seminary, 1919.

Wilson, Woodrow. "Making the World Safe for Democracy: Woodrow Wilson Asks for War." Sixty-Fifth Congress, Session 1, Senate Document 5. History Matters: The U.S. Survey Course on the Web. Online: http://historymatters.gmu.edu/d/4943/.

Wise, Daniel. *The Convert's Counsellor Respecting His Church Relations: or Popular Objections to Methodism Considered and Answered: with Reasons Why Methodist Converts Should Join a Methodist Church.* Boston: Magee, 1856.

Wood, Gordon S. *The Radicalism of the American Revolution.* New York: Vintage, 1993.

Woodruff, George W., editor. *Journal of the General Conference of the Methodist Episcopal Church, Held in Baltimore, MD., 1876.* New York: Nelson & Phillips, 1876.

————. *Journal of the General Conference of the Methodist Episcopal Church, Held in Cincinnati, OH, 1880*. New York: Phillips & Hunt, 1880.

Women's Home Missionary Society. *First–Thirty-Ninth Annual Reports of the Board of Managers of the Woman's Home Missionary Society of the Methodist Episcopal Church for the Years 1881–1920*. Cincinnati: Western Methodist Book Concern Press, 1882–1911; Methodist Book Concern, 1912–1920.

Year Books for the Years Ending April 30th, 1902–1906 Containing the Thirty-Sixth–Fortieth Annual Reporst of the New York City Church Extension and Missionary Society of the Methodist Episcopal Church. New York: New York City Church Extension Society and Missionary Society, 1902–1906.

Index

Made in the USA
San Bernardino, CA
20 June 2014